# The Critic as Amateur

# The Critic as Amateur

*Edited by Saikat Majumdar and Aarthi Vadde*

BLOOMSBURY

NEW DELHI • LONDON • OXFORD • NEW YORK • SYDNEY

BLOOMSBURY INDIA
Bloomsbury Publishing India Pvt. Ltd
Second Floor, Building No. 4
DDA Complex LSC, Pocket C – 6 & 7
Vasant Kunj, New Delhi 110070
www.bloomsbury.com



**First published in India 2020**
First published in the United States of America 2020


Cover design by Pinaki De

This edition published with permission from Bloomsbury Publishing Plc,
50 Bedford Square, London, WC1B3DP, UK



British Library Cataloguing-in-Publication Data
A catalogue record for this book is available from the British Library.

Library of Congress Cataloging-in-Publication Data
A catalog record for this book is available from the Library of Congress

ISBN: 978-93-89391-06-0

For sale in the Indian subcontinent only

Typeset by Integra Software Services Pvt. Ltd.
Digitally Printed and bound in India by Replika Press Pvt. Ltd. In 2019.

# CONTENTS

# LIST OF CONTRIBUTORS

**Derek Attridge** is Emeritus Professor at the University of York, UK, and a Fellow of the British Academy. His many books range from literary theory to South African writing, James Joyce, and poetic form. The most recent is *The Experience of Poetry: From Homer's Listeners to Shakespeare's Readers* (2019). He has taught in England, Scotland, and the United States.

**Emily Bloom** is Associate Director of the Society of Fellows and Heyman Center for the Humanities and Lecturer in the Department of English and Comparative Literature at Columbia University. She specializes in late modernism with a focus on the interrelations between media institutions and transnational literary networks. Her book, *The Wireless Past: Anglo-Irish Writers and the BBC, 1931–1968* (2016), was awarded the Modernist Studies Association's First Book Prize.

**Rosinka Chaudhuri** is Director and Professor of Cultural Studies at the Centre for Studies in Social Sciences, Calcutta (CSSSC). She was also the first Mellon Professor of the Global South at the University of Oxford, 2017–18. She has written *Gentlemen Poets in Colonial Bengal* (2002), *Freedom and Beef Steaks* (2012), and *The Literary Thing* (2013) and edited *Derozio, Poet of India* (2008), *The Indian Postcolonial* (co-edited, 2010), *A History of Indian Poetry in English* (2016), and *An Acre of Green Grass and Other English Writings of Buddhadeva Bose* (2018). She has also translated and introduced *Rabindranath Tagore: Letters from a Young Poet* (2014).

**Christopher Hilliard** is Professor of History at the University of Sydney. His research focuses on literature and literary criticism in popular intellectual life. His recent work, on freedom of expression and crimes involving the written word, has taken him into legal history and social history. He is the author, most recently, of *The Littlehampton Libels* (2017) and *English as a Vocation: The "Scrutiny" Movement* (2012). Other books include *The Bookmen's Dominion* (2006) and *To Exercise Our Talents* (2006).

**Tom Lutz** is the founding editor and publisher of *Los Angeles Review of Books* and teaches at the University of California, Riverside. He is the author most recently of *And the Monkey Learned Nothing* (2016) and *Drinking Mare's Milk on the Roof of the World* (2016), two collections of anecdotes from a life of obsessive travel. His other books include *Doing Nothing* (2006), *Cosmopolitan Vistas* (2004), *Crying* (1999), *American Nervousness, 1903* (1991), and the forthcoming *Born Slippy: A Novel* (2020).

**Saikat Majumdar** is Professor of English and Creative Writing at Ashoka University, and the author of three novels, including *The Scent of God* (2019), and *The Firebird* (2015; published in the United States as *Play House*, 2017), one of *Telegraph*'s Best Books and a finalist for the Bangalore Literature Festival Best Fiction Award in 2015, and for the Mumbai Film Festival Word-to-Screen Market in 2016. He has also published a general nonfiction title, *College: Pathways of Possibility* (2018), on liberal arts education in India, and a monograph on global modernism, *Prose of the World* (2013), a finalist for the Modernist Studies Association Book Award in 2014.

**Peter D. McDonald** is Professor of English and Related Literature at the University of Oxford and a Fellow of St. Hugh's College. He writes on literature, the modern state, and the freedom of expression; the history of writing systems, cultural institutions, and publishing; multilingualism, translation, and interculturality; and the promise of creative criticism. His publications include *British Literary Culture and Publishing Practice, 1880–1914* (1997); *Making Meaning*, co-edited with Michael Suarez (2002); *The Literature Police* (2009); and *Artefacts of Writing* (2017). He is currently part of a research team working on PEN and the freedom of expression.

**Melanie Micir** is Assistant Professor of English at Washington University in St. Louis. She teaches courses on modern and contemporary British literature and gender and sexuality studies. Her work has been published or is forthcoming in *MLQ*, *JML*, *Modernism/modernity*, and several edited collections. Her first book, *The Passion Projects: Modernist Women, Intimate Archives, Unfinished Lives*, is forthcoming from Princeton University Press.

**Zlatina Nikolova** recently completed her PhD at Royal Holloway, University of London. Her PhD focused on the stylistic and thematic features of the autobiographical prose and film criticism of the modernist author Bryher. She has presented papers on the parallels between Bryher's and H.D.'s autobiographical prose, on stereotypes of femininity in Bryher's *Two Selves*, the female experience of the Great War, and on the parallels between Sergei Eisenstein's film theories and women characters in *Borderline*. Her research interests include the writing produced by the POOL Group, early film culture, and women's autobiographical writing.

**Ragini Tharoor Srinivasan** is Assistant Professor of English at the University of Arizona, where she works on contemporary South Asian Anglophone and Asian/American literatures and cultural theory. She has also taught at the University of Nevada, Reno, and at the University of California, Berkeley, where she earned a PhD in Rhetoric in 2016. An award-winning journalist and former magazine editor, she contributes essays and reviews to international scholarly, public, and semi-public outlets. Visit www.raginitharoorsrinivasan.com.

**Chris Townsend** is Professor of the History of Avant-Garde Film in the Department of Media Arts, Royal Holloway, University of London, and Department Chair. He specializes in the relationships between film, writing and painting in high modernism. Recent work includes a study of Duncan Grant's *Abstract Kinetic Collage Painting* as part of a digital project with Tate Britain. A study of the membership of POOL Group will appear in a special issue of *Papers on Language and Literature* in 2019. He is working on a book about the relationship of the inter-war modernist avant-garde and new media industries.

**Aarthi Vadde** is Associate Professor of English at Duke University. Her research focuses on the relationship of literature and media to globalization. She is the author of *Chimeras of Form: Modernist Internationalism beyond Europe, 1914–2016* (2016), winner of the American Comparative Literature Association's 2018 Harry Levin Prize. A special forum on the book was convened in *The Cambridge Journal of Postcolonial Literary Inquiry.* She has also published numerous articles in such venues as *Comparative Literature*, *Modern Fiction Studies*, *Modernism/modernity*, *New Literary History*, *NOVEL*, and *Public Books*.

**Mimi Winick** is Postdoctoral Fellow in the English Department at Virginia Commonwealth University, where she is at work on a monograph provisionally titled *Fantastic Scholarship*. Her research concerns the intersections of the history of the humanities, new religious movements, and imaginative prose in nineteenth- and early twentieth-century Britain. Her essays have appeared in journals including *Nineteenth-Century Literature* and *Modernism/ Modernity*.

**Kara Wittman** is Assistant Professor of English and Director of College Writing at Pomona College. She works on the philosophical experience of wonder in literature, rhetoric, and pedagogy and has also published on "small" forms of communication: small talk, phatic speech, marginalia.

# ACKNOWLEDGMENTS

*Docendo discimus*. By teaching, we learn. The same goes for editing. We are most grateful to our contributors for all their work has taught us. Without them, this collection would not be possible. Their enthusiasm for and belief in the project made even the most mundane editorial tasks worthwhile. Haaris Naqvi at Bloomsbury has been an excellent source of advice through the production of this book. The anonymous readers he found offered intelligent and generous suggestions in the early stages of design and later stages of revision. Kathleen Burns provided much appreciated editorial assistance. We are proud to note that this collection on the critic as amateur has been a genuinely transnational endeavor. With contributors based in universities across Australia, India, the UK, and the United States, we can say for certain that we have ventured outside our usual professional circuits and been rewarded in kind.

# Introduction: Criticism for the Whole Person

*Aarthi Vadde with Saikat Majumdar*

Why a collection on the critic as amateur now? After all, we are living in a great age of anger, mistrust, and vengeance against professional experts and the institutions that shelter them. Our political fates worldwide are being shaped by a euphoria and passion for the anti-establishment candidate—the iconoclast, the outsider, and perforce, the amateur. Such a figure embodies, with equal strength, hope for radical change and cynicism with the technocratic elite. Calls to "blow it up" and "burn it down" augment political despair with populist anger. In the minds of many voters on the right and the left, it is not such a bad idea to blow up a world of career operators driven more by self-preservation than by public service. "Burn it down" is the lament of a populace tired of propping up institutions, cultural and educational as well as political, which seem to perpetuate inequality rather than diminish it.

This collection turns to the critic as amateur not to endorse the backlash against experts but to recover a story of literary study and institutional crossover that might combat it. Our contributors reexamine the professionalization of modern literary study from the point of view of the amateur. Yet, from the outset, point of view is misleading because "the amateur" is not a uniform position so much as an assortment of perspectives on the practice and purpose of criticism. Some of our contributors take the amateur as the default identity of the untrained reader—akin to the common reader—but passionate enough about books to want to talk and write about them. Others see the amateur emerging as a legible identity via the requirements of formal education. Overlapping strongly with the category of the student (high school, undergraduate, graduate, and adult learner are among the varieties addressed here), the amateur emerges in several essays as both a curricular artifact and a retrospective identity created through professional initiation. Indeed, thinking about the critic as amateur yields a double-consciousness of specialist training as some contributors make cases for revitalizing literary criticism by returning to those moments before its conventions of reading and writing were second nature.

Still, in an even wider ambit, the critic as amateur designates a range of impulses that have historically been at odds with the disciplinary confines of academic literary study in particular and the consolidation of a cloistered expert culture in general. Our contributors use a focus on the amateur to think about the place of authority in the literary field, and they ask when it makes sense to forgo demonstrable knowledge for demonstrable ignorance. They understand that specialists in one area of literary study might be novices in another, and they explore the disciplinary specificities of professional expertise to build bridges across literary and nonliterary, academic and nonacademic venues of criticism. In the process, several essays reconsider the reduction of criticism to the scholarly monograph or peer-reviewed article and instead advocate for a wider and more various understanding of critical activity. Genres like the radio script and journalistic review garner newfound importance while institutional and do-it-yourself (DIY) acts of collection, curation, and distribution appear as overlooked sites of criticism more broadly conceived.

It is not surprising that attention to criticism should draw humanities professors, which all our contributors are, into a reflection upon best practices for the fields of literary and cultural study. Our contributors are scholars as well as critics, which is to say, they take an interest in the histories of their disciplines, participate in methodological debates, and contribute to knowledge. What is surprising is how frequently amateurism emerges in considerations of professional identity across all levels of the professoriate. Amateurism, for example, is an elective affinity for such luminaries as Roland Barthes and Edward Said, both of whom saw it as a riposte to professional insularity and routine. Barthes's emphasis on pleasure and Said's on moral courage, while taking the critic as amateur in diverging directions, nonetheless share the mark of aristocracy. Both invoke amateurism from positions of extraordinary accomplishment—not so much rejecting professionalism as transcending the field and gaining its fealty in return. Yet amateurism as an elective affinity need not come only from the upper-echelons of academia. Historically, as essays on Pramatha Chaudhuri, Vernon Lee, and Dorothy Richardson show, it has also been the posture of the eclectic writer-critic regarded as eccentric in the wake of the academic division and professionalization of the arts. Being difficult to categorize talents, Chaudhuri, Lee, and Richardson get their due in this collection. These amateurs turn out to be key players in the very cultural networks that, upon cohering into distinct disciplines (literature, psychology, film), would render them anomalous.

In essays broaching the beleaguered state of the humanities today, amateurism becomes a gesture of authenticity made under conditions of structural duress. For humanities PhDs facing a decimated job market, the casualization of academic labor, and institutional inhospitality to activist projects (antiracist, feminist, queer, trans, to name a few), categories like "independent scholar" and "labor of love" take on newly politicized dimensions. Fewer jobs and bad working conditions are forcing excellent critics out of the academy, but some are also choosing to leave in order to pursue otherwise unsustainable modes of inquiry. For such critics, the amateur is essential to explaining those forms of work that bear proximity to a calling. Theirs are passions that will be pursued even in the absence of institutional recognition and monetary compensation.

Indeed, the entanglement of passion with knowledge characterizes our contributors' shared interest in the critic as amateur. The amateur's ignoble fate over the twentieth century and even more ignoble rise in the twenty-first-century resurgence of right-wing populism speaks to how deeply riven specialist and popular cultures have become. Despite differing perspectives on how to restore the bonds of communication, we uniformly assert that the energies of amateurism are too potent to cede to those who would reject professional expertise outright, sew division, and exploit others' ignorance while masking their own. This collection therefore embraces amateurism out of the desire to understand criticism as exceeding the strictures of professionalism even when professionals are the ones doing it. We believe that the professional study of literature and culture will benefit from its practitioners yielding to their amateur impulses. Moreover, we find that amateurism, in its various guises, has driven the study of the humanities forward in under-credited ways.

The essays that follow this introduction make good on this conviction by taking three major paths. They explore and question the genealogies of expertise rather than simply taking authority for granted. They face rather than repress the contradictions that arise from studying aesthetic experience via what can be limited disciplinary vocabularies. They value disparate and lively critical cultures populated by students, radio hosts, film spectators, small press publishers, book collectors, and bloggers. Such a motley crew replaces the construct of the ideal or imagined reader with living, breathing, rough-around-the-edges critics.

## Amateurism and the making of literary expertise

The long and varied history of the critic as amateur becomes newly salient within a knowledge society where expertise is paramount, but professional experts are often maligned. When sociologists use the term "knowledge society" to characterize the present, they are not suggesting that knowledge has never played a role in social organization. Rather, they are crediting the production, distribution, and reproduction of knowledge with being the "constitutive mechanism" of contemporary society.[1] As societies become more knowledge-dependent, the ability to claim expertise becomes more aligned with power, profit, and influence. However, the tendency to concentrate expertise in a narrow subset of the population—the professional-managerial class—faces challenges from the very sociotechnical milieu that has brought the knowledge society to fruition. At the center of this milieu is the internet.

It is now commonplace to observe that the internet has made information more accessible. This is more of a truism than a truth, but it is fair to say that the internet has enabled lay people—amateurs—to do knowledge work that rivals professional institutions in certain arenas. Crowdsourced websites like Wikipedia, social media platforms like Facebook and Twitter, and software packages like Photoshop and Final Cut Pro enable amateur users to develop and share often self-taught skills (what some sociologists call "lay expertise"); become "influencers" in fields from fashion to politics; and develop modes of collaboration (what some media theorists call "networked expertise") that have transformed how print-based industries like publishing do business.[2] We mention these developments not to overstate the power of digital amateurs or trumpet the equalizing force of Web 2.0 participatory culture, but to argue that multiple models of expertise are in play on the internet in highly visible ways.[3] It is the place where abstract claims about the knowledge society feel most palpable.

Knowledge is a form of currency for everyday users on social media as well as for traditionally knowledge-based industries striving to adapt to digital media. Information is a commodity for the technology companies operating the platforms and services that keep internet culture afloat. Yet, as knowledge becomes increasingly central to entrepreneurialism, self-management, occupational advancement, and economic growth, our actual understanding of the concept grows more remote. Knowledge: the black box at the center of everything.

What would it mean to claim the mantle of the amateur as a way of understanding knowledge better? Can the amateur, so central to internet culture, also help us imagine an outside to the sociotechnical milieu of the knowledge society? We get one powerful answer from the writer Pankaj Mishra whose amateurism seems informed by and yet in direct contradiction to both networked and professionalized forms of expertise. Mishra, writing in 1998, recounts sitting in Benares in 1988 and reading authors far removed from his time and place without knowing anything about their contexts. Such unscholarly and "disconnected" reading led to new revelations, not only about these authors' works but strangely also about his immediate surroundings.[4] In other words, reading with minimal resources enabled a literary engagement that the mandates of professional scholarship and the power of the search engine (in popular use by 1994) would have inhibited. The gaping lack of historical knowledge, cultural affiliation, and information access kept Mishra from entering the social context of nineteenth-century France; consequently, he conjured a new life for Flaubert's Frédéric Moreau as a character entering late twentieth-century rural Uttar Pradesh. Neither such ignorance nor such flights of fancy seem as plausible or sincere in the age of the Google search, mobile devices, and always-on computing. And that is the point.

What started as a technological phenomenon—digital connectivity—has now snowballed into an entire system of values that prizes more rather than less; more information, we imagine, will necessarily lead to better knowledge and more freedom. More information and more informed opinion also necessarily lead to disputes over cultural authority. The magazines and journals described in Mishra's essay—the *TLS, Partisan Review*, and the *New York Review of Books*—rare surprises in 1980s Benares, are now easily available in any part of the world with an internet connection, sometimes behind a paywall but often not. Yet, at the same time, the influence of these traditional arbiters of literary value is offset by digital literary cultures that increasingly arbitrate their own set of values separate from or in competition with these prestigious periodicals. Think *Goodreads*, Amazon book reviews, blogs like *Book Slut* and *Moorish Girl*, and born-digital highbrow forums like the *Los Angeles Review of Books* and *Public Books*.[5] A review in *The New York Review of Books* is still an important thing but far less so than it was ten years ago. Who knows what the next ten years will do to its circulation or cultural capital?

We are not bemoaning the state of legacy media so much as noting a major shift. For over a decade now, we have witnessed the move of reader/viewer traffic away from traditional news venues to sites like Buzzfeed and ScoopWhoop to take just two examples from the United States and India. Although recent research shows a small number of this readership returning to the websites of traditional news venues, such as *CNN*, *Fox News*, *Washington Post*, and the *New York Times*, the more important fact is the mass migration of readership online.[6] The proliferation of born-digital media—blogs, magazines, social media platforms, news feeds—and algorithmically driven recommendation systems (whether for the *New York Times* or Buzzfeed) makes it possible for individuals and whole groups to dwell in restricted information ecologies while at the same time believing they have more and better access to information than ever before. More people now get their news and opinions about the world entirely from the groups they choose and the groups that search engines, social media feeds, and recommendation algorithms choose for them. Hence, the contradictory effects of empowerment and confirmation bias: users banding together can call out and hold accountable professional experts who think they know better, but users banding together can also ignore or discredit organs of news and culture that actually do know better.

The way we understand the evolution of literary studies, as a specialized field rooted in print modernity, is now inseparable from the political and epistemological conflicts internal to a digitally driven knowledge society. The assumption that knowledge is less a disciplinary domain than a circulating currency, while obviously thorny in the ways mentioned above, also places needed pressure on the academic disciplines as we have inherited them from the Enlightenment projects of the nineteenth century. If natural philosophy did fine as a term with Isaac Newton, the post-Enlightenment practitioners of the Newtonian disciplines were going to need the pointed specificity of the word "science," and subsequently, "scientists," to distinguish their specialties from the amorphous, all-encompassing ambition of philosophy. The rational logic of modernity, the modern nation-state, and in some instances, the project of colonialism would consolidate many of the human and social sciences in the distinct forms of disciplinary expertise in which we possess them today. The imperial project, it is now understood, also had much to do with the inauguration of literary curricula in the colonies, especially in nineteenth-century India, though it would not be until Leavisite Cambridge in the early twentieth century that English literature would attain its full disciplinary significance.

The nineteenth century also saw the rise of the modern research university (inspired by the Humboldtian model of higher education) in Europe and North America. As universities and graduate schools became the primary province of literary study, amateur practitioners like "the man of letters" found themselves discredited. Whereas the man of letters drew his literary-critical authority from individual prestige and perceived moral and intellectual superiority, the professional specialist who would supplant him based the capacity for literary judgment upon systematic training and knowledge acquisition.[7] By the 1920s, John Middleton Murry referred to the gentlemanly amateur in damning terms: "No amount of sedulous apery or word-mosaic will make a writer of the dilettante belletrist."[8]

But as we in this volume argue, amateurism's demise was never complete even if the amateurs themselves were shunted out of disciplinary origin stories. The narrative that emerges from these essays is that of the amateur's simultaneous coexistence with the credentialed expert—sometimes harmonious, other times uneasy but always illuminating of literary study's diverse configurations beyond the discipline of "literary studies." Not before the explosive growth of digital participatory culture has the amateur drawn so much attention or had so much voice. Yet the rise of the digital amateur, polarizing as such a figure might be, leads us to point out the myriad ways amateurism and expertise had already been entwined from the turn of the twentieth century onward.

We argue that the dominant narrative of this period, which chronicles the rise and consolidation of the professions as well as the rise and consolidation of academic literature departments, overlooks the ways that amateurs and professionals forged partnerships and rivalries.[9] Such entanglements at times prefigure the lay and networked expertise of internet cultures and at other times query the very definition of and attitudes toward knowledge operative within knowledge societies. We find that amateurs occasionally do lay claim to expertise, but more often than not, as with Mishra, they complicate what it means to be knowledgeable, wield facts, and perform authority. Spotlighting the history of amateurism, our collection yields alternative vocabularies for describing the nature of literature and literary expertise.

* * *

It would seem that the more subjective the domain of knowledge, the stronger the ability of an amateur to rival a professional expert. It is far easier to ignore the gatekeepers of literature than those of cancer research, where access to equipment is prohibitively expensive and the consensus around findings more concrete and substantial.[10] While such an admission might be disturbing to some readers, we readily ask: Is literature with a capital "L" even a domain of knowledge?

Professional scholars certainly need literature to be institutionally recognized as knowledge for our livelihoods, but that need does not do justice to what literature, as a subset of imaginative and finely written works, actually is. As Michael Wood writes, literature in its modern sense is difficult to pin down. It "offers something harder—in the sense of 'hard' sciences—than understanding and something softer than we often imagine knowledge to be."[11] In drawing this conclusion, Wood builds on Stefan Collini's pairing of understanding and knowledge as related terms with distinct connotations. For Collini, knowledge connotes "accumulated stock" while understanding—less physical, more processual—emphasizes the role of human activity in creating knowledge.[12] Wood regards literature in sensuous terms as harder than understanding but softer than knowledge. Literary study is not cancer research, yet its experts have acquired something specific from it, namely knowledge "on holiday." With this metaphor, drawn from mixing Barthes and Ludwig Wittgenstein, Wood argues that literature teaches us to adjudicate knowledge as a given category by presenting all of its knowledge hypothetically. A set of possibilities rather than a store of facts, literature "creates a new zone between work and play."[13] Its liminality solicits readers to consider even the most outlandish possibility as operative and consequently takes flight where statistical norms would ground us in the likely, the predictable, the known.

Knowledge on holiday might sound odd. However, just as professors of literature realize we must justify our vocation via a claim to knowledge, we are equally prepared for the accusation, made more with unwitting condescension than malice, that what we do is not real work. We're not curing cancer after all. Deidre Lynch argues that the practices of criticism and pedagogy native to literary studies remain eccentric within the post-Enlightenment formation of the disciplines (despite literary criticism's subjection to it) precisely because professing literature demands a personal touch.[14] Professors of literature are expected to love their object of study. Their vocation is not to eliminate pleasure but to ensure its proper administration; hence, the discipline's deviation from the norms of "publicness and impersonality" that govern other professional occupations.[15] Interestingly enough, Lynch's emphasis on the *propriety* of pleasure casts the literature professor as a descendant of eighteenth-century periodical founders like Joseph Addison and Richard Steele. Addison and Steele famously turned to journalism and the genre of the essay in particular to bring "philosophy out of closets and libraries, schools and colleges, to dwell in clubs and assemblies, at tea-tables and in coffee-houses."[16] What is less remembered about this democratizing claim, however, is their emphasis on using journalistic criticism to regulate the sociability of the coffeehouses. Periodicals like *The Tatler* and *The Spectator* may have rejected the pedantry of scholasticism and the insularity of the court, but they were equally opposed to the frivolity of coffeehouse society where "newsmongers," idlers, and gossips threatened to lead each other astray in temperament and values.[17]

In their role as journalists and essayists, Addison and Steele, like literature professors to come, turned to criticism to initiate a restive and autodidactic collective into the conventions of polite conversation and debate. Whether we are talking about eighteenth-century coffeehouse patrons or a twenty-first-century group of undergraduates, the assumption is that transforming opinion into insight and pleasure into politesse is the work of the trained professional with a flair for play. Blurring the boundaries between the workaday and the holiday, the literary professions paradoxically must stay in proximity of amateur sensibilities, if only to regulate them properly. The amateur, from the Latin "*amare*," to love, remains essential to the legitimation of professional literary expertise.

This point seems extendable to other disciplines that comprise an aesthetic education simply because art, music, and film also inhabit the zone between work and play in the fully administered world of late modernity. In the parlance of undergraduate advisors, "passion majors" cover the arts rendered up for disciplinary study while "parent majors" cover the natural and social sciences that feed into clear-cut professional paths. The anxiety over the idea and practice of the professional path is instructive, since it is usually cast in opposition to the indulgence of private passion. But contradiction is exactly how the disciplinary and professional contours of literary study take shape—through a fascinating dialectic of the individual passion and the collective standard.[18]

The implicit standards of professing literature in the university come into sharp relief when creative writers take up the task of teaching without awareness of ongoing scholarly conversations or membership in the professional associations that grow up around the study of literature. Roman Jakobson defended professors in no uncertain terms when he compared Vladimir Nabokov teaching literature to an elephant teaching zoology. While we all enjoy the joke, we should by now be convinced that Jakobson is, *at the very least*, half wrong. Unsurprisingly, many poets and novelists have been far better at criticism than objects and forces have been at playing physicists or elephants at playing zoologists. Creative writers have been at least as good as politicians at playing political theorists, and they are significantly ahead of the subjects of auto-ethnography engaging in its disciplinary practice, a relatively young development in the field of anthropology.

This point about the object of study becoming the agent of study goes beyond the simple fact that poets and novelists have written works of literary criticism. It pertains to the very spirit of critical writing as a creative practice with possible kinship to poetic, narrative, and dramatic utterances. If the poetic, narrative, and dramatic generally distinguish the art of the literary writer from that of the scholarly critic, then they also have the potential to distinguish the deliberate idiosyncrasy of the amateur from the necessary conventionality of the professional commentator on literature. The amateur assumes a private and particular voice—in keeping with the individualized style demanded of creative writers—rather than subordinate herself to the collective voice of the profession. If one were to simplify (and therefore also vulgarize a bit), at the heart of the Jakobson-Nabokov feud is the creative writer versus the community of scholars. The goal of the scholar is to meet the collective standard and consequently to subordinate (though not necessarily eliminate) the peculiarities of voice. The goal of the creative writer as critic is the consolidation of a rich and unique private voice fortified as much with the power of imagination as with scholarship.[19] In practice, the work of the critic overlaps with the work of the scholar. In spirit, the critic as amateur seeks the singular voice of the poet or fiction writer. Roland Barthes brings this point home when he talks of attempting a novel: "the world no longer comes to me as an object but as a writing, i.e. as a practice. I proceed to another type of knowledge (that of the Amateur)."[20]

Barthes's distinction between knowing the world as an object and knowing it as a writing practice informs our distinction between the critic's particularized voice buoyed by invention and the scholar's specialized one grounded in the sharing of an object of study with professional peers. These theoretical propositions, while always threatening to collapse in real-world situations, nevertheless have important implications for how we explain the various overlaps readily apparent in amateur and professional commentary on literature. Contributors such as Christopher Hilliard and Melanie Micir, for instance, have foregrounded persuasive instances of communal amateurism—or for that matter, amateur communities. But, as their essays show, the professional is far more defined by her membership in an established community with set standards than the amateur, who works on her own in irregular time intervals and by affiliating with loosely regulated groups.

In turn, amateurs and professionals alike address audiences who share their interests and structures of address; yet, in the absence of systematic training, amateurs refine their voices in comparatively unruly ways to those credentialed by a degree program. A critic or a scholar can be either amateur or professional; they can also find themselves shifting affiliations depending on the context or task at hand. With full recognition of this fluidity, our formulation regards criticism as more likely to be amateur in ethos than scholarship, which necessarily becomes professional in ethos in the course of satisfying the requirements of university assessment and academic publishing.

It is, of course, clear that neither literature nor the study of it can altogether dispense with the power or the centrality of the individual voice, just as it is clear that a proper historical or technical understanding of literature is impossible without the specialist standards of scholarship. The dialectic of the individual and the collective is as essential to literary studies as it is to literature itself, yet we in the discipline have given short shrift to those boundary zones between the particularized and the specialized, the private and the communal upon which amateurism alights. This collection is the first sustained attempt by a group of intellectuals to locate the rifted place of the amateur in literary thought. It is more empirical than normative—a long and wide look at what has been rather than what should be, though the latter too stirs at places, sometimes directly and sometimes through implication.

We have come to think of this collection as more of a mixtape than a reference guide. It imparts feeling as well as knowledge and attempts to inject something of the private voice into what is fundamentally a collaborative endeavor. Amateurism's secret history within disciplinary literary study surfaces through theoretical argument, personal reminiscence, historical case study, and interdisciplinary conversation across literary and media studies. Although we have concentrated our study of amateurism within the field of English-language literature, we have given a sampling of amateurism in other disciplines (film, book history, media studies) and another linguistic culture (Bengali). As with any good mixtape, the order of the essays matters and the effect, we believe, is ultimately cohesive if inevitably selective. Our hope is that this collection will bring more like-minded projects in its wake and compel readers of whatever stripe to dig further into the archives we open up (especially in Parts II and III) as well as identify new ones. Most of all, in circulating this book, we wish to extend the pleasures we have found in making amateurism our professional concern.

Which brings us to the question: Isn't this a professional study of the amateur? That's what Tom Lutz suspects in his contribution. Lutz is Professor of Creative Writing at University of California–Riverside and the editor of the *Los Angeles Review of Books*, so it's hard to say his intervention—as that of the volume on the whole—is not quite professional. Yet, as Lutz's essay shows, you can take the boy out of the country, but you can't take the country out of the boy. We find it just as hard to take the amateur out of literary criticism, no matter how much one tries to professionalize its practice. This point is partially indebted to the overtly politicized language of feminist and multicultural criticism in the late 1980s–1990s. During the height of the canon wars, proponents of identity-based critique questioned the "objectivity" of academic criticism. Instead of aspiring to impersonality, they turned to personal and autobiographical writing as tools for dismantling, or at least refusing to reproduce, a normatively white and patriarchal culture of knowledge production.[21]

In identity-oriented work, professionalism became a byword for the silencing of marginalized and deviant voices, and it is not surprising that defenses of professionalism emerged among those critics looking to defend the relative autonomy of literature from perceived political jockeying. Stanley Fish cynically saw the rejection of professionalism as one of the finest and most final marks of professionalism: "*Anti-professionalism is professionalism in its purest form*."[22] Derek Attridge will have more to say about Fish's accusation in his contribution, but, for now, we ask whether the elision of the amateur as such from these polarized debates detracted from attention to literary criticism as a genre that entwines rather than divides disciplinary and activist imperatives. In our collection, we submit for consideration a post-professional rather than an anti-professional approach to the critic as amateur.

* * *

In the history of literary criticism, the amateur appears in some expected places and in some unexpected ones. Since the essays in this collection focus, for the most part, on the late nineteenth century and beyond, the collective story that emerges here is of a period in which literary studies becomes a discipline enshrined in the university. Literary criticism, when it appears beyond the university's ambit (mostly in nonacademic media venues, print, or otherwise), dwells in breathing distance of its edifice of professionalism, though that distance varies from time to time.

Our collection opens with four essays that variously reflect upon and epitomize the enlightened innocence of amateurism. Each performs to differing degrees the unlearning of learned behaviors with respect to critical reading and writing. Taken as a group Derek Attridge's, Tom Lutz's, Ragini Tharoor Srinivasan's, and Peter McDonald's contributions could also be said to offer schematic assessments of the state of literary studies. After all, they respectively address the professionalization of literary criticism, the systematic training of eclectic readers into scholars with specialties, and the metrics of productivity used by university administrators to assess the worth of their faculty. Yet schematics is precisely what these critics chafe at, and their writing styles resist the summary description attempted here. They weave together intellectual biography with intimate anecdote, confident technical analysis with the searching desire for experiences of reading and writing that remain beyond codification.

Derek Attridge's essay "In Praise of Amateurism" reveals how deeply entangled amateurism and professionalism are by explaining how individual responses to literature underpin collective standards of reading. For Attridge, an individual response to a literary work always retains elements of the amateur. It is the uniqueness and intensity of reading as an event that inspires the entire apparatus we call professional or academic criticism. Recognizing the unpredictability of literary experience, Attridge champions what he calls "critical amateurism," a phrase that recalls Edward Said's celebration of "critical humanism" as the kind of practice that feels enabling after the onslaught on traditional humanism by high theory and the radical political culture surrounding it. "Critical amateurism," Attridge says, "would carry the impulse of the amateur reader into the professional arena; both acknowledging and seeking to enhance the singular experience of the literary work that lies at the heart of the institution to which we—students, teachers, critics, and scholars alike—belong."

Tom Lutz's visceral account of his growth and development as a young American man in a provincial location privileges the personal, even the idiosyncratic. In doing so, it also provides the crucial backstory of the shaping of an influential academic and public intellectual through his very intimate, and one might say, autodidactic relation to literature. Especially striking is the way Lutz engages with the story of a provincial youth in a far-flung corner of postcolonial India to tell his own tale of eclectic education as a curiously similar figure in the United States.

Ragini Tharoor Srinivasan locates the tussle of the amateur and the professional in a place that seems unlikely at first but which, upon deeper inspection, makes serious and urgent sense: interdisciplinary humanities study in the contemporary US academy. Anecdotally speaking, Srinivasan is fond of saying that she has two degrees in "nothing": a BA in Literature from the critical-theory inflected program at Duke—essentially a degree in theory and cultural studies—and a PhD in Rhetoric from the University of California, Berkeley. Is such interdisciplinary study the privilege of a rarefied professionalism or an ambitious form of amateurism? Further complicating this question is the range of institutional responses to interdisciplinarity: some regarding it as a prestigious line of inquiry and others dismissing it as an illegitimate form of scholarship. As she chronicles the refinement of her own critical ethos, Srinivasan comes to reexamine such responses and ultimately question their location and assumptions. Her approach fittingly follows interdisciplinarity out of the university into the experimental spaces of independent scholarship, the broad church of journalism, and the inwardness of theoretically infused life writing.

Although based in Oxford, Peter McDonald looks away from the established canons of Anglo-American criticism as he seeks to find a critical discourse and idiom sustainable for the field in the long run. He places two iconic thinkers, Rabindranath Tagore and Maurice Blanchot, into an innovative conversation that explains as well as performs his model of "creative criticism." For McDonald, creative criticism justifies itself in anti-scholastic terms as it foregrounds immediate experience over accumulated erudition. It resists the straitjackets of scholarly writing—the move to define terms, defend theses, and yield reproducible results. In the course of describing the affinities between Tagore's and Blanchot's accounts of the creative process, McDonald acknowledges both the evasiveness and utopianism inherent to creative criticism. Yet, in dark times for higher education, he contends that its very slipperiness might be inspiration for true curricular innovation.

Part II of the collection turns to historical case studies that decenter the dominant story of literary criticism's professionalization within the university in the first half of the twentieth century. The essays in this part follow familiar disciplinary practices into unfamiliar territory and recover key intellectual figures whose contributions to criticism are "amateur" insofar as they stand at a remove from the university or actively dissent from influential academic schools and styles of writing. Christopher Hilliard's essay shows how the critical and pedagogical methods of canonical figures F. R. Leavis and I. A. Richards were taken up and recontextualized by educators working with adult learners, high school students, and aspiring creative writers. His essay reveals the feedback loop of amateurism and professionalism as the institutionalization of practical criticism in a variety of classrooms created the opportunity for more amateurs to learn and alter its methods. Hilliard's wide net captures the dissemination of practical criticism as a far from trickle-down phenomenon. English teachers and student-amateurs of varying class backgrounds and interests had to renegotiate their relationship to Leavisian standards as they adapted techniques forged in the elite college classroom to their classrooms and self-made study spaces.

Rosinka Chaudhuri's essay on Bengali critic Pramatha Chaudhuri, the only one in this collection to engage at length with criticism in a non-Western language, enters deeper into the context of South-Asian aesthetics and literary thought opened by McDonald's essay. Chaudhuri's celebration of "the critic as *rasik*" in Pramatha's personality and practice is a very important one, if only because it introduces a hard-to-translate category of amateur sensibility into what is primarily a collection of engagements with Western and English-language criticism. It is possible to translate *rasik* as "aesthete," but it would be a poor and inadequate translation. There are endless shades of play, humor, and even eroticism that do not necessarily come alive in the term "aesthete," particularly with its Pre-Raphaelite connotations in the context of English literary criticism. While its etymology goes back to the classical Sanskrit idea of *rasa*, literally meaning "juice" or "taste" but really implying aesthetic flavor, the *rasik* in Bangla implies something of a bon vivant, of the arts as much as of life. Chaudhuri situates Pramatha, who distanced himself quickly from university life, within the booming sphere of Bengali letters where he became an influential writer, editor, and publisher. In reassessing his career, she simultaneously reflects upon the relation of the *rasik* to concepts of amateurism, criticism, and de-professionalization as espoused by Barthes and Theodor Adorno.

For Mimi Winick, "sophisticated amateurism" flavors the critical style of androgynous intellectual, Vernon Lee. Drawing on queer theories of sophistication, Winick argues that Lee cultivated a highly self-conscious mode of authority that foiled the gendered male consolidation of professional expertise taking place in the university. Sophisticated amateurism stands in oblique relationship to the academy by introducing aberrant forms of affection and attachment into scholarship's scientific methods and specialist vocabularies. Notably, such strategies also differentiate themselves from a naive amateurism incapable of recognizing that even ordinary, untrained engagements with literature and culture can come to exhibit distinct patterns and conventions. Winick's reappraisal of the continuities between Lee's criticism and fiction shows how Lee positioned herself against, among others, William James, one of the most esteemed scholars of her era. Attacking his philosophy of pragmatism as a spurious redefinition of truth, Lee deploys sophistication against what she takes to be the sophistry of pragmatist argument.

Part III of *The Critic as Amateur* remains oriented to critical figures and networks that bring amateurism and professionalism into unpredictable configurations. However, it also focalizes the entanglements of high- and middlebrow culture as each essay brings the history of criticism into conversation with the history of media. Zlatina Nikolova and Christopher Townsend's essay on Dorothy Richardson and *Close Up* shows us how a prominent little magazine brought modernism and mass culture together by recruiting writers from the literary avant-garde and the nascent commercial film industries. Like Lee, Richardson is a critic better known for her fiction, yet Nikolova and Townsend urge us to see her through the very particular lens of her film criticism. Rather than simply declare Richardson an amateur film critic, Nikolova and Townsend's essay opens into an extensive accounting of the amateur and professional exchanges forged by *Close Up*. Their argument rejects the premise that amateurism and professionalism can be fixed identities in a milieu where "contributors from diverse fields exchanged or intercalated roles." Such contributors include women like Richardson, whose criticism derived from combining their experience as professional writers with their unschooled positions as film spectators, and (mostly) men who worked in filmmaking as cinematographers and editors but had little experience in writing for publication. Nikolova and Townsend compare the styles of criticism that evolve through the little magazine and find that Richardson's style assumes a more anthropological than aesthetic mode of interpretation. By emphasizing reception over production, she becomes an important anthropologist of popular film culture in Britain in the 1920s.

When Nikolova and Townsend centralize Richardson's film criticism, they at once contribute new understandings of her reputation to two fields—literary studies and film studies. They argue that the influence of cinematic techniques on her modernist fiction is overstated given the lack of demonstrable interest in those techniques in her film criticism. In turn, they find that Richardson's style foreshadows a professionalized journalistic film criticism that would contrast the specialized criticism taking shape among industry technicians. Such a mainstream criticism traded technical expertise in the medium for camaraderie with lay audiences who regarded "the movies" as a novel topic of conversation and consumption.

We see a similar rise of the middlebrow over and against the professionalization of disciplinary literary study in Emily Bloom's essay on the BBC radio program "New Judgment." Working at the intersection of communications studies and literary studies, Bloom turns to the airwaves to get beyond the disciplinary circuits of the university and explore possibilities for a popular literary criticism directed at mass audiences. Attentive to how a new medium, in this case radio, pushed writers like Stephen Spender, Elizabeth Bowen, and Seán O'Faoláin outside their comfort zones, Bloom absorbingly details how a radiogenic literary criticism demanded new genres of critical writing, like the feature broadcast, and more relatable models of authority than the ivory tower professor.

If radio and film made early-to-mid-twentieth-century literary critics amateurs in new media, Melanie Micir shows how feminist small presses have survived since the 1970s thanks to amateur forms of labor in the venerable medium of print. Such forms of labor are rooted in "energy and enthusiasm" rather than "expertise or even experience." They also demand a volunteerism that can be at odds with the priorities of professional recognition, advancement, and compensation. Micir's comprehensive foray into feminist publishing projects—presses, subscription services, collections— broadens the definition of criticism to include the judgments entailed in literary curation, recovering and publishing out-of-print titles and collecting rare books by women. Her expanded definition of criticism calls into question the university's or even journalism's monopoly on it and points to a number of alternative routes by which feminist publishers thrive on a shoestring budget. Their intimate publics meet up with crowdsourced digital platforms; their print audience grows thanks to their agility with digital forms of opinion sharing: blogs, social media posts, and monthly recommendations sent right to one's inbox.

Finally, Kara Wittman's essay on the undergraduate student stands as the epilogue to the entire collection. The undergraduate—even the one specializing in literature—is an amateur by almost any definition. Wittman's essay provides insight into how teachers may make rich use of that amateurism. Is undergraduate training meant to initiate a shift away from amateurism? Or does such training preserve amateurism as a tabula rasa for the kind of originality that quickly becomes jaded within the established practices of academic training? Wittman's identification of the paradoxes surrounding original argument in literary studies throws into relief the various convictions professed across the arc of the collection. By returning to the trenches of the classroom, she finds a deep connection between the practices of criticism outlined in previous essays and the desire to experience something again for the first time.

## The purpose of criticism

Time after time, this volume raises questions of purpose and motivation. "What is it all for?" asks Peter McDonald. "Why do we love what we love?" asks Tom Lutz. In their own ways, each of these essays broaches the project of criticism as a matter of education. And education is never reducible to acquiring a technique or mastering a skill set. It is about meeting our emotional as well as intellectual needs. It is about finding meaning in what we do over a lifetime. In that sense, as Kara Wittman puts it, we are all in some way beginning regardless of our stage in school, professional achievements, or phase of life.

"Treating the whole person" is an approach gaining more and more traction in modern psychology and integrative medicine. It represents a turn to mind-body health that is actually a professional acknowledgment of modern medicine's limited toolbox. Treating symptoms, managing diseases, and prescribing drug therapies are what physicians primarily do, but even they are returning to categories like "well-being" and "holistic health" in their practices. Well-being, as humanists know all too well, has its Western origins in Aristotle's concept of *Eudaemonia*, a kind of thriving that is impossible to define scientifically or measure empirically. Certainly, what sounds progressive in the medical profession might sound like old hat to liberal humanists—all the way from the conservative wing of the discipline to the left-leaning humanists trained in "the historicist-contextualist paradigm."[23] Regardless of one's stance on literary study's capacity to mold better or happier people, ruling out the capacity of literature to console, rile up, or provide ethical direction is to miss out critically on the myriad ways whole people read and what they read for.[24]

This collection might alternatively have been called "Criticism for the Whole Person" because we are aiming to bring the professionalized practice of criticism back to its foundations in the experience of reading, the search for understanding, the finding and refining of one's own voice, and the lending of that voice to social advocacy. If humanities scholars ignore or implicitly diminish these foundations, we will see ourselves quickly usurped by professionals all too eager to make the whole person their bread and butter. Beth Blum writes of the "intelligent self-help" industry as rivaling the university by claiming to supply the cure for what ails us. Such promises would embarrass or incense most university-based scholars of the humanities.[25] Her primary example is Alain de Botton whose anti-academic polemics exploit the friction between high- and middlebrow culture. De Botton baldly states:

> Our most celebrated intellectual institutions rarely consent to ask, let alone to answer, the most serious questions of the soul.

> Oprah Winfrey may not provide the deepest possible analysis of the human condition, but her questions are often more probing and meaningful than those posed by Ivy League professors in the humanities.[26]

This from an article titled "Can Tolstoy Save Your Marriage?" published in *The Wall Street Journal*. De Botton plays to a conservative audience's attraction to the classics and plays off a middlebrow sensibility responsive to the notion that practical use outweighs disinterested study.

Indeed de Botton's alternative educational institution, *The School of Life* continues in the traditions of such middlebrow institutions as Oprah's Book Club and its predecessor The-Book-of-the-Month Club, which as Janice Radway argues, imagine and foster a community of "general readers" often in direct opposition to an academic readership judged "focused, professional, technical, and specialized."[27] Radway's ethnography of the club shows how middlebrow culture evolves into a counter-practice against the properly administered passion (to recall Lynch) of disciplinary literary studies and the aloofness of high culture periodicals like *The New Yorker, The Nation*, and the *Partisan Review*. An organization born in the United States in 1926 and still in operation today, the-Book-of-the-Month Club, in Radway's Althusserian vocabulary, "hailed" its members as "subjects with pressing emotional needs and desires produced by their particular historical situation."[28] De Botton's appeal takes much the same form but, despite the invocation of Oprah, carefully de-feminizes self-help by making it "intelligent."

De Botton appeals to the great, mostly male, authors and proclaims his categorical alliance with—and the university's abdication of—the highest values: "The modern university has achieved unparalleled expertise in imparting factual information about culture, but it remains wholly uninterested in training students to use culture as a repertoire of wisdom."[29] Wisdom. This is a notoriously difficult word to define. For de Botton, it aligns truth with that which is "inwardly beneficial."[30] Not many literature professors would subordinate the truth to that which makes us feel good. Yet de Botton is not wrong about the tension between a university humanities education and middlebrow desires; nor is he wrong about the tension between culture as an object of study and culture as a repertoire of wisdom.

Talcott Parsons, sociologist and Max Weber's English-language translator, foreshadowed this incompatibility back in 1939 when he identified the peculiar structure of professional authority. Such authority, he argued, derives not from a manifestation of "superior 'wisdom' in general or of higher moral character. It is rather based on the superior 'technical competence' of the professional man."[31] For Alfred North Whitehead, "the discoveries of the nineteenth century were in the direction of professionalism, so that we are left with no expansion of wisdom and with greater need of it."[32] Such an accentuation of technical competence is what currently divides the scholar from the critic in Joseph North's estimation.[33] If the scholar is the one who analyzes culture and the critic is the one who intervenes in it, it is fair to say that when we act as critics, we are making a generalized bid for wisdom that exceeds our technical competence in a particular theory, period, or geography. When we cast ourselves as amateur, and study past intellectual figures who have claimed the mantle of amateurism, we return what we know as scholars "on holiday" to the generality of life.

Reclaiming the general might be one way in which this collection echoes the early twentieth-century paradigm of criticism, which North traces via I. A. Richards and F. R. Leavis, and characterizes as a particularly successful yoking of specialist techniques to matters of widespread concern.[34] Leavis made so successful a case for humanistic criticism as the core of a liberal arts education precisely because he was able to satisfy simultaneously the technical demands and ethical rationales of the modern research university. *The School of Life* smuggles the highbrow generality of criticism into the middlebrow desires of the general reader. The aim of this happy synthesis is to fill the vacuum created by the technocratic turn of humanities education in the university. Yet, as Blum shows, the corporate university is all too happy to marry technocracy to a commodified notion of well-being by jumping on the self-help bandwagon. She cites the creation of wellness centers on campus, the redesign of undergraduate courses in a therapeutic and instrumental "how to" vein, and the permeation of all sectors of the university with "complex advice networks" aimed at mitigating the "effects of deeper systemic problems: intensifying competition, a fractured tenure system, racial inequity, and ever-expanding job precarity."[35]

In this brave new world of university life, wisdom, truth, and love grow more elusive not from having disappeared from the discourse on education but from having proliferated through so many rival advice networks. Our collection takes some of these networks as case studies in the process of trying to regain a grip on the relationship between disciplinary knowledge and general states of human flourishing. Such a task has involved, contra de Botton, reflecting on the ways in which our objects of study might become repertoires of genuine wisdom in a work culture bent toward entrepreneurial innovation and quantifiable proof of productivity. *The Critic as Amateur* affirms the need for literary and cultural critics to use what is specialized about our work—our professional expertise—to reach people where they live. Such outreach may take the form of teaching undergraduates in general education courses, undertaking journalistic projects, founding small presses, forging networks between the university and other institutions of education, or simply making a case in written form for the necessity of an aesthetic education. This book shows how much humanities professionals are already doing by way of criticism in an expanded register, but it also proposes we might be doing our best work when we feel at our most amateur.

What is it all for? Why do we love what we love? Writing about the critic as amateur has released these questions into a collection made primarily for an academic audience, but with the hope that general readers will find some value in it too. We invite whoever picks up this book to think with us about how the relationship between the academic and the general reader evolved into one of mutual suspicion. Most importantly, we look to the following essays for a criticism that injects vulnerability, passion, and even ignorance into expertise.

## Notes

1 Nico Stehr, *Knowledge Societies* (London: Sage Publications, 1994), 6.

2 For an early and influential example of celebratory rhetoric about the web, see Clay Shirky, *Here Comes Everybody* (New York: Penguin, 2008). For explanations of lay expertise and networked expertise, see Reiner Grundmann, "The Problem of Expertise in Knowledge Societies," *Minerva* 55, no. 1 (2017): 25–48 and Henry Jenkins, *Convergence Culture: Where Old and New Media Collide* (New York: New York University Press, 2006).

3 For a discussion of this phenomenon with respect to contemporary literature specifically, see Aarthi Vadde, "Amateur Creativity: Contemporary Literature and the Digital Publishing Scene," *New Literary History* 48, no. 1 (2017): 27–51.

4 Pankaj Mishra, "Edmund Wilson in Benares," *New York Review of Books*, April 9, 1998. Available online: https://www.nybooks.com/articles/1998/04/09/edmund-wilson-in-benares/.

5 For more on these outlets, see Lisa Nakamura, "Words with Friends: Socially Networked Reading on *Goodreads*," *PMLA* 128, no. 1 (January 2013): 238–243; Houman Bareket, Robert Barry, and David Winters, eds., *The Digital Critic: Literary Culture Online* (New York: OR Books, 2017); Evan Kindley, "Little Magazines, Blogs, and Literary Media," in *American Literature in Transition*, ed. Rachel Greenwald Smith (Cambridge: Cambridge University Press, 2018), 345–359.

6 Rani Molla, "Buzzfeed is Losing Website Traffic as Readers Head for More Traditional News Media," November 30, 2017. Available online: https://www.recode.net/2017/11/30/16709310/buzzfeed-losing-web-traffic-readers-layoffs-uniques-prefer-news-over-viral-sites. The decline in Buzzfeed's traffic is as follows: "69.8 million U.S. readers in October [2017], a 10 percent drop from the 77.4 million readers it drew in October 2016, and a 12 percent drop from 2015 when it had 79.3 million readers, according to comScore data."

7 Josephine M. Guy and Ian Small, "The British 'Man of Letters' and the Rise of the Professional," in *The Cambridge History of Literary Criticism*, ed. A. Walton Litz, Louis Menand, and Lawrence Rainey (Cambridge: Cambridge University Press, 2000), 7:385. As Rónán McDonald argues, anxieties over literary criticism's association with "the dilettantism and impressionism of the amateur critic" continue to this very day. Such fears led many of its leading practitioners (for example, I. A. Richards and Northrop Frye) to devise methods that would "scientize the field." Rónán McDonald, ed., *The Values of Literary Studies* (Cambridge: Cambridge University Press, 2015), 8.

8 Quoted in Marjorie Garber, *Academic Instincts* (Princeton, NJ: Princeton University Press, 2001), 15. Ironically enough, Guy and Small dub Murry an amateur critic in the tradition of the man of letters precisely because he drew on his personal authority to make such rhetorically flamboyant judgments.

9 In making these claims, we join scholars like Jonathan Rose and Rachel Sagner Buurma and Laura Heffernan who have advocated for a disciplinary history of English literary study that restores the centrality of non-elite institutions and learners. See Jonathan Rose,

*The Intellectual Life of the British Working-Classes* (New Haven, CT: Yale University Press, 2002) and Rachel Sagner Buurma and Laura Heffernan, "The Classroom in the Canon: T.S. Eliot's Modern English Literature Extension Course for Working People and *The Sacred Wood*," *PMLA* 133, no. 2 (2018): 264–281.

10 The cost of scientific research, admittedly, has not stopped climate change deniers, groups against vaccination, and other skeptics of established scientific findings. However, such groups' narratives are more likely to be classified as misinformation or politicized propaganda than the literary opinions of nonexpert readers are.

11 Michael Wood, *Literature and the Taste of Knowledge* (Cambridge: Cambridge University Press, 2005), 54.

12 Ibid., 52.

13 Ibid., 59.

14 Deidre Lynch, *Loving Literature* (Chicago: University of Chicago Press, 2015), 4.

15 Ibid., 5.

16 Joseph Addison, *The Spectator*, ed. Donald F. Bond, 5 vols. (Oxford: Oxford University Press, 1965), 10, I:44.

17 See Brian William Cowan, "Mr. Spectator and the Coffeehouse Public Sphere," *Eighteenth-century Studies* 37, no. 3 (2004): 352–353 and Jon Mee, *Conversable Worlds* (Oxford: Oxford University Press, 2011), 39.

18 Helen Small examines this dialectic between individual response and collective standards in all its philosophically contentious detail in *The Value of the Humanities* (Oxford: Oxford University Press, 2013), 162.

19 Saikat Majumdar, "The Critic as Amateur," *New Literary History* 48, no. 1 (2017): 1–25.

20 Roland Barthes, "Longtemps, je me suis couché de bonne heure ...," in *The Rustle of Language*, trans. Richard Howard (Berkeley: University of California Press, 1989), 289.

21 For an influential example of such criticism, see Diane P. Freedman, Olivia Frey, and Frances Murphy Zauhar, eds., *The Intimate Critique: Autobiographical Literary Criticism* (Durham, NC: Duke University Press, 1993).

22 Stanley Fish, *Doing What Comes Naturally: Change, Rhetoric, and the Practice of Theory in Literary and Legal Studies* (Durham, NC: Duke University Press, 1989), 245.

23 Joseph North, *Literary Criticism: A Concise Political History* (Cambridge, MA: Harvard University Press, 2017).

24 There is, of course, an ongoing conversation about the merits of critique and postcritique in literary studies. Michael Warner's

"Uncritical Reading," in *Polemic*, ed. Jane Gallop (New York: Routledge, 2004) and Rita Felski's body of work from *The Uses of Literature* (Oxford: Wiley-Blackwell, 2008) onward are key guides for integrating middlebrow styles of reading into new reading methods like uncritical reading or postcritique. In this collection, we are also interested in the ways that middlebrow reading refuses to be assimilated into professional practices. Merve Emre facetiously calls such reading practices bad in *Paraliterary: The Making of Bad Readers in Postwar America* (Chicago: University of Chicago Press, 2017).

25 Beth Blum, "The Self-helpification of Academe," *The Chronicle of Higher Education*, July 8, 2018. Available online: https://www.chronicle.com/article/The-Self-Helpification-of/243861?key=d70YTgktpgcK7_T5bad8tW_q9Vg3M9PbtHLjGTx5g7rXjhWW06_jJI0_00EPRb_vQVZvY3RrdGdJeE05T0pTUjBZWTM3cFZuN1U5SkxxYjZXWkUzSlJ5NW5Yaw.

26 Alain de Botton, "Can Tolstoy Save Your Marriage?" *The Wall Street Journal*, December 18, 2010. Available online: https://www.wsj.com/articles/SB10001424052748704828104576021713651690094.

27 Janice Radway, *A Feeling for Books* (Chapel Hill and London: UNC Press, 1997), 10.

28 Ibid., 263.

29 de Botton, "Tolstoy," n.p.

30 Ibid.

31 Talcott Parsons, "The Professions and Social Structure," *Social Forces* 17, no. 4 (1939): 460. For more on Parsons in relationship to the critic as amateur, see Melanie Micir and Aarthi Vadde, "Obliterature: Toward an Amateur Criticism," *Modernism/Modernity* 24, no. 3 (2018): 511–543.

32 Alfred North Whitehead, *Science and the Modern World* (1925; New York: Free Press, 1967), 198.

33 North, *Literary Criticism*, 12.

34 Ibid., 180.

35 Blum, "Self-helpification," n.p.

# Bibliography

Addison, Joseph. *The Spectator*. Edited by Donald F. Bond. 5 vols. Oxford: Oxford University Press, 1965, 10, I:44.

Bareket, Houman, Robert Barry, and David Winters, eds. *The Digital Critic: Literary Culture Online*. New York: OR Books, 2017.

Barthes, Roland. "Longtemps, je me suis couché de bonne heure …." In *The Rustle of Language*, trans. Richard Howard. Berkeley: University of California Press, 1989.

Blum, Beth. "The Self-helpification of Academe." *The Chronicle of Higher Education*. July 8, 2018. Available online: https://www.chronicle.com/article/The-Self-Helpification-of/243861?key=d70YTgktpgcK7_T5bad8tW_q9Vg3M9PbtHLjGTx5g7rXjhWW06_jJI0_00EPRb_vQVZvY3RrdGdJeE05T0pTUjBZWTM3cFZuN1U5SkxxYjZXWkUzSlJ5NW5Yaw (accessed August 18, 2018).

Buurma, Rachel Sagner and Laura Heffernan. "The Classroom in the Canon: T.S. Eliot's Modern English Literature Extension Course for Working People and *The Sacred Wood*." *PMLA* 133, no. 2 (2018): 264–281.

Cowan, Brian William. "Mr. Spectator and the Coffeehouse Public Sphere." *Eighteenth-century Studies* 37, no. 3 (2004): 345–366.

De Botton, Alain. "Can Tolstoy Save Your Marriage." *The Wall Street Journal*. December 18, 2010. Available online: https://www.wsj.com/articles/SB10001424052748704828104576021713651690094 (accessed August 18, 2018).

Emre, Merve. *Paraliterary: The Making of Bad Readers in Postwar America*. Chicago: University of Chicago Press, 2017.

Felski, Rita. *The Uses of Literature*. Oxford: Wiley-Blackwell, 2008.

Freedman, Diane P., Olivia Frey, and Frances Murphy Zauhar, eds. *The Intimate Critique: Autobiographical Literary Criticism*. Durham, NC: Duke University Press, 1993.

Garber, Marjorie. *Academic Instincts*. Princeton, NJ: Princeton University Press, 2001.

Grundmann, Reiner. "The Problem of Expertise in Knowledge Societies." *Minerva* 55, no. 1 (2017): 25–48.

Guy, Josephine M. and Ian Small. "The British 'Man of Letters' and the Rise of the Professional." In *The Cambridge History of Literary Criticism*, edited by A. Walton Litz, Louis Menand, and Lawrence Rainey, 377–388. Vol. 7. Cambridge: Cambridge University Press, 2000.

Jenkins, Henry. *Convergence Culture: Where Old and New Media Collide*. New York: New York University Press, 2006.

Kindley, Evan. "Little Magazines, Blogs, and Literary Media." In *American Literature in Transition*, edited by Rachel Greenwald Smith. Cambridge: Cambridge University Press, 2018.

Lynch, Deidre. *Loving Literature*. Chicago: University of Chicago Press, 2015.

Majumdar, Saikat. "The Critic as Amateur." *New Literary History* 48, no. 1 (2017): 1–25.

McDonald, Rónán, ed. *The Values of Literary Studies*. Cambridge: Cambridge University Press, 2015.
Mee, Jon. *Conversable Worlds*. Oxford: Oxford University Press, 2011.
Micir, Melanie and Aarthi Vadde. "Obliterature: Toward an Amateur Criticism." *Modernism/Modernity* 24, no. 3 (2018): 511–543.
Mishra, Pankaj. "Edmund Wilson in Benares." *New York Review of Books*. April 9, 1998. Available online: https://www.nybooks.com/articles/1998/04/09/edmund-wilson-in-benares/ (accessed June 9, 2018).
Molla, Rani. "Buzzfeed Is Losing Website Traffic as Readers Head for More Traditional News Media." *Recode*. November 30, 2017. Available online: https://www.recode.net/2017/11/30/16709310/buzzfeed-losing-web-traffic-readers-layoffs-uniques-prefer-news-over-viral-sites (accessed June 9, 2018).
Nakamura, Lisa. "Words with Friends: Socially Networked Reading on *Goodreads*." *PMLA* 128, no. 1 (January 2013): 238–243.
North, Joseph. *Literary Criticism: A Concise Political History*. Cambridge, MA: Harvard University Press, 2017.
Parsons, Talcott. "The Professions and Social Structure." *Social Forces* 17, no. 4 (1939): 457–467.
Radway, Janice. *A Feeling for Books*. Chapel Hill and London: UNC Press, 1997.
Rose, Jonathan. *The Intellectual Life of the British Working-Classes*. New Haven, CT: Yale University Press, 2002.
Shirky, Clay. *Here Comes Everybody*. New York: Penguin, 2008.
Small, Helen. *The Value of the Humanities*. Oxford: Oxford University Press, 2013.
Sontag, Susan. *Against Interpretation and Other Essays*. New York: Picador, 2001.
Vadde, Aarthi. "Amateur Creativity: Contemporary Literature and the Digital Publishing Scene." *New Literary History* 48, no. 1 (2017): 27–51.
Warner, Michael. "Uncritical Reading." In *Polemic*, edited by Jane Gallop. New York: Routledge, 2004.
Whitehead, Alfred North. *Science and the Modern World*. 1925. New York: Free Press, 1967.
Wood, Michael. *Literature and the Taste of Knowledge*. Cambridge: Cambridge University Press, 2005.

# PART ONE

# The Amateur Impulse

# 1

# In Praise of Amateurism

*Derek Attridge*

## Amateurism vs. professionalism

The figure designated by the term "amateur" has been the object of both praise and blame for two centuries. At first (in the late eighteenth century) a neutral term close to its French meaning, "lover" or "devotee," it wasn't long before it was being used to make a distinction between those who carry out an activity as professionals and those who don't—and this distinction led to the possibility of a pejorative sense for the word and thence to the emergence in the second half of the nineteenth century of the distinctly derogatory term "amateurish." The more obvious the need for professional expertise in a particular activity, the stronger the criticism implied in calling someone an amateur: an "amateur train-spotter" is almost a tautology, an "amateur actor" carries a hint of disparagement, and "amateur surgeon" is wholly condemnatory.

But there is also a long history of assuming that the nonprofessional is to be *preferred* to the professional. This idea is much older than the word "amateur" itself. It is there in Plato's representation of the rhapsode Ion in the dialogue of that name in which Socrates makes fun of the professional performer of Homeric epic who claims to be an expert but can't say what it is he is an expert in; it is reflected in the many self-deprecating comments made by poets from antiquity to the present (the rhetorical trope of *recusatio* is one version of this apologetic stance); it governs the Renaissance ideal of the gentleman who carries out difficult tasks with easy *sprezzatura*. In this latter instance, its close association with class is evident: as a gentleman (and it was unquestionably a masculine accomplishment) you demonstrated your superiority to the lower echelons of society by doing naturally what they had to work diligently and obviously at.

These class implications lingered until the recent past and perhaps linger still in certain quarters. Sport is one example. I grew up in South Africa playing rugby union, a strictly amateur game, and was expected to regard the professionals who played the rugby league version of the sport as distinctly ill-bred. The slow acceptance of professional athletes into the Olympic Games during the course of the twentieth century testifies to similar class issues. Looked at from this angle, only those who can afford to pursue a sport or a study project without financial recompense are able to be true amateurs.[1] Praise of amateurism may not be as unprejudiced a posture as it seems.

A related phenomenon is the mistrust of the expert.[2] Here is the blurb for a recent book as it appears on Amazon:

> Modern life is being destroyed by experts and professionals. We have lost our amateur spirit and need to rediscover the radical and liberating pleasure of doing things we love. In *The Amateur*, thinker Andy Merrifield shows us how the many spheres of our lives—work, knowledge, cities, politics—have fallen into the hands of box tickers, bean counters and rule followers.[3]

This mistrust was disastrously evident in the campaign in favor of Brexit, when predictions of the dire economic effects of Britain's departure from the European Union were dismissed by populist politicians on the grounds that they were the not-to-be-believed utterances of experts, and similar rejections of available knowledge have proved politically useful on a number of other occasions around the world, not least in the most recent US presidential campaign as well as in denials of the human responsibility for climate change

The prizing of the amateur has been in evidence in British culture (and many other cultures) over a long period. The enduring Romantic ideal of organic wholeness influentially advanced by Schiller is opposed to the specialization that cultivates only one aspect of human potential, while Wordsworth's related attack on the meddling intellect that murders to dissect has had numerous echoes since the beginning of the nineteenth century. The Victorian age was the great era of the prominent amateur; the men we call the "Victorian sages" did not acquire their eminence through any professional association or endorsement but through their own achievements.

The field of literary study has been particularly marked by this tendency. Doubts about literature as an academic subject produced much opposition to its acceptance as a legitimate subject for university study, and the hostilities did not end when its supporters were victorious. In 1937, for instance, Stephen Potter published *The Muse in Chains*, whose title gives a clear pointer to its argument, and in 1969 John Gross brought out, to wide acclaim, *The Rise and Fall of the Man of Letters* in which he lamented the disappearance of the taste-making literary colossus under the onslaught of academics and experts.[4] Exactly when this was supposed to have happened remains unclear; Gross asserts that the founding of *The Review of English Studies* in 1925 indicated that "the academic *apparatchiks* were in full command" (189), but he also finds professionalism rearing its blood-drained head in earlier centuries. Some of the most heavy-hitting literary critics of the mid-twentieth century, F. R. Leavis, R. P. Blackmur, and Kenneth Burke among them, had a queasy relationship with academic specialisms,[5] and the widespread resistance to the influx of theoretical writing in the latter part of the same century often reflected a distaste for technical terminology deemed to be distant from the simpler and more genuine expressions of literary appreciation.[6]

Echoing these diagnoses, but from a very different perspective, Terry Eagleton argues in the *Function of Criticism* that "the founding of English as a university 'discipline' [...] entailed a professionalization of literary studies which was quite alien to the [Victorian] sage's 'amateur' outlook, and more resolutely specialist than the man of letters could afford to be."[7] He continues, "Criticism achieved security by committing political suicide; its moment of academic institutionalization is also the moment of its effective demise as a socially active force." Within academic English, the conflict between "amateur" and "professional" was to continue, transposed into a quarrel between "criticism" and "scholarship" (65). *In Loving Literature: A Cultural History*, Deidre Shauna

Lynch traces the history of the idea that literary works are things we might love, and, although she stops her narrative just before the introduction of English literature into the university curriculum, she notes the tension between the two conceptions of literary study embodied in its academic institutionalization:

> Our pursuits of rigor or campaigns for a new professionalism have often been shadowed by expressions of nostalgia for a past ostensibly readier to acknowledge that the project of really understanding literature necessarily eludes the grasp of expert cultures—readier to acknowledge that literature involves readers' hearts as well as minds, and their sensibility as well as training.[8]

Some commentators on this tension between heart and head regard it as not simply an opposition between two very different approaches to literature but as the manifestation of a more complicated relationship. One such was Stanley Fish, who, in a set of essays collected in *Doing What Comes Naturally* (1989), set his sights on the question of the bad odor into which the idea of professionalism appeared to have fallen.[9] Of these essays, the one most fully relevant to the question of amateurism bears the title "Anti-professionalism" and reaches the characteristically Fishian conclusion that "anti-professionalism is professionalism in its purest form" (245): in other words, expressing antagonism toward the inroads of the bean counters and box-tickers, the narrow specialists and the promotion-seeking game-players, is a quintessential gesture of the academic professional. Furthermore, Fish argues that this apparently self-contradictory state of affairs is not one we should object to, since it is a manifestation of the paradox by which we live our lives, wholly determined by the conditions and conventions of our place and time yet unavoidably operating on the assumption that we are not. Amateurism understood in this way, to extrapolate from Fish's argument, is the belief that we can best function as fully active and astute human beings by trusting in our own free exercise of powers and shunning the narrowness of disciplinary formations and the lure of financial reward. And this belief is, Fish claims, at the center of our professional activities and principles, since not to hold it would be to surrender to helplessness in the face of our determining context.

Bruce Robbins also argues that it is too simple to oppose the amateur, in the guise of the "public intellectual," to the professional. "There are no more intellectuals today, we are told," he writes in *Secular Vocations*, or else there soon will be none, largely because there is no longer room for them in our compartmentalized, commodified, bureaucratized society. Society today makes room only for professionals—credentialed carriers of institutionally defined expertise who sell their commodity on the market, academic or otherwise, and are thus constitutionally incapable of carrying on the intellectuals' public, independent, critical functions.[10]

Robbins's challenge to this view begins with two chapters that complicate the simple opposition between the amateur intellectual and the professional academic, the first an analysis of the film western *The Professionals* and the second, partly in response to Fish, a discussion of the "professionalizing of literary criticism."[11] Although he is more receptive to the possibility of political action on the part of the professional academic than Fish (or Eagleton), Robbins, too, sees the stance of anti-professionalism as an aspect of professionalism. Professional literary critics, he argues, "adopt [...] an anti-professional point of view which seems capable of representing and bestowing the legitimacy they fear they lack," concluding that "anti-professionalism is a ritual of professional legitimation" (74).

Marjorie Garber echoes these refusals of an absolute distinction between amateur and professional, though in a more sweeping manner: "What is most fascinating is the way in which these terms circulate to make the fortunes of the one rise higher than the fortunes of the other, while determinedly resisting the sense that one is always the necessary condition for the other." And she adds a further twist: "Not only are they mutually interconnected. Part of their power comes from the disavowal of the close affinity between them."[12] It would be impossible to intertwine the two apparently opposing attitudes more intimately than this.

## The amateur impulse

To write in praise of amateurism in literary studies, then, is to plunge into this already full stream of debate and dissension. My aim is to identify what might be valuable about the amateur impulse without making myself complicit either with the naïve view of the professional and the expert as blights on the living organism of literary appreciation or with the sophisticated view that to do so is merely a typical expression of professionalism. It is easy but not very interesting to condemn the excesses of professionalism, such as the overuse of technical terminology, the slavish following of critical fashion, or the prioritizing of peer recognition and financial reward over genuine inquiry, and this kind of objection, as Fish, Robbins, and others have shown, is indeed part and parcel of the discourse of professionalism itself. If to be professional in one's dealings with literature is to be aware of these dangers while acknowledging, and attempting to embody in one's work, such virtues as objectivity, careful argument, scrupulous and thorough research, responsible treatment of sources, and honorable behavior vis-à-vis one's colleagues, it is a label I willingly own up to. How, then, is it possible to praise the amateur impulse in literary studies without falling into either of the traps I have sketched and doing so in a way that avoids undervaluing the real virtues of professionalism?

Let us first consider the vast professional edifice that has grown up around literature. Very familiar are the various institutions involved in the publishing industry, producing both works of literature and works about literature: the agents who mediate between authors and publishers, the teams of editors, designers, production managers, proofers, indexers, and others who convert manuscripts into books ready for the press, the printing and distribution industry that produces and disseminates the book once it is made, the marketers who advertise it, the booksellers who get it to the reading public, the reviewers who assess it, and the lawyers who guard its copyright and pounce on anyone they deem guilty of plagiarism. Then there is the academic arena: the scholars who undertake research into literature or use literature as evidence, the journals that publish reviews and articles on literary topics, the libraries that hold copies of books for general reading and materials for scholars to consult, the universities that house and foster literary research, the academies, institutes, and subject associations that promote literary study, the workshops, conferences, and invited talks at which literature and the investigation of literature are discussed. A further huge field is that of education: the teachers, students, examiners, administrators, and writers of textbooks who enable works of literature to reach each successive generation, and the schools and colleges in which literary education takes place. We may add to all these the second-hand bookshops and auction houses selling rare manuscripts and editions that find their way into collectors' and libraries' holdings. Literary works also play a major role in the world of theater, which employs actors, directors, designers, and front-of-house staff, and the world of cinema, which has an even larger array of employees. All these activities require buildings to be built, serviced, and maintained; finances to be organized and maintained; and personnel to be trained and provided with the necessaries of employment. This list, lengthy though it is, is far from exhausting the catalog of occupations and institutions that make possible the circulation, consumption, and study of literature.[13]

Now let us visualize a series of scenes: a man sitting on a bench on a sunny afternoon with an engrossing novel in his hands; a woman in her living room reciting a favorite poem to a visiting friend; a theatergoer convulsed with laughter at a witty riposte from a character on stage. And let us assume that these people are not associated with one of the institutions listed in the previous paragraph or any other branch of literary professionalism: each of them qualifies as an amateur responding to a literary work. What is the connection between these scenes and the massive enterprise that constitutes the literary profession? My answer is straightforward: the latter would not exist without the former.[14] Were it not for the experience of an individual reading, hearing, or seeing a literary work, an experience repeated countless times through history and across geographical spaces and social classes, there would be no libraries of literary works; no literature classes or degrees; no funding for literary research; no call for literary editions, histories, biographies or exegeses; no literary academics, journals, or presses.

I've taken the case at the opposite pole of the professional engagement with literary works, the out-and-out amateur, but there is no reason why we should regard an amateur response as limited to this category: professionals in the literature business, and I include myself, when not grubbing in libraries, holding forth in classrooms, speaking at conferences, writing our articles and books, and so on, may well pick up a novel to read for the pleasure it brings, enjoy a colleague's recitation of a poem, or laugh at a comic retort on stage, without doing so in what might be thought of as a "professional" manner. The individual in question may be an expert in stylistics or literary history or practical criticism, and he or she may be a professor or a journalist or a reviewer, but in the moment of engagement with the words of the text this expertise takes second place to the singular, intimate, unpredictable response to the literary work.

This is the point at which it is important to bear in mind the inadequacy of the view that the amateur is opposed to the professional and the expert through being untainted by external influences and free to act as a completely autonomous being. It would be wrong, and retrograde, to regard the moment of individual engagement with the text as a moment of pure literary appreciation, the subject liberated from the constraints of culture and convention interacting with the words, or the genius, of the author. Every reading act, which is also a reading event, is undertaken by an entity constituted by a complex of cultural knowledges, habits, predilections, and aversions; though we would normally call this entity a subject or a self, I prefer to call it an *idioculture*, a neologism I have ventured elsewhere on the model of *idiolect*, the unique version of a language spoken by an individual.[15] The reader or hearer is a singular nexus in the network of cultural processes and products, and the amateur experience I have described, whether by a professional or a nonprofessional, is an encounter between a subjectivity constituted by that cultural nexus and the equally complex cultural web that comprises the literary work. Neither of these is an organic, unchanging whole; on the contrary, it is their self-dividedness and internal tensions that make creative engagements possible.

The idioculture of a literary academic, or agent, or editor, will include elements derived from their profession, and it would be foolish to try to exclude these in order to achieve a "pure" response to a work of literature. I bring to my engagement with John Donne the residue of my many forays into Renaissance literature, my study of English meter, my somewhat shaky grasp of British history, my knowledge of Early Modern English, and so on, but this does not prevent my experience in reading or reciting from memory, say, "A Valediction, Forbidding Mourning," from being an amateur one in the sense I want to advance. The man on the park bench with no links to literary institutions also brings a richly complex idioculture to bear on the work, some aspects of which may be more germane to the novel he is reading than anything he could have acquired from such institutions.[16] The best reviewers of literary works in the mass media may have little in the way of professional background but they bring to their task the knowledge of a wide range of literary works as well as other kinds of information, and sometimes the practical awareness gained from their own creative efforts. The development of the internet has made available an enormous, and enormously hospitable, venue for critical responses to literary works, allowing readers with greatly varying intellectual and cultural resources to join the discussion.[17]

Crucially, however, an amateur reading, no matter by whom, involves an openness to whatever the work, on a particular occasion, will bring—a readiness to have habits and preconceptions challenged and a willingness to be changed by the experience. A professional reading in the narrowest sense of the word, by contrast, will approach the text instrumentally, scrutinizing it for such things as evidence of some historical trend, an insight into the psychology of the author, signs of the influence of a precursor, or examples of a stylistic device.[18] Both kinds of reading, no doubt, bring pleasure, but the pleasure of the scholar who has added to a bank of data is different from the pleasure generated by a reading of the work as literature, which is to say as the product of an author's (or authors') creativity.

Reading or hearing a literary work, or seeing one performed, is a multifaceted activity, and the contrast I have drawn between two varieties, amateur and professional, is, of course, a simplification. I can read "Goblin Market" for the sheer pleasure of its sounds and images while at the same time making a mental note of its metrical oddities or the impress on it of Victorian capitalism, and I can be cognizant of the use of plot conventions in *The Importance of Being Earnest* while chuckling at the comic repartee. Nevertheless, even though both kinds of reading may operate simultaneously, both often occur on their own. The distinction will allow us to pursue the implications of amateurism further.

## Roland Barthes, amateur

One writer who had a particular interest in the figure of the amateur was Roland Barthes. In his autobiographical jottings, *Roland Barthes by Roland Barthes*, Barthes compares his own piano-playing and painting in watercolors to the genteel pursuits of the nineteenth-century maiden who "produced uselessly, stupidly, for herself, but *she produced*: it was her own form of expenditure," and this comment is followed by a paragraph headed "The amateur," which explores briefly the kind of production in question.[19] Though Barthes is not talking about the amateurism of reading, it is worth noting his emphasis on the noncompetitive, non-heroic, self-pleasing nature of the performance of the amateur. An engagement with literature on this model would be noninstrumental, undertaken not in order to achieve financial gain or professional advancement but for the sake of the pleasure and insight provided by the experience itself. In *Camera Lucida*, Barthes again addresses the question of the amateur:

> Usually the amateur is defined as an immature state of the artist: someone who cannot—or will not—achieve the mastery of a profession. But in the field of photographic practice, it is the amateur, on the contrary, who is the assumption of the professional: for it is he who stands closer to the *noeme* of Photography.[20]

The amateur photographer is not trying to produce a work of art but simply recording what is there. Again, we see the absence of a motive beyond the most immediate impulse, and it is not difficult to extrapolate from this scenario to an amateur engagement with literature.

The figure of the amateur was more than a passing concern for Barthes; it was central to his thought, as Adrien Chassain shows in an essay that traces this fascination through several phases of his career.[21] For Barthes, the discourses of the lover (*l'amoureux*) and the amateur are related: both are outside fashion, politics, and theory.[22] But, Chassain argues, the idea of the amateur eventually changed for Barthes from a simple descriptive category to a figure that he placed at the center of his utopian thought. In "Vingt mot-clés sur Roland Barthes," Barthes—echoing the famous passage in Marx's *German Ideology* on the distribution of labor that will allow someone to fish, hunt, herd cattle, and write criticism at different times of the same day—notes: "I can imagine a society of the future, completely unalienated, which, in terms of writing, would know only the activities of the amateur."[23] In a note that did not make it into the published version of *Roland Barthes by Roland Barthes*, he relates his adolescent dream of the "the role of a universal amateur, capable of all types of writing."[24] Although Barthes is still thinking of production rather than of consumption, this utopian vision of the supremacy of amateurism is an appealing picture that is worth adapting for reading practices. In fact, as I have been arguing, it is already widespread, since only the most died-in-the-wool fact-chaser does not, at times, read for the sake of amateur pleasures.

## Critical amateurism

What, then, are the implications of the notion of amateur reading for critical practice? I am not, let me say at once, making an argument for the cessation of scholarly work in such fields as literary history, ideology critique, stylistics, or biography, even though some of these activities may not be directly concerned with the primary amateur experience of literature. I am arguing, rather, for a recognition that none of these fields would exist were it not for that primary experience, and for a better balance between the amateur impulse and the professional apparatus in the academic study and teaching of literature than exists at present. Recent decades have been dominated by what Joseph North has termed the "historicist/contextualist paradigm," which he describes as "the production of cultural and historical knowledge for an audience of specialists."[25] Tom Eyers, in a further telling critique of the ascendancy of empirical methods, identifies the rise of the "digital humanities" as another culprit in the drift away from the particularity of literary experience.[26] These two new books are among the signs of a heartening rebalancing in literary studies; as Eyers himself puts it, "The years since the turn of the millennium have seen a number of calls for a moratorium on the primacy of historical and empirical methods, and for a return to the question of what makes literature, literature" (11).

The obstacles to such a recalibration are significant, however. A large number of academics in literature departments today were trained as historians rather than as literary critics, and graduate students are still urged to find topics that involve empirical research rather than an engagement with the literary qualities of the works they are studying or a theoretical reflection on the operation of literature. The attraction of empirical approaches can be understood partly as the availability of an immense storehouse of subjects for PhD dissertations, articles, conference papers, and monographs, often requiring only a modicum of literary sensitivity and very little breadth of literary knowledge. There is no limit to the nooks and crannies of cultural history that can be examined, or the manuscripts and printed publications that can be edited, or the ephemera that can be counted and classified. The marketization of higher education has gone hand in hand with a privileging of science and technology, and the humanities are now expected to demonstrate the same subservience to the world of facts as the scientific disciplines. Funding bodies look more favorably on data collection than literary criticism, researchers are encouraged to work in teams, and, in the UK at least, jobs are increasingly likely to go to applicants who can demonstrate their skill at "grant capture" rather than their ability to understand and appreciate novels, poems, and plays. The very word "research," with its scientistic overtones, pushes the literary scholar into empirical zones. The term "professional" sometimes gets attached to this understanding of what constitutes literary study (a misuse of the term, to my mind), and no one who is under its sway would reach for the word "amateur."

The best hope for a new emphasis on the amateur impulse in literary studies, perhaps, lies in the classroom.[27] The zeal for positivist and empiricist approaches, it is true, has made itself felt in high school and undergraduate teaching; a couple of decades ago teachers of A-level English in England found themselves directed to include attention to "context" (in an unavoidably impoverished form), and many undergraduate students find themselves being introduced to obscure corners of literary history at the expense of more central works. The welcome expansion of the canon over the past fifty years has sometimes led to a neglect of questions of literary value in pedagogy, and students who are made to study poorly executed literary works, which provide little in the way of enjoyment, are not going to become the best critics. Nevertheless, the primary activity in these classrooms still, I believe, is the training of young people to become good readers of outstanding literary works—readers, that is, who are sensitive to the formal properties of works, alert to their handling of meaning, cognizant of their relations to other works (contemporaneous, earlier, and later), and, as I've stressed already, open to being surprised and changed by what they experience. There is no reason why these skills should be left behind by those few who go on to graduate study and the even fewer with aspirations to join the academic profession.

It is, at the very least, a useful exercise to imagine what the academic study of literature with full acknowledgment of the importance of the amateur impulse might look like. For a start, the employment of literature purely to advance historical knowledge would be left to history departments, unless it was the history of literature that was being examined. Graduate students would be encouraged to choose topics that involve the close study of literary works (assuming these are works that merit such study); promotion and funding committees would be as open to critical studies as to data mining, archival research, and contextual investigation; more academic books would foreground specifically literary issues and fewer would be confined to a narrow historical period. Critical commentary, instead of being driven by the need to say something ingenious and unprecedented, would aim at an accurate reflection of the critic's experience.[28] Perhaps a stronger sense would emerge of the literary work as an event to be lived through rather than an object to be examined, and formal features, which are often either ignored or treated as static structures, would be understood as an important part of the happening of the work.[29] There might develop a greater overlap between the categories of "scholar" and "critic," and the idea of "research" in the humanities would become more flexible. There would be fuller recognition of the role of literary criticism in affirming and sustaining the best literature—and in continuing to question the meaning of "best" in this context. The classroom would become less a place where information is conveyed and interpretations from different approaches assessed and more a place where students are inspired to let literary works affect them directly and individually.

As one illustration of the importance of amateurism, I will take the study of meter. Generations of students have found this a subject of forbidding complexity and one that bears very little relation to their own experience of poetry. It is a highly professionalized neck of the academic woods: there are long books sporting arcane symbols and lists of forbidding Greek terms, and journals feature lengthy disputes about the way to divide up particular lines or analyze familiar rhythmic patterns. Having perpetrated some of this material myself, I am not going to say it is a waste of time; it is not for all comers, however. Much more valuable to the student who wants to savor poems in regular meters to the full is the amateur appreciation of rhythm, by which I mean the familiarity with patterns of beats and offbeats that comes from listening to thousands of examples of metrical song, as most young people will have done by the time they are in college. Hip-hop in particular inculcates a sophisticated, bodily understanding of the relation between a regular beat and the accentual patterns of the language, but all popular song relies on a metrical form that allows departure and return, tension and release, in an onward pulsing movement. If students can harness this understanding in responding to poems, they need only the simplest technical methods to record it on the page and discuss it with one another.

Critical amateurism, then, would carry the impulse of the amateur reader into the professional arena, both acknowledging and seeking to enhance the singular experience of the literary work that lies at the heart of the institution to which we—students, teachers, critics, and scholars alike—belong.

## Notes

1 On the class distinctions implicit in the amateur/professional distinction in sport, see Marjorie Garber, *Academic Instincts* (Princeton: Princeton University Press, 2001), 5–9.

2 Ezra Pound, interestingly, makes a clear distinction between the professional and the expert in the matter of poetry criticism, preferring the amateur "quite often" to the professional but upholding the expert against the amateurs who are trying to "drown out the masters." The expert, for Pound, gains mastery from experience. See A. Walton Litz and Lawrence Rainey, "Ezra Pound," in *The Cambridge History of Literary Criticism*, volume 7, eds. A. Walton Litz, Louis Menand, and Lawrence Rainey (Cambridge: Cambridge University Press, 2000), 66.

3 Andy Merrifield, *The Amateur: The Pleasures of Doing What You Love* (Second edition, London: Verso, 2018).

4 Stephen Potter, *The Muse in Chains: A Study in Education* (London: Jonathan Cape, 1937); John Gross, *The Rise and Fall of the Man of Letters: Aspects of Literary Life since 1800* (London: Weidenfeld & Nicolson, 1969).

5 One of Blackmur's best-known declarations was "Criticism, is, I take it, the formal discourse of an amateur" (*Language as Gesture* [New York: Harcourt Brace, 1952], 372).

6 For one book-length example of this resistance, see David Bromwich, *Politics by Other Means: Higher Education and Group Thinking* (New Haven: Yale University Press, 1992).

7 Terry Eagleton, *The Function of Criticism: From "The Spectator" to Post-structuralism* (London: Verso, 1984), 65.

8 Deidre Shauna Lynch, *Loving Literature: A Cultural History* (Chicago: University of Chicago Press, 2015), 2.

9 Stanley Fish, *Doing What Comes Naturally: Change, Rhetoric, and the Practice of Theory in Literary and Legal Studies* (Durham: Duke University Press, 1989).

10 Bruce Robbins, *Secular Vocations: Intellectuals, Professionals, Culture* (London: Verso, 1993), ix–x.

11 Chapter 2 of *Secular Vocations* is titled "Culture and Distance: On the Professionalizing of Literary Criticism."

12 Garber, *Academic Instincts*, 5.

13 Although the focus of this chapter is on literature, a similar picture could be drawn of the institutions and practices pertaining in the other art forms; the visual arts, in particular, have spawned a vast speculative market driven by monetary appetites. The argument that follows is equally applicable to these other branches of art.

14 As Garber would insist, the dependence operates in the other direction as well: it is hard to imagine a reader who is immune from the influence of such institutions as education and publishing. (Indeed the very medium by means of which the work has reached the reader carries the traces of several professional bodies.)

15 See Derek Attridge, *The Singularity of Literature* (Abingdon: Routledge Classics, 2017), 28–30 and *passim*, and *The Work of Literature* (Oxford: Oxford University Press, 2015), 33 and *passim*.

16 In "The Critic as Amateur," Saikat Majumdar gives an eloquent account of the knowledges every reader brings to the act of reading. "It can be any kind of knowledge," he writes, "—that of child-rearing, sports, furniture design, nature, banking, or, for that matter, the affective knowledge of love, grief, or boredom" (*New Literary History*, 48 (2017): 1–25, citation on p. 6).

17 The purchase of the comment site Goodreads by Amazon in 2013 signaled its success as a repository for amateur opinion, and in April

2016 it was reported that the site had hosted 50 million reviews (https://the-digital-reader.com/2016/04/07/goodreads-reaches-new-milestone-fifty-million-reviews/).

18 Reading instrumentally is not limited to professionals, however: an amateur may read for the purpose of self-help or comfort—though unless this purpose is wholly dominant, the work is always capable of providing more (or less) than the reader bargained for. My thanks to Aarthi Vadde for this point.

19 Roland Barthes, *Roland Barthes by Roland Barthes*, trans. Richard Howard (New York: Hill and Wang, 1977), 52. A book-length version of Barthes's observation is Wayne Booth's account of his own amateur cello-playing in *For the Love of It: Amateuring and Its Rivals* (Chicago: University of Chicago Press, 1999).

20 Roland Barthes, *Camera Lucida: Reflections on Photography*, trans. Richard Howard (New York: Hill and Wang, 1981), 98–99. By the *noeme* of photography Barthes means its essence, which he defines as "That-has-been."

21 Adrien Chassain, "Roland Barthes: 'Les pratiques et les valeurs de l'amateur'," *LHT Fabula*, 15 (October 2015). Available online: http://www.fabula.org/lht/15/chassain.html (accessed May 23, 2018). Although Chassain finds a similarity between Barthes's praise of the amateur and Brecht's, the latter's approval of amateur acting had more to do with the alienation produced by a certain clumsiness.

22 See Roland Barthes, *A Lover's Discourse: Fragments*, trans. Richard Howard (New York: Hill and Wang, 1979).

23 "Je peux imaginer une societé à venir, totalement désaliénée, qui, sur le plan de l'écriture, ne connaîtrait plus que des activités d'amateur." Cited in Chassain, "Roland Barthes," from "Vingt mots-clès sur Roland Barthes," in *Oeuvres Complètes*, vol. 4, *Livres, Textes, Entretiens, 1972–1976*, ed. Eric Marty (Paris: Seuil, 2002), 861.

24 "le role d'un amateur universal, apte à toutes les écritures." Roland Barthes, *Le lexique de l'auteur: Séminaire à l'Ecole pratique des hautes études 1973–1974 suivi de Fragments inédits du « Roland Barthes par Roland Barthes, »* ed. Anne Herschberg Pierrot (Paris: Seuil, 2007), 261.

25 Joseph North, *Literary Criticism: A Concise Political History* (Cambridge: Harvard University Press, 2017), 81, 115. North provides a trenchant account of this turn, though he is less convincing in his account of the critical practice he would like to see in its place.

26 Tom Eyers, *Speculative Formalism: Literature, Theory, and the Critical Present* (Evanston: Northwestern University Press, 2017). Eyers offers a critique of the digital humanities as a "new positivism," with particular attention to the work of Franco Moretti and Stephen

Ramsey (34–56). He refers elsewhere to "the strangulating hegemony of historicism in the literary disciplines," "Theory over Method, or In Defense of Polemic," *Critical Inquiry* 44 (2017): 139.

27 See the essay by Kara Wittman in this volume for a discussion of the undergraduate experience of literature.

28 For a discussion and examples of such "minimal interpretation," see Derek Attridge and Henry Staten, *The Craft of Poetry: Dialogues on Minimal Interpretation* (Abingdon: Routledge, 2015).

29 This sentence crystallizes one of the main arguments in Attridge, *The Singularity of Literature* and *The Work of Literature.*

# Bibliography


Attridge, Derek, and Henry Staten. *The Craft of Poetry: Dialogues on Minimal Interpretation*. Abingdon: Routledge, 2015.

Attridge, Derek. *The Singularity of Literature*. 2004. Routledge Classics. Abingdon: Routledge, 2017.

Attridge, Derek. *The Work of Literature*. Oxford: Oxford University Press, 2015.

Barthes, Roland. *Camera Lucida: Reflections on Photography*, trans. Richard Howard. New York: Hill and Wang, 1981.

Barthes, Roland. *Le lexique de l'auteur: Séminaire à l'Ecole pratique des hautes études 1973–1974 suivi de Fragments inédits du « Roland Barthes par Roland Barthes,»* ed. Anne Herschberg Pierrot. Paris: Seuil, 2007.

Barthes, Roland. *A Lover's Discourse: Fragments*, trans. Richard Howard. New York: Hill and Wang, 1979.

Barthes, Roland. *Oeuvres Complètes*, vol. 4, *Livres, textes, entretiens, 1972–1976*, ed. Eric Marty. Paris: Seuil, 2002.

Barthes, Roland. *Roland Barthes by Roland Barthes*, trans. Richard Howard. New York: Hill and Wang, 1977.

Blackmur, R. P. *Language as Gesture*. New York: Harcourt Brace, 1952.

Booth, Wayne C. *For the Love of It: Amateuring and Its Rivals*. Chicago: University of Chicago Press, 1999.

Bromwich, David. *Politics by Other Means: Higher Education and Group Thinking*. New Haven: Yale University Press, 1992.

Chassain, Adrien. "Roland Barthes: 'Les pratiques et les valeurs de l'amateur'." *LHT Fabula*. 15 (October 2015). Available online: http://www.fabula.org/lht/15/chassain.html (accessed May 30, 2018).

Eagleton, Terry. *The Function of Criticism: From "The Spectator" to Post-structuralism*. London: Verso, 1984.

Eyers, Tom. *Speculative Formalism: Literature, Theory, and the Critical Present*. Evanston: Northwestern University Press, 2017.

Eyers, Tom. "Theory over Method, or in Defense of Polemic." *Critical Inquiry* 44 (2017): 136–143.

Fish, Stanley. *Doing What Comes Naturally: Change, Rhetoric, and the Practice of Theory in Literary and Legal Studies*. Durham: Duke University Press, 1989.

Garber, Marjorie. *Academic Instincts*. Princeton: Princeton University Press, 2001.

Gross, John. *The Rise and Fall of the Man of Letters: Aspects of Literary Life since 1800*. London: Weidenfeld & Nicolson, 1969.

Litz, A. Walton and Lawrence Rainey, "Ezra Pound." In *The Cambridge History of Literary Criticism*, volume 7, edited by A. Walton Litz, Louis Menand, and Lawrence Rainey. Cambridge: Cambridge University Press, 2000, 57–92.

Lynch, Deidre Shauna. *Loving Literature: A Cultural History*. Chicago: University of Chicago Press, 2015.

Merrifield, Andy. *The Amateur: The Pleasures of Doing What You Love*. Second edition. London: Verso, 2018.

North, Joseph. *Literary Criticism: A Concise Political History*. Cambridge: Harvard University Press, 2017.

Potter, Stephen. *The Muse in Chains: A Study in Education*. London: Jonathan Cape, 1937.

Robbins, Bruce. *Secular Vocations: Intellectuals, Professionals, Culture*. London: Verso, 1993.

# 2

# In the Shadow of the Archive

*Tom Lutz*

*The Critic as Amateur*: immediately one recognizes the prompt, a good idea for an essay, an excellent occasion for a collection of essays, and the time seems right for reasons easy to uncover. For those of us in this volume, though, it's hard not to notice that we've been given a contradictory task. The phrase can't really apply to us since we are all professional readers, professional critics, or we wouldn't be here. Most of us started as amateurs—at least I have yet to meet the person who decided to become a professional reader the way one might decide to become a stockbroker, or an orthodontist, as a career choice that could marry talent and ability to income and status, as a rational, economic choice. People become tax attorneys for all sorts of reasons, but rarely because they were reading IRS regulations under the covers with a flashlight as children. Radiologists don't begin their lives in love with reading X-rays, and no one reads X-rays as a hobby, as a pleasure divorced from professional duties. But people almost always love reading novels or poetry long before they have any professional relation to them. We readers are amateurs before we are anything else. We become critics, at least in part, as a result.

They say everyone's a critic, but they don't mean everyone writes criticism. Writing criticism, being a critic, is much more like being an orthodontist. We don't do it without a professional reason. We might have opinions about a book and share them; we might even blog about them, chat about them, bring them up at dinner parties. But criticism—criticism recognized as such by other critics—is something else. It's not for amateurs.

Even now, as I write this, I find myself wandering away from any love I have for the object—reading, books—toward various professional goals, as if, much as I would like to talk about what I love, the reading I love, the novels I'm reading right now that I love, the novel that, as a boy, made me realize that I loved novels (*The Black Stallion*)—much as I would like to talk about love, I almost never get to it; I wander away. I'm pulled toward professional business, toward criticism, toward those concerns that have little to do with my life as a lover, pulled toward the thing I do after I have been moved by a piece of writing or after I have failed to be moved by a piece of writing: *this*, I watch myself thinking, *this is your mind on criticism.*

I wander around the net following my Google search of the phrase "the critic as amateur" and see what Saikat Majumdar has to say about it—Majumdar's essay is a reading of "Edmund Wilson in Benares," an autobiographical essay by Pankaj Mishra about his reading life as a young man. I see what he says that Pankaj Mishra has to say about it; I read Mishra, see what he feels Edmund Wilson has to say about it, and then back to Majumdar's piece, where he talks about how Bruce Robbins and Marjorie Garber help us understand Mishra's postcolonial moment.[1]

And then, a few Google entries down, I come upon a piece Leslie Fiedler published back in 1950, "Toward an Amateur Criticism," in *The Kenyon Review*: "The discrepancy," he writes there, "between the metaphors typical to the creative mind and those typical to the critical mind in our world (and this is true often in the single individual who practices both as poet and critic) indicate a quietly desperate cleavage."[2] I begin to feel situated as I read these things, I begin to feel like a critic, I begin to lose the object. I am cleaved, I am whole.

* * *

I loved *The Black Stallion* as much as I loved horses back then, the horses I loved before I read the book, despite the fact that the book was as close to a horse as I had ever been. Conjuring those heady days of first, complicated literary engagement, I remember the taste, the flavor, the rich visuality, the overfull experience of that reading. I loved *that* beautiful, complicated, brilliant horse, which the boy and the trainer go to pick up halfway around the world; I loved the boy; I loved the world of the book, its density, its artistry, its astounding ability to intertwine its visions with my own desires—none of this, of course, even close to articulable for me at the time. And ever since, I have fallen in love over and over again, first with my sisters' Nancy Drew books and Sherlock Holmes and *Fail-Safe*, then Jack Kerouac, and Joseph Heller and Philip Roth and Grace Paley and Flannery O'Connor, and somehow I began reading Apuleius and Rabelais and Emily Brontë and Borges—all of that and so much more when I was still an amateur, before I had tasted criticism any farther than the *New York Times Book Review*, before I knew the professional meaning of *canon* or *context* or *narrative* or *genre*, before I had learned to think like a critic. Like Mishra in Majumdar's essay (and maybe I should mention that I found myself, just now, flirting with amateurism, wanting to say not *Mishra in Majumdar's essay* but *Pankaj in Saikat's essay*, because when I was an amateur, authors and narrators felt real, not like markers, not like ideas, or territories, or stand-ins for critical concepts, but like, well, people, people who "talked" to me, who told me stories)—at any rate, like Pankaj Mishra, I'll say, I was an autodidact. I was a prickly, rebellious youth: reactive, Oedipal. I knew nothing and knew everything, especially knew that I didn't need *the man* to tell me what to read, didn't need *college*, didn't need *the establishment*. The names and ideas that flashed by me in the pages of the *Book Review* undoubtedly had some impact, and I had a job in high school as a page at the public library and saw a lot of books go by. My mother read literary novels, and before I was a page I would see her stack of books sitting on the dryer waiting to be taken back to that library and register the names on the spines. Some would repeat, like Malamud and Bellow, and so I intuited they had value. I remember nothing from my English classes in high school, the high school from which, like Spicoli, I rolled out of in a cloud of marijuana smoke—did we even read books in those classes? I don't know. But on my own I read rapaciously, insatiably, before and through those years and beyond. I remained wildly undereducated and undisciplined but not unexposed to our field, not entirely lacking some idea, however inchoate, of the literary. And perhaps that notion, that there is a subset of books that are literary, is the first slip down the slide from amateur to critic.

* * *

My evolving canon, during my twenties, was formed by the used bookstore. For a few years I lived near Iowa City, and I bought books from Alandoni's on South Dubuque St. near the railroad tracks, books that, I surmised later, had been used by students at the Writers Workshop, an institution I hadn't heard of yet. For fifty cents or a dollar a piece I was thus accidentally introduced to the stuff writers read. Alandoni, long-haired, bearded, and bespectacled, was noticeably proud of his operation, and I understood, although I didn't have the words or concepts for it yet, that he was proud of his curation. He was a sophisticated reader with strong tastes that ran to the metafictional, so I read Barth, Barthelme, and Pynchon, and wow, was I in over my head, and wow, did I love it. I appreciated the parodic mimicry of *The Sot-Weed Factor* somehow, despite never having read a single word written in the eighteenth century.

I spent some of this time speed-dating authors, some of it as a serial monogamist—reading all of Hesse in a row, then all of Nabokov—and I reached new levels of ecstatic bewilderment reading *Ada*. The French and Russian and German sprinkled through that book was thrilling, and now it makes me wonder: how much reading pleasure is like that, aspirational, aloft in the cloud of unknowing, full of the promise of some future self that might read a book like that and understand it, a future self that could read French, German, and Russian?—after all, this guy, this Vladimir, he could read and write them all, it was possible, it was doable, it was within reach. I loved thinking of myself as the kind of person who one day could really read the book I was reading.

So, an amateur. A lover. Very much not a professional. And as I write about that time in my life I find myself having little flashes of dread—my readers here, that is, the readers of this chapter, this volume, are all critics, all careful analysts, all alert to my missteps. They will immediately know that I'm just wandering around, drifting, meandering around the subject, not getting anywhere, not scoring any points, hardly professional even now. So, in a panic,

I look for a citation, something that will justify me, something to shore against my ruins. I grab this from Leslie Fiedler's essay, as he tries to explain why criticism will never be a science:

> The primary act of faith which makes criticism possible compels the critic under any circumstances to speak *as if* to men and not to specialists. The compulsory comprehensibility of the critic is not a matter of pandering to indolence, prejudice or ignorance, but of resisting the impulse to talk to himself or a congeries of reasonable facsimiles of himself. In an age of declining sociability and the widespread failure of love, it is difficult to be an *amateur.*[3]

I love that, but it doesn't help my cause much. Even Fielder, in defense of the amateur, tells me not to do what I'm doing: I'm writing *as if* to readers, yes, but very much to congeries of myself, too. Maybe I can't be a critic and an amateur at the same time?

Perhaps it's impossible, and perhaps that means that this whole volume's premise is a problem, not a proposition? I wonder if what I should do is act like a critic, write like a critic, think like a critic as I praise the amateur, elevate the amateur, pretend that a critic can—despite *the widespread failure of love*—indeed love the amateur, appreciate the amateur, explain the amateur. Because at least, if nothing else, we can be the amateur's critic; schooled in the tools of appreciation, we can perhaps appreciate the amateur.

Majumdar's piece on Mishra, Saikat's on Pankaj, is this, in part: an appreciation. He reads Mishra's amateurism as a lack of professionalism, which, to be fair, is how Pankaj presents it himself. But Saikat's essay is not just about amateurism, not just about reading; it is about the world and about the relation of reading to the world. He makes us feel the oddity, the fish-out-of-water tentativeness of Pankaj, this provincial autodidact, sneaking into the library of a quasi-provincial university in what Mishra would go on, years later, to call "the ruins of empire," fueled by, in Majumdar's words, a "vague but ineluctable" desire to read, a desire that is always also a yearning for an achieved cosmopolitanism, reading being, it turns out, for Pankaj, for me, for so many, the sweet price of acquiring cosmopolitan identity.[4]

***

My own provincialism at the age of eighteen was intense, despite how physically close I was to the center of empire, growing up an hour outside of New York City. Pankaj, 8,000 miles away, was reading the *TLS*, *Partisan Review*, and *New York Review of Books*, none of which I had ever heard of, even though the latter two were published within thirty miles of my house. The shadow of empire is cast very close to its center, cast there perhaps not dissimilarly to the way it shades its outposts; that is, as I read Majumdar's piece, I felt an absolute kinship with Pankaj. We both read compulsively, both felt our provincial stain, both consorted with desperate and criminal characters in our reading and our lives, both craved an arrival that was textual—we weren't looking for money (except to eat) or careers, we were looking for some transcendence we had endowed literature with the power to bestow. The boy in *The Black Stallion* was not me, really—he had a horse, he traveled to "Arabia"—but Pankaj, the boy with the cosmopolitan longing in Varanasi, trying to quench that thirst by reading, yes, *c'est moi.* "The dream of cosmopolitanism conceived in the provincial periphery"? Yes, that was my dream, the offstage prize I fumbled toward, marooned in my own ignorance on the suburban periphery, then on the Midwestern periphery, working with my hands at building sites, at farms, at restaurants—Mishra's cosmopolitan dream was my dream, the achievement of it promising to lift me not out of my socioeconomic position, but out of my witlessness.

Mishra, as we know, quickly became a professional: no amateurs publish regularly in the *New York Review of Books*. Mishra's route to professional reading was, again like my own, circuitous, though he had several years of college under his belt by the time he was having trouble understanding Edmund Wilson. Among my odd jobs in my amateur years was one cooking breakfast and lunch for students at a small college in Dubuque, Iowa. I was an anomaly there, the one young man working with a half dozen middle-aged women, and they quite religiously enforced our coffee and lunch breaks on the precise right minute each day, at which point I would pull out a book and read while they talked about their lives, lives of husbands and kids that had very little overlap with my own countercultural debauchery. They thought I was an oddball, but we were all quite friendly. The used bookstores in Dubuque were not as strenuously curated as Alandoni's, but most used bookstores result in a coherent curriculum of sorts: a combination of the shopowner's taste, the books that ended up in someone's library before death caused their boxing up and dropping off, the books that sold enough copies that at least some were likely to survive the ravages of time, the books that were assigned in courses so had a better than average chance of still being on a shelf.

And we used bookstore buyers develop a keen sense of our own. Certain bindings draw the aficionado of beach reads, certain trim sizes stand out to the avant-gardist, and since shopping often means wandering down uncategorized shelf after haphazard shelf, taste culture becomes physicalized, the shopper becoming like a gold panner, sifting through stacks to spy the ore. I had gone on a Freud and Nietzsche kick, and when the school's financial aid director saw me reading *Beyond Good and Evil* during one of the kitchen staff's coffee breaks, he stopped and asked me what my story was. Not sure what he was asking, I just said: Story? Yes, he said, I see what you're reading every day. Are you a college graduate? No, I said and laughed, no, never went to college, and I wondered how much of my complex emotions about that I betrayed—it was both the chip on my shoulder and the self-conferred epaulet that covered it. He said, well, you could go here for free if you wanted.

College after all. It turned out, I realized later, he was just looking for warm bodies to attach Pell Grants to, another camel to transport Pell Grants across the small college desert, but at the time I was, well, honored, flattered, and I agreed. For the next couple years I cooked from 5:00 AM to 1:00 PM and then went to classes in the afternoons and evenings. I very quickly realized that there were people, called professors, who talked about books for a living, read books for a paycheck. I wanted a job like that, a job that involved no piles of grilled cheese sandwiches, a job where reading was not just lunch-break enthrallment but work, a calling, a living. I started to become a professional, almost from my first day as long-in-the-tooth undergraduate; I started to become a critic.

* * *

Of course now this chapter has devolved into a somewhat boring story, which would probably be told much better by someone else and would no doubt be much more captivating if it was about somebody else, preferably a famous writer. I worry that, so far, the story is not particularly compelling, however to the point it might be, and we know that, as Fiedler says, "The critic's unforgivable sin is to be dull." My professional self put that line in, again suddenly desperate for a citation, a source, an authority, and it's a paltry offering, since Fiedler was such a disreputable professional, such a renegade figure, writing against professionalism and in favor of pornography, so committed to being a maverick it appeared contrived. Still, I feel the need to buttress this all with some critical concepts and references, and he's better than nothing. I need to demonstrate my fealty to the archive, as Majumdar says the professional must, even as I try to understand how I came to read without one. I find myself wondering, as I muck about in the residue of those years, why Nietzsche? Freud made sense—he was the world's most famous psychologist; I was screwed up and needed help. But Nietzsche? How did I come upon him? Then I realize: someone must have talked about him in another book—yes, that's it; my syllabus was generated intertextually. Aha! A concept. An archive! I'm making some progress!

Until I started taking courses in my late twenties, the closest I came to having an archive I recognized as such was the board-and-cinder-block shelf full of books I had read and about which I was overweeningly proud. It was possible, I was told as I registered for classes, to get credit for outside learning and skip some requirements; I needed just to bring a list of books to a professor, who would examine me on them and give me credit for a corresponding course. I put together a list of all the novels I had read and was again quite pleased with myself. It was a long list, a hundred books or more. I asked to be given credit for a survey of English literature. The professor looked at it and smiled. All but three or four of these books were published in the last fifty years, he said. Okay, I thought, wondering why he thought that might be worth saying and also marveling that I had never noticed it. Very few of them are British, he added, and many are translations. He smiled again, finding me an interesting specimen. I'm very glad you've read all these books, he added, it's all very impressive, but it is not a survey of English literature; it's a survey of the mid-twentieth-century American novel with some translations and random texts thrown in. There is no poetry, no nonfiction, nothing between Beowulf and Virginia Woolf. (There was no Beowulf or Virginia Woolf, either, he just couldn't resist the joke, which I filed away to understand later.) I'm afraid, he said, I can't exempt you from the survey course for this.

And so my reading started to be professionalized, even in retrospect. I understood there were historical periods, and that they mattered. There were national boundaries, and they mattered. There were original languages, and that mattered. Everything in my little archive shifted. Marjorie Garber claims that the terms *amateur* and *professional* "produce each other and they define each other," but that doesn't feel exactly right.[5] The professional simply redefines the amateur object. My amateur reading was being transformed, retroactively, by professional categories.

But perhaps not completely transformed. I remained undisciplined (and remain so yet). I managed to find a new university that allowed me to design my own major and then went on to a do-it-yourself, interdisciplinary PhD program that allowed me to continue my amateur recklessness. Mishra writes, in the original *NYRB* essay (how it eases my professional panic to call on him to say what I want to say): "I read randomly, whatever I could find, and with the furious intensity of a small-town boy to whom books are the sole means of communicating with, and understanding, the larger world."[6] And Majumdar (ditto, what a relief to have him pitch in here) understands the autodidactic impulse and its frustration with curricula, and that frustration's relation to provincial self-fashioning and provincial self-loathing. I spent my time in these schools never losing my sense of being a rube, my self-identification as the working-class kid who didn't go to college—and, indeed, I emerged from that decade of immersion with a Stanford PhD feeling as unsophisticated and frightfully undereducated as ever, with no field to call my own, no sense of mastery, no worldliness, no sense of arrival, the yearning and desire to be at home in the world as fresh as it had ever been.

My self-image was fictional, full of contradictions: how can a kid who didn't go to college have a PhD? Well, as it turns out, it is easy to hold such contradictions—it's just me; it's me in my own deepest story. How can someone still feel like an outsider after four years at Stanford as a TA, however transient that position is? And then I spent three years in the belly of that institution as a full-time lecturer. But in my story, I remained unschooled, and being inside did nothing to alleviate the feeling of being outside. Even these many years later, officially a Distinguished Professor, I still feel like I don't belong, that I am not like the other Distinguished Professors, that I am an autodidactic, undereducated, not-very-well-brought-up, etiquette-challenged, insufficiently professionalized poseur, an imposter in academic regalia.

But this chapter can't go on being about me and my little quandaries, can it? Where's the central idea? Where's the disciplinary context? What is the critical theory validating this excursus? Like the idea that Shakespeare is the greatest writer because he never appears in his text (Iris Murdoch: "He's the most invisible of writers"), most forms of criticism shun the personal, certainly the confessional, the anecdotal, because we understand the paucity of the personal, the fallacy of the affective, and so we mostly ignore the feeling of what happens when we read—unless, of course, we happen to be writing about "the reader," which, in critical discourse, always means the amateur reader, not the professional.[7] In any case, if so many authorities agree, it must be right: the author should disappear. Flaubert: "The artist must make posterity believe he never lived." And so should the critic. Kundera: "The archive's ideal: the sweet equality that reigns in an enormous common grave."[8] I hope it is clear I am upping the RPM now, the references per minute, as a defense against the eruption of personal feeling, a defense against the anecdote. And I hope it is clear that I mean it to be a little funny.

Because all of this is always already (wink) personal, always situated in experience, as Majumdar reminds us. Like Mishra, Nirad C. Chaudhuri was a provincial autodidact, and also a "polymath," a label that is an honorific form of "undisciplined." Chaudhuri's distaste for specialization and the curricular structure of the university, according to Majumdar, was a form of active resistance to the colonial project, which it very well may have been, and yet, Chaudhuri, *c'est moi, aussi.* His "absurdly utopian desire to become a polymath scholar"? Everything I've done, from the motley assortment of books I've written, all of which manage to slip through multiple disciplinary cracks, to *Los Angeles Review of Books*—all my work has been wayward and resistant to specialization, all of it displays utopian polymathic tendencies. I am, if anything, a hopeless encyclopediac, and this undoubtedly is, again, a cosmopolitan desire. Perhaps it is also a very understandable *méconnaissance*: the archive as crooked mirror. C. L. R. James, V. S. Naipaul, Chaudhuri, Mishra—all these postcolonial writers of the former British empire teach themselves a polymathic relation to the archive rather than a specialized one, and for Majumdar this is central to their resistance. I suppose that, since America housed some of the earliest postcolonial subjects, it is not surprising that we have consistently sprouted autodidact polymaths (Benjamin Franklin, Herman Melville, Walt Whitman, Frederick Douglass, Abraham Lincoln, Mark Twain, Booker T. Washington, Charlotte Perkins Gilman, Thomas Edison, Emma Goldman, Frank Lloyd Wright, Malcolm X, Steve Jobs) and autodidact writers (Louisa May Alcott, Edith Wharton, Theodore Dreiser, Ernest Hemingway, F. Scott Fitzgerald, Laura Ingalls Wilder, William Faulkner, Maya Angelou). Autodidacticism can be the result of a desire lacking means of fulfillment—that is a lack of educational opportunity—or it can be a quirk, a choice, a resistance. What determines the idiosyncrasies of our *méconnaissance*? Why do some of us allow our amateur lives to be erased by professionalism? Why do some resist the very professionalism that pays our rent?

Perhaps it is a bit like asking why some of us love Gertrude Stein while she leaves others cold. Why do some of us, never having met a horse, fall in love with horses? Why do some of us embrace nationalism, or a region, or a race, while others desire cosmopolitanism, the more tenuously rooted the better? Why do we love what we love, whatever our profession? And of whom should we ask these questions? The amateur, the scholar, the critic? The rootless cosmopolitan in me says: all three.

* * *

We wandering cosmopolitans in the shadow of the archive desire nothing more than to devour it, piece by piece, to assimilate the object of our enrapturement. The scholar and the critic pretend to have already ingested it all, pretend to a comprehension that we know—that we even explicitly argue—is unachievable. The black stallion glistens in the morning light; the Arabian desert stretches out, consumes my life, my bed, my world, my night, as the bright low rising Middle Eastern sun makes of me a different boy, a boy who has left New Jersey forever, who lives in some larger world, who partakes of so much more than my little postage stamp of soil can offer. The stallion is afraid of the boat that will take him across the sea, afraid of the storm. The horse's trainer, the professional, tries to calm him, to help him venture into new worlds, help him cross the immeasurable ocean to his new home, but the stallion is inconsolable. Can it be that only the boy knows how to touch the animal, that only he knows how to caress the sleek beast's wildness?

Yes: only the untutored boy, it turns out, in his boundless yearning, knows how to become one with the steed, how to bring him home, how to allow for the squalls and waves smashing and shuddering the hull (*they are not real!* he tells the horse), how to allow for the messiness, for glorious incomprehension, for incommensurability, for love, under the covers, falling into a dream.

## Notes

1 See Pankaj Mishra, "Edmund Wilson in Benares," *New York Review of Books*, April 19, 1998. Available online: https://www.nybooks.com/articles/1998/04/09/edmund-wilson-in-benares/ and Saikat Majumdar, "The Critic as Amateur," *New Literary History* 48, no. 1 (2017): 1–24.

2 Leslie A. Fiedler, "Toward an Amateur Criticism," *The Kenyon Review* 12, no. 4 (1950). Available online: https://www.kenyonreview.org/kr-online-issue/kenyon-reviewcredos/selections/leslie-a-fiedler-656342/.

3 Ibid.

4 Majumdar, "Critic," 24.

5 Marjorie Garber, *Academic Instincts* (Princeton: Princeton University Press, 2001), 5.

6 Mishra, "Edmund Wilson," n.p.

7 Iris Murdoch, "The Sublime and the Beautiful Revisited," in *Existentialists and Mystics: Writings on Philosophy and Literature*, ed. Peter Conradi (New York: Penguin, 1997), 262.

8 Gustave Flaubert, quoted in Milan Kundera, *The Art of the Novel*, trans. Linda Asher (New York: HarperCollins, 1998).

## Bibliography

Fiedler, Leslie A. "Toward an Amateur Criticism." *The Kenyon Review* 12, no. 4 (1950): 561–574. Available online: https://www.kenyonreview.org/kr-online-issue/kenyon-review-credos/selections/leslie-a-fiedler-656342/.

Garber, Marjorie. *Academic Instincts*. Princeton: Princeton University Press, 2001.

Mishra, Pankaj. "Edmund Wilson in Benares." *New York Review of Books*. April 9, 1998. Available online: https://www.nybooks.com/articles/1998/04/09/edmund-wilson-in-benares/.

Majumdar, Saikat. "The Critic as Amateur." *New Literary History* 48, no. 1 (2017): 1–24.

Kundera, Milan. *The Art of the Novel*, trans. Linda Asher. New York: HarperCollins, 1998.

Murdoch, Iris. "The Sublime and the Beautiful Revisited." In *Existentialists and Mystics: Writings on Philosophy and Literature*, edited by Peter Conradi. New York: Penguin, 1997.

# 3

# "It's All Very Suggestive, but It Isn't Scholarship"

*Ragini Tharoor Srinivasan*

> It is essential to emphasize that there is nothing definitive here ... I have done scarcely more that put down some preliminary markers for more detailed future investigations. My concerns are heuristic and my conclusions are strictly provisional.
>
> —Paul Gilroy[1]

> It is the power of suggestion that one most misses, I thought, taking Mr B the critic in my hand and reading, very carefully and very dutifully, his remarks upon the art of poetry. Very able they were, acute and full of learning; but the trouble was, that his feelings no longer communicated; his mind seemed separated into different chambers; not a sound carried from one to the other.
>
> —Virginia Woolf[2]

I was preparing for my doctoral qualifying exams. The professor and I were discussing Paul Gilroy's 1993 work of diaspora theory, *The Black Atlantic: Modernity and Double Consciousness*. I take meticulous notes (notetaking, a practice in which I have no training, only practice, has always been my primary research methodology) and so I know that it was March 25, my mother's birthday.

I also know that my responses to the Gilroy were organized around the following subjects, central to the book: tradition, modernity, culture, diaspora, music, the self. These were mammoth assemblages, transnational and transhistorical, necessitating both Gilroy's interdisciplinary approach to literary and cultural studies and his idiosyncratic archive, spanning subjects and texts like the late nineteenth-century Fisk Jubilee Singers, Richard Wright's reconfiguration of black authorship, and Toni Morrison's 1987 novel, *Beloved*.

Gilroy's method in *The Black Atlantic* is associative, cocreative, analogical, comparative. In order to theorize the transatlantic black diaspora, he draws connections across genre and time. He offers, as quoted in the first epigraph, "nothing definitive." This self-description situates Gilroy, who received his PhD from the Centre for Contemporary Cultural Studies at the University of Birmingham in 1986, and worked as an editor and columnist before becoming an academic, in the tradition of the bricoleur, who puts to page the "preliminary markers" that are ready to hand (the song he has just heard, the novel he has just read). His conclusions are "provisional." He "does not confine himself to accomplishment and execution … [he speaks] through the medium of things: giving an account of his personality and life by the choices he makes between the limited possibilities."[3]

Neither Gilroy's archive nor approach troubled me. I had arrived at Berkeley's interdisciplinary PhD program in Rhetoric from Duke's interdisciplinary program in Literature, where "Introduction to Cultural Studies" was a required undergraduate course. In between degrees, I worked as a magazine editor. I was accustomed to moving across fields, to marshalling motley objects in service of my subjects. I was jazzed about Gilroy's theorizations of "tradition as a changing same," "countercultures of modernity," "anti-anti-essentialism," the "magic" audibilities of music, and the generatively homonymic "roots" and "routes" that structure diasporic sensibilities. I was making connections to a wide range of thinkers, including Benedict Anderson, Rey Chow, Inderpal Grewal, and Stuart Hall.

After listening for some time to my exuberant exegesis of the text, the professor's nod gave way to a qualified dismissal. "Yes, yes," he said, cutting me off. "It's all very suggestive, but it isn't scholarship."

## It's all very suggestive

Because that's what I was supposed to be learning: how to be a scholar, conduct research, and approach the literary text as an object of knowledge qua knowledge through accepted disciplinary methodologies. How to master the text, become an expert, or at least, perform expertise. Gilroy's "preliminary markers for more detailed future investigations" apparently didn't cut it, and that exchange over *The Black Atlantic* has stayed with me for nearly a decade. If *The Black Atlantic*, published by Harvard University Press, no less, wasn't scholarship, what was it? And what was its relation to a constellation of adjacent genres, like literature, journalism, creative nonfiction, and criticism? While withholding a direct critique of cultural studies, the professor was calling into question the interdisciplinary and political thrust of Gilroy's writing. In specifying "suggestion" as the opposite of scholarship, he further implied the following: first, that a text's associative threads, however finely knitted, did not constitute a scholarly archive; second, that a text's ability to provoke its reader did not count as a contribution to scholarship; third, that a scholarly text was one that offered instruction, not interlocution.

Association. Provocation. Interlocution. Each of these qualities characterizes a mode of writing that resounds with what Virginia Woolf memorably calls "the power of suggestion." These words, quoted in the second epigraph, appear in the final chapter of *A Room of One's Own* in which Woolf considers Coleridge's theory of the "resonant and porous" androgynous mind that "transmits emotion without impediment; that ... is naturally creative, incandescent, and undivided."[4] Mr B's remarks on poetry, by contrast, emerge from a wholly masculine mind; "acute and full of learning" though they are, they do not transmit emotion and are neither creative nor undivided. "Thus," Woolf continues, "when one takes a sentence of Mr B in to the mind it falls plump to the ground—dead."[5]

Woolf's has always seemed to me the best description of the highest aspiration of writing: that it lives. Granted, I am taking liberties by moving from the juxtaposition of suggestion and scholarship, anecdotally offered, to Woolf's discussion of gendered criticism. But I am inferring from Woolf's negative description of Mr B that he is guilty of precisely that which Gilroy avoids and which the professor's ideal "scholarship" offers: definition, mastery, avowals of expertise. Mr B is guilty, in other words, of thinking he is thinking great thoughts, which, to cite poet Kay Ryan, "do not nourish / small thoughts / as parents do children." "Like the eucalyptus," Mr B's plump, dead sentences "make the soil / beneath them barren. / Standing in a / grove of them / is hideous."[6]

Mr B's criticism, in contrast to Gilroy's, leaves the reader unmoved, unnourished. Unlike Coleridge's androgynous sentences, his words do not "[give] birth to all kinds of other ideas"; they lack "the secret of perpetual life."[7] They present on the page, but midwife nothing. This is not only a defect of nonfiction. Reading a celebrated novel by Mr A, Woolf criticizes the inspiration-blocking egocentrism of its first-person narrative: "the dominance of the letter 'I' and the aridity, which like the giant beech tree, it casts within its shade. Nothing will grow there."[8] Mr A's is an "I" that divides and directs, instructs and describes, leaving the soil beneath it barren. It is significant that the writers under consideration are *Misters* A and B, along with Mr Galsworthy and Mr Kipling, who Woolf identifies as "crude and immature," lacking the "spark of the woman," which also means lacking (crucially, for our purposes) "suggestive power." "And when a book lacks suggestive power," Woolf continues, "however hard it hits the surface of the mind it cannot penetrate within."[9]

Arid, barren, lifeless: the text lacking in suggestive power, the masculine text. Incandescent, undivided, nourishing: the androgynous text, resonant with suggestive power. For Woolf, it is the female principle that cocreatively enables the latter to "penetrate" the mind of the reader. Importantly, however, this is not the kind of penetration that feminist writers like Trinh T. Minh-ha describe as a scientistic will to knowledge that "perforate[s] meaning by forcing … entry," "a mentality that proves incapable of touching the living thing without crushing its delicateness."[10] The mode of penetration Woolf describes does not force entry into the object to be known; instead, it goes below the surface of the mind of the knower-reader in order to plant there a seed. To give life to new thought. To suggest.

"Suggestion" (n): *the process by which an idea brings to the mind another idea by association or natural connection; a prompting from within.*

Suggestive, not scholarship, the professor said: as if the text's ideas, quotable nuggets and Easter eggs, redolent coinages, were impure, unearned, products of spontaneity not rigor.

"Suggestion" (n): *the putting into the mind of an idea, an object of thought, a plan; the insinuation of a belief or impulse into the mind of a subject by words, gestures, or the like.*

Suggestive, not scholarship: as if the text were planting wayward seeds within its reader, which might sprout into beanstalks but only at the risk of her losing herself in the clouds.

It was all very suggestive, but it wasn't scholarship. And why not? Because there was "nothing definitive here." No "definition" (n): *the setting of bounds or limits; limitation, restriction; determination, decision; the action of making definite.* No "precise statement of the essential nature of a thing." No "stating exactly what a thing is, or what a word means."

Definition is singular. Suggestion, plural. Definition is pledge. Suggestion, potential. Definition is closed and bound. Suggestion open, unbound.

To define is to fix, to render timeless, to answer. To suggest is to lay bare the contingent, to inhabit the temporal, to question.

To define is to master; there is no definition without knowing. To suggest is to wager, to suspend the pretense.

Definition avows certainty over suggestion's possibility.

To define is expert. To suggest, amateur.

And yet.

Without the power of suggestion, no sound carries.

Without the power of suggestion, no unification of meaning.

Without the power of suggestion, death.

## But it isn't scholarship

After the exchange over *The Black Atlantic*, I passed my exams, earned a PhD, and became faculty in an English department. But I am still thinking through the professor's distinction between "suggestion" and "scholarship." On the one hand, it was neither strictly negative (scholarly vs. non-scholarly) nor simply about credentials (scholar vs. layperson). On the other hand, it was a clearly damning judgment of interdisciplinary criticism that spans the academic, journalistic, and creative. In what follows, I examine instances of such criticism in a range of institutional contexts in order to situate Gilroy's forgoing of the definitive in the broader context of a "critical amateurism" that characterizes suggestive writing across genres.

I am an academic who identifies as a "writer" more than as a "scholar." This is in part because of my background in journalism. I started submitting letters to the editor and personal essays to local outlets as a preteen. When my classmates were aspiring doctors, I said I would be "an essayist." At fifteen, I began writing a regular column for *India Currents*, a features and opinions magazine that had been a mainstay for California's Indian American immigrants since the late 1980s. After graduating from college, I became the chief editor of that magazine. Once in graduate school, I freelanced for venues on three continents, from international standard-bearers like *The New Yorker* and *The Caravan*, to a range of publications at the intersection of academic and public writing, like the *Los Angeles Review of Books*, *Public Books*, and *Guernica*.

My editorial and journalistic work was often directly related to my doctoral research; on many occasions, I was edited by other academics. But as the language of my public and creative essays began to cross-pollinate with that of my dissertation, some faculty chafed. I was cautioned against being journalistic ("This introduction reads like a movie trailer"). I was told to return to the literature, not labor to produce my own. As I wrote myself into treatments of texts by which I felt hailed, I was urged to desist. "What are you doing? ... Is what you are doing scholarship, or are you moonlighting? ... To whom are you writing these hybrid texts?"[11] Write scholarship, not journalism. Write scholarship, not literature. Write scholarship, not creative nonfiction.[12]

I was participating in what *LARB* editor Evan Kindley describes as "a boom in public writing by younger academics."[13] This boom has been widely discussed in relation to two concurrent phenomena: the evisceration of the tenure track and adjunctification of higher education, which leads many graduate students into journalism, first as an "alt-ac" side gig and then as a profession,[14] and the rise of a new culture of public intellectualism and the advent of hybrid "little magazines" welcoming to academics "hungry for new audiences and broader forms of intellectual exchange."[15] My aims were somewhat different. It wasn't a new audience I was after exactly, nor publicity as such, and I was not audaciously pursuing the mantle of public intellectual. Rather, I sought opportunities to publish in what Lili

Loofbourow and Philip Maciak term "semipublic" forums because of the form of writing such outlets afford.[16]

For Loofbourow and Maciak, semipublic writing is like "giving a public lecture, starting a colloquium series, or organizing a conference."[17] For Sharon Marcus, editor of *Public Books*, semipublic writing is "teacherly": "[it] does not avoid difficult ideas or terms; it explains them ... adopt[ing] a pedagogical stance."[18] I find the term "semipublic" useful as a qualification of Kindley's "public writing." The semipublic bridges critical and scholarly genres, public and academic audiences, and the institutional contexts of journalism and the university. Stylistically, this might mean that endnotes are permissible, yet spare. References to scholarly texts abound but are explained. Professional academics are valued but not privileged addressees. Unlike writing that seeks the widest possible public address, the semipublic informs a relatively rarefied audience. By that same token, it is more collaborative than scholarly writing: multiple editors are typically involved, and the swift publishing pace enables timely reader feedback.

Semipublic writing is one example of what I am calling critical amateurism. It approaches Gilroy's and Woolf's descriptions of the non-definitive and suggestive. It pursues moments of re-cognition, values readerly pleasure, catalyzes experiences of understanding, and renews positions of enunciation. It opens something up in and for its readers. It "turn[s] around a foreign thing or turn[s] it around to play with it ... while [respecting] its realms of opaqueness."[19] Broadly speaking, these are the aims of all my writing, whether for journalistic, literary, or academic outlets, and whether for ethnic, public, or disciplinary audiences (which are not, I should stress, necessarily discrete). Although the style of my writing is modulated by its intended audience (I might use Hinglish colloquialisms in personal essays; I lead with a hypothesis in journal articles), I strive to maintain a consistently amateur approach to my subjects. I present problems with multiple possible resolutions or none. I take artistic license and brandish the authority of biography. I try to create space in the text for the reader. I invite response, qualification, refutation, noise. I do not presume to know.

My identification as a "writer," as opposed to "scholar," stems from my journalism background. But this is only part of the story. I also have an interdisciplinary PhD, which is a bit like saying I don't have one.

Anyone who has been in an interdisciplinary program—whether in Area Studies, Identity Studies, or "Critical Studies"[20]—knows that there can be real anxieties among professors and students about the legitimacy of such training. If, to borrow Saikat Majumdar's description, "the scholar is defined by his commitment to his archive of study," then what of the scholar who promiscuously tracks between archives? If the professional scholar is one who "comes from an organized community that has institutionalized elements and traditions of knowledge held to be essentially allied to its archive of study,"[21] then what of the scholar who comes from a plurality of communities, each differently institutionalized as a counter-traditional and canon-busting knowledge project? What of the writing of this scholar, untethered from disciplinary constraints? Is such a scholar, an interdisciplinary scholar, an amateur? And if so, when is interdisciplinary scholarship scholarly enough? Such questions were at the heart of the professor's ambivalent response to *The Black Atlantic*, itself a richly interdisciplinary text written by a scholar variously described as a historian, sociologist, social theorist, and cultural critic.

Although times are changing, faculty in interdisciplinary programs like those in which I was trained typically hold doctorates in disciplines like English, philosophy, and history. For such faculty, interdisciplinarity is earned through a rejection of disciplinary location and re-housement in programs that largely didn't exist in their present configurations until the late twentieth century.[22] For their students, interdisciplinarity is a given; yet, in order to produce legible scholarship, they must establish second homes in traditional disciplines. That's how I became an English professor, despite holding no English degree.

To be clear: interdisciplinarity is not new, and Gilroy's training at the Birmingham School is a case in point. What is relatively recent is the widespread phenomenon of institutional reverse migration in which my generation has participated. My faculty moved from English to cultural studies and media, philosophy to feminist theory, and history to history of consciousness. I, one of the congenitally interdisciplined, moved from cultural and critical theory (back) into English. I am not a canon-schooled, archive-committed scholar now doing canon-busting, archive-expanding work. I was trained in canon-busting and archival promiscuity, and my writing necessarily reflects that mode of intellectual formation.

Over and above intervening in traditional disciplines, it is apparent now that interdisciplines are themselves tradition constituting and enabling of particular forms of scholarship. Recent investigations into the institutional histories of interdisciplinary fields bear this out. I am thinking, for example, of Robyn Wiegman's critical interrogation of the desires for social justice that animate identity knowledges and Mark Chiang's work on how the symbolic capital of race intersects with the cultural capital of literature in the production of Asian American Studies as a field contradictorily animated by desires for representation within the academy and for autonomy from it.[23] Both Wiegman and Chiang ask how institutional affiliations, in addition to disciplinary locations, variously enable and constrain the creative criticality of scholarship. What forms of scholarly writing do the disciplines enable, versus the interdisciplines? For that matter, what form of scholarship might it only be possible to produce outside the academy? Is there a relationship between interdisciplinary scholarly formation and the production of independent scholarship by researchers without academic posts?

I do not claim a definite correlation between interdisciplinary training and a rise in the number of independent scholars; such a statement would require empirical research beyond the scope of this discussion. But it is certainly the case that some scholars become "independent" because of the illegibility of interdisciplinary work. The cultural theorist E. Dawson Varughese finished her PhD in 2007 and taught until 2011 in a UK university. She then resigned in order to conduct research that "did not sit easily within extant research cultures." Despite her university's professed commitment to "real interdisciplinarity," Varughese told me, her work "confused" other academics: "She's not a 'proper' literary studies academic and yet, not a 'true' social scientist either." Varughese also craved more creative outlets: "My desire to work with the public through literary arts and visual cultures was going to be difficult to enact as part of my academic role. Part of becoming an independent scholar was to pursue that drive towards the creative industries." Since leaving the academy, Varughese has written four monographs and numerous articles, while founding an international literary-arts organization, *Karvan*. She attends conferences, serves on academic editorial boards, and has held visiting fellowships in India and the UK. "I don't think that I could have pursued my research interests to the extent that I have," Varughese says, "if I had been in a formal academic post."[24]

There are other reasons to leave the academy, as in the case of the feminist scholar Sara Ahmed's 2016 resignation from Goldsmiths College, London, as a protest against the university's failure to adequately address the problem of sexual harassment. Ahmed's most recent book, *Living a Feminist Life*, was written after her resignation; it offers accessible, semipublic glosses on each of her previous books along with creative meditations on its titular subject. "A bruise can lead to a wall; a bruise can be a break," Ahmed writes in a typical passage. "When a stone breaks, a stone becomes stones. A fragment: what breaks off is on the way to becoming something else. Feminism: on the way to becoming something else."[25] Even as Ahmed offers visions of feminism, she questions the knowability of the category itself. Some sections read like a series of Zen koans, rhetorical devices meant to focus the mind: "What is already willed is not encountered as willful"; "To be in question is to question being"; "We can refuse to miss what we are deemed to be missing."[26] Such elliptical, aphoristic statements serve to crystallize Ahmed's key arguments, while also demonstrating their inherently paradoxical nature: in order to be a feminist killjoy, one must have joy; to take a stand in the academy, Ahmed stands outside it.

Alexis Pauline Gumbs, who identifies as "poet, independent scholar, and activist" as well as "Black feminist love evangelist," maintains her independence from the academy in part "to fortify the efforts of teachers of all kinds," not just those within "institutions of higher education."[27] Gumbs has published two books of poetry and theory which each respond to a single work of scholarship (all the endnotes in her 2016 *Spill* refer to Hortense Spillers's *Black, White, and in Color*; in her 2018 *M Archive*, they refer to M. Jacqui Alexander's *Pedagogies of Crossing*). Here is Gumbs's description of Spillers: "Again and again, there were phrases in her work *that did far more than make her point*. They made worlds. They invited affect."[28] For Gumbs, *Pedagogies of Crossing* "works to create textual possibilities for inquiry *beyond individual scholarly authority.*"[29] Her sustained responses to these suggestive texts evidence a pedagogical ethic consonant with that of Jacques Rancière's "ignorant schoolmaster," who ignores the inequality between writer-pedagogue and reader-student so as not to stultify the latter with avowals of her ignorance relative to the former's expertise.[30] As Gumbs says, "Transformative education is not about transforming students. It is about being present for their inherent brilliance and assisting them in transforming their and our relationship to oppressive institutions."[31]

Reading Gumbs, I find myself asking if a junior scholar on the tenure track would have been able to respond to Spillers's invitation to "affect" or Alexander's invitation to forgo "authority" with such generically hybrid, formally experimental work. The question is whether or not such work would count as scholarship. Are books that engage established archives and theoretical apparatuses scholarship by default? Is Varughese's research, produced outside the academy, legible as academic? Would Ahmed's and Gumbs's recent books be judged by a university review committee as merely "suggestive"? Might they be profitably read as works of critical amateurism instead?

The questions to be asked about independent scholarship are akin to those I posed earlier about interdisciplinary work. Do "scholars" always produce "scholarship"? Must scholarship be disciplinarily legible or institutionally housed? The conventional story about interdisciplinary and independent scholars is that they do double duty: they know what they know and what the traditional scholars know. But the reality is that those of us who've been schooled in interdisciplines, like those who work outside the academy, know differently. We've read more of certain things than scholars in disciplines, and we've also read less than those scholars in the areas in which they're trained and actively working. We are not canon-bound, which may mean we are not versed in canon, but as Melanie Micir (this volume) observes of contemporary feminist publishing, repeating the past you don't remember can actually be a good thing. Any account of the tradition-busting, paradigm-moving potential of interdisciplinary and independent work thus has to take seriously that one of the qualities we bring to the table is ignorance. Non-knowledge is an enabling condition of our work. If we don't know what we don't know, we are free to know otherwise. We may not define, but we are free to suggest.

## Writing against knowing

We are free to be amateurs.

Amateurism is not, of course, ignorance. It is not strictly non-knowledge, either. It is a mode of thinking, being, and writing untethered to formal license or qualification. It is also the disposition that motors suggestion. Three recent performances of amateurism by a novelist (Jhumpa Lahiri), journalist (Mark Greif), and poet (Brian Blanchfield), each of whom also holds a professional academic post, bear out its critical and creative capacities.

First, however, a note on the romance of amateurism. During my editorial tenure at *India Currents*, I solicited essays from writers with varying levels of journalistic experience. A particularly memorable contributor was investment banker Keerthik Sasidharan, who followed that foray into journalism (I was, he says, his first editor) by contributing to numerous international venues. A decade later, now a well-known public writer with a contract for a three-volume work on Hindu mythology and history, Sasidharan describes his amateur impulse:

> [I] am often reminded of my father's friends, who, after listening to K.J. Yesudas' singing or Nikhil Banerjee's sitar, decided to learn music or purchase a sitar. As a child, I found their efforts mystifying. After all, they would never perform in front of an audience. Nor would they be any good at it compared to a child half their age ... Their exertions seemed like an indulgence ... But now ... I have begun to see what they truly were after: soak themselves in the warm afterglow of something they intuited as larger than themselves ... they were the first amateurs I had met in my life; individuals who weren't overwhelmed by the enormity of the journeys they had embarked on ... they were like how I am with my own efforts — relieved to just be without any pressure to be smart, clever, or have profound insights. I plod along, perhaps for the pleasure of plodding itself. It is this which distinguishes the amateur from the professional: to travel with no intention of reaching the destination.[32]

Sasidharan voices here an amateurism of pleasure and following one's inclinations. Politics, literature, art, philosophy, physics: whatever escaped his attention during his education and professional training he now explores with gusto. As an amateur, he need not have "profound insights." Free of the pressure to be original, he can be citational: in the "warm afterglow" of each subject he pursues, he imitates, references, and tries on for size.

The romance of amateurism finds expression in each of the works I am about to discuss but with an important qualification. For Sasidharan, and as the old saying goes, it's the journey that counts, not the point of arrival. Note that this commonplace preserves the destination as out there somewhere, reachable for some professional others, if not the amateur. For Lahiri, Greif, and Blanchfield, by contrast, "it's the journey that counts" because there is no destination. These amateurs plod along not as an alternative to achieving profundity but as the only possible mode of knowing once they've dispensed with the illusion of the profound.

Take for example Lahiri's 2016 *In Other Words*, which the Pulitzer-winning English-language fictionist wrote in Italian. The memoir recounts Lahiri's decision to move to Rome and read and write only in Italian, which she has long loved. The move is "a choice … a risk," "an act of demolition, a new beginning."[33] Having achieved international literary renown in the Anglophone world, Lahiri decides to strip herself of skill and become an amateur in the field in which she is already a celebrated professional. This renunciation of linguistic expertise enables her to experiment with being an "author" who doesn't "feel authoritative."[34]

Lahiri's project bears some of the "indulgence" Sasidharan first suspects of his father. The writer has financial resources, contacts, and editorial support that few others could match. Moreover, Lahiri's amateurism is compelling precisely because she is no amateur. The fascination of *In Other Words* is the opportunity to read bad writing by a master writer, to revel in the knower's knowing engagement with not knowing. That said, it would be a mistake to read Lahiri's project solely in these terms. As she explains, she is after a sustained condition of partial, "useful" ignorance.[35] Thus, if she should ever become as fluent in Italian as she is in English, the game would be up: "If it were possible to bridge the distance between me and Italian, I would stop writing in that language."[36] The appeal of writing in Italian is that she can never become an Italian writer.

Lahiri's experiments in amateurism are instructive. For one, by trading "certainty for uncertainty," she is able to "[learn], again, to write."[37] "My knowledge of English is both an advantage and a hindrance," she explains. "I rewrite everything like a lunatic until it satisfies me, while in Italian, like a soldier in the desert, I have to simply keep going."[38] Whereas Lahiri's English prose bears the burden of her mastery, her Italian is free to be imperfect, awkward, peculiar. In short, her Italian lives and allows her to feel alive. Her English, condemned to perfection, "no longer appeals to [her]" and falls plump to the ground.[39] Ironically, writing in Italian has the unintended effect of improving Lahiri's English. The journey into non-knowledge reconfigures the knower.

Lahiri's writing career has involved a series of moves away from scholarship qua scholarship—from credentialed academic dissertation in Renaissance Studies, to English-language creative fiction, to Italian-language writing that revels in ignorance—though she is also a professor of creative writing at Princeton. My next example of critical amateurism is by Mark Greif, a cofounder of *n+1* who was at the vanguard of the "little magazine" movement credited with energizing the semipublic writing discussed above. Greif is also a professor of English at Stanford, and his work tracks between the modes of scholarly, journalistic and academic.

Around 2009, Greif resolved to learn how to rap. Barack Obama had just become president, and, Greif writes, "The feeling I had at his election was that I ought to change, too. I ought to learn something."[40] He developed a method of approach: he would learn only "the classics ... songs I could live with forever."[41] Greif had no intention of mastering the art of rap or becoming a rapper; he vowed not to write original pieces or perform in public. Like Sasidharan and Lahiri, he aimed at a deeply internal reconfiguration of the self that would involve both complete "detachment" and "immersion."[42] "I just had the idea," he writes, "that I could fix myself, privately."[43]

"Learning to Rap," the essay that recounts this effort, is included in Greif's 2016 *Against Everything*, which collects his widely circulated takes on exercise, Radiohead, and Octomom. The rap essay is a comparatively minor piece, but it illuminates Greif's larger concerns with knowledge and cults of authority. In an essay "On Food," Greif queries the value of experience in relation to expertise, asking, "Could there be anything I know that the usual food critics ... don't?"[44] In an essay on Thoreau, he confesses that the philosopher became for him "the most important thinker" before he had even read his work.[45] This is the way in which we often "know" what we know: not as books read, but as books to be read; not as what we have learned, but as what others have told us; not as who we are, but as who we sense we ought to be.

*Against Everything* is really against knowing, against thinking one knows, and against thinking one knows without thinking about why one thinks one knows. "Learning to Rap" is full of such cautions: "Even I, knowing nothing ..."[46] As Greif grapples with rap's intricate lyricism, he acknowledges that he is struggling belatedly with things "all hip-hop listeners already know."[47] But his point is not to offer some original theory of rap, not to know better than others, nor even to know differently. Rather, Greif aims to also know, to almost know, and to approximate knowing. Deferring knowledge in this way is an amateur's tactic, one that allows Greif to focus on the desires, anxieties, and experiences that propel his quest—that is, the "why" of knowing, as opposed to the "what."

Approximating knowing is also the project of poet Brian Blanchfield's *Proxies: Essays Near Knowing*, my last example of critical amateurism. The book offers a series of short essays on topics ranging from foot washing to tumbleweeds. Each is a proxy for knowledge of its titular subject, "a stand-in" liable to be asked "on what authority" it performs its approximations.[48] For Blanchfield, who is a professor of creative writing and literature at the University of Idaho, the appeal of the proxy is that it "expresses a kind of concession to imprecision, a failure"; in the sciences, he notes, proxy is "the word for a subject you choose to study to produce data that can *approximate* the data you'd get from the actual, desired subject, if it were not prohibitively hard to apprehend."[49] As he engages his surrounds and revisits formative texts, Blanchfield offers readings that suggest what one might know about the "actual, desired subjects" of literature and the world, if they were not always just beyond reach.

Like Erich Auerbach, who wrote *Mimesis* without access to a research library, Blanchfield writes without looking anything up.[50] Unlike Auerbach, Blanchfield refuses access to that which he might easily obtain. It is a tactical deferral of knowledge like Greif's that allows him to explore the epistemological value of error. "I wrote these essays with the internet off," he explains. "I determined not to review again the books and other works I consulted in memory, and I did not ... verify assertions or ground speculation or firm up approximations."[51] If scholarship is the product of research-based conclusions, Blanchfield's essays are deliberately "unresearched ... analytic but nonacademic."[52] He quotes without verifying quotations, cites without confirming sources, and paraphrases with impunity. *Proxies* closes, however, with an extended "Correction" that revises the primary text. In some cases, the corrections are factual: North Carolina's state tree is the longleaf pine, not the flowering dogwood. In others, however, they are nuanced qualifications that deepen the original text.

In "On Reset," an essay that begins with Blanchfield watching a series of videotaped soap opera auditions and ends by meditating on poetry, Blanchfield quotes Muriel Rukeyser:

> Choose your poet here, or, rather, do not choose but recall ... the light of a new awareness that was not something you *learned* but something rather that you seemed to *remember*.
>
> This is the multiple time-sense in poetry, before which your slow mortality takes its proper place.[53]

These lines bolster Blanchfield's argument that poetry does not teach the reader so much as it renews for her what she already knows, enabling a form of self-return that in turn constitutes the reader as poet. This is a theme developed throughout *Proxies*: that the best writing enables the reader to discover "as though remembering"; that Blanchfield's own writing will "[lay] the propitious conditions for others to come into their own as though it were a return."[54] But Rukeyser's actual words are these:

> Remember what happened to you when you came to your poem, any poem whose truth overcame all inertia in you at that moment, so that your slow mortality took its proper place, and before it the light of a new awareness was not something new, but something you *recognized*.
>
> That is the multiple time-sense in poetry, that is the ever new, which is recognized as something already in ourselves, but not discovered.[55]

There are subtle differences between the two passages, including the difference between remembrance and recognition. In the first iteration, the reader does not learn from a poet or poem but is moved to recollection of former knowledge by the work in question. In the second iteration, the reader is already poet; poetry is in and constitutive of the truth of the self. Whereas the multiple time-sense in the first iteration is external to the self, in the second, it is a property of the self. By offering the corrected quote fifty pages after its misquotation, Blanchfield invites the reader to query not only Rukeyser's theory of poetic awareness but also the functioning of our memories in relation to the readings we carry within us. What we know, we only ever know in fragments. What we write is always taken up in pieces, refracted variously by our addressees. This is a theory of life as much as it is a theory of critical amateurism and a first premise for scholarship worthy of the name.

* * *

As a professional academic, I am invested in the question of what "scholarship" is—thus, my lengthy response, years in the making, to the professor. As a writer who strives to infuse my work with the amateurism of suggestion, I am even more interested in what it could be. What kinds of scholarship would we produce if we pursued our subjects the way Lahiri pursues Italian: "as if [it] were a book that, no matter how hard [we] work, [we] can't write"?[56] What if we proceeded from the premise that we are not experts, will never be experts, but rather, in Greif's words, "slow learners"?[57] We would be content that our work be brought to fruition by others. We would be willing, to quote Blanchfield's reading of Roland Barthes, to "[open] the dossier wherein much more lies, should anyone wish to pursue it."[58] And we would recognize that at its suggestive best, scholarship, too, is "always unfinished, always being remade."[59]

This is, at the time of writing in 2018, yet another "the sky is falling" moment for humanistic inquiry. Political upheaval, economic and social divestment from public education, rampant anti-intellectualism—and that's only to state the obvious. But crises also present opportunities for us "to engage in experiments that will allow us to shift and adapt to new ecosystems."[60] Critical amateurism at the intersections of scholarship, journalism, and creative writing is one such experiment that humanists can embrace in our pursuit of renewal, both within and outside the academy. Writing toward a horizon of mastery that is always already deferred by the knowledge of knowing's impossibility, we will demonstrate how ignorance can be a creative asset, as opposed to an alibi. We will show how "near knowing" is epistemology, and expose when it masks not knowing at all.

That is, in any case, the kind of scholarship I aim to write. Call it amateur. Call it criticism. Call it—what was that word again?—well, you know.

# Notes

1 Paul Gilroy, *The Black Atlantic: Modernity and Double Consciousness* (Cambridge: Harvard University Press, 1993), xi.
2 Virginia Woolf, *A Room of One's Own* (1929: New York: Harvest, 1989), 101.
3 Claude Lévi-Strauss, *The Savage Mind*, trans. George Weidenfeld and Nicolson, Ltd. (1962: Chicago: University of Chicago Press, 1966), 21.
4 Woolf, *Room*, 98.
5 Ibid., 101.
6 Kay Ryan, *Say Uncle: Poems* (New York: Grove Press, 2000), 46.
7 Woolf, *Room*, 101.
8 Ibid., 100.
9 Ibid., 102.
10 Trinh T. Minh-ha, *Woman Native, Other: Writing Postcoloniality and Feminism* (Bloomington: Indiana University Press, 1989), 48–49.
11 Lili Loofbourow and Phillip Maciak, "Introduction: The Time of the Semipublic Intellectual," *PMLA* 130, no. 2 (2015): 439.
12 These positions are not uniformly shared by senior scholars. Sharon Marcus, Dean of Humanities at Columbia University, argues, "The ability to be intellectually bilingual, by which I mean the ability to translate specialist knowledge into more accessible terms, should never detract from a junior scholar's merits…public writing is a positive contribution to knowledge." See Sharon Marcus, "How to Talk about Books You *Have* Read," *PMLA* 130, no. 2 (2015): 478.
13 Evan Kindley, "Growing Up in Public: Academia, Journalism, and the New Public Intellectual," *PMLA* 130, no. 2 (2015): 471.
14 There are many more writers who fit this bill than I can list here; what follows is a partial and idiosyncratic list. For examples of PhDs-turned-journalists, see Aaron Bady, Jacob Brogan, Sarah Kendzior, Jo Livingstone, and Lili Loofbourow. Many scholars maintain formal perches in the academy while engaging in semipublic writing. See, for example, Jelani Cobb, Merve Emre, Eve Ewing, Hua Hsu, Amitava Kumar, Emily Lordi, Kate Manne, Namwali Serpell, Richard Jean So, and Amia Srinivasan (see also graduate students Marissa Brostoff, Andrea Long Chu, Jane Hu, and Clint Smith). Finally, there are

numerous PhDs who are also creative writers. To name a few from my research field of South Asian Anglophone literature, see Amit Chaudhuri, Amitav Ghosh, Jhumpa Lahiri, and Saikat Majumdar.

15 Loofbourow and Maciak, "Introduction," 441.

16 As I was completing this essay, and observing the radical incompleteness of note 14, I began to wonder if Kindley's "boom" has not been more directly implicated in the ongoing "bust" of the academic humanities in the United States than is typically acknowledged. In addition to the semi-public outlets and little magazines I mention above, there are numerous institutions now devoted to channeling academic writers into the public sphere, like The OpEd Project, The Conversation, The Immanent Frame, and Arcade. Numerous peer-reviewed journals now also publish semipublic content online (for example, *boundary2* has *b2o, Social Text* has *Periscope, Post45* has *Contemporaries*, and *Public Books* is affiliated with *Public Culture*). Contributing to public and semipublic outlets seems to be becoming a new norm in the academy, not the exception. This is in part because of the swelling ranks of PhD-holding editors, whose academic interests motor both the content they solicit and the writers to whom they turn. Then, there is the fact that academic writers are a knowledgeable, reliable source of creative and critical content who are, in most cases, otherwise salaried and therefore willing to write for free. Does this movement represent an amplification of academic writing or its displacement? This is a question to be explored at length elsewhere. Here, I wish to underscore that my call for a critical amateurism of suggestion is intended to deepen and extend the category of scholarship, not to evacuate, nullify, or replace it.

17 Ibid., 445.

18 Marcus, "How to," 476–477.

19 Trinh, *Woman*, 48.

20 What I am provisionally calling "Critical Studies" programs include those in which I studied, Berkeley Rhetoric and Duke Literature, as well as the University of Chicago's Committee on Social Thought, Brown's Modern Culture and Media, NYU's Social and Cultural Analysis, History of Consciousness at Santa Cruz, Culture and Theory at Irvine, Comparative Studies in Discourse and Society at Minnesota, and Modern Thought and Literature at Stanford.

21 Majumdar, "The Critic as Amateur," *New Literary History* 48, no. 1 (2017): 1–24.

22 While the pioneering Birmingham School was founded by Richard Hoggart in 1964, departments like Duke Literature and Berkeley Rhetoric were not refashioned as cultural studies and critical theory programs until the 1980s and 1990s. For a discussion of Duke

Literature, albeit a polemical one, see David Yaffe, "The Department That Fell to Earth," *Lingua Franca* 9, no. 1 (1999): 24–31.

23 See Mark Chiang, *The Cultural Capital of Asian American Studies: Autonomy and Representation in the University* (New York: New York University Press, 2009) and Robyn Wiegman, *Object Lessons* (Durham: Duke University Press, 2012).

24 E-mail correspondence with Varughese, June 10, 2018.

25 Sarah Ahmed, *Living a Feminist Life* (Durham: Duke University Press, 2017), 186.

26 Ibid., 113, 134, 185.

27 Heather Laine Talley, "Brilliance Remastered: An Interview with Alexis Pauline Gumbs," *Feminist Teacher* 22, no. 2 (2012): 165.

28 Alexis Pauline Gumbs, *Spill: Scenes of Black Feminist Fugitivity* (Durham: Duke University Press, 2016), xi, my emphasis.

29 Alexis Pauline Gumbs, *M Archive: After the End of the World* (Durham: Duke University Press, 2018), ix, my emphasis.

30 Jacques Rancière, "The Emancipated Spectator," *ArtForum* 45, no. 7 (2007).

31 Talley, "Brilliance Remastered: An Interview with Alexis Pauline Gumbs," 165.

32 Keerthik Sasidharan, "In Praise of Amateurs in an Age of Professionals," *The Hindu*, January 14, 2018. Available online: http://www.thehindu.com/opinion/columns/in-praise-of-amateurs-in-an-age-of-professionals/article22437509.ece (accessed May 21, 2018).

33 Jhumpa Lahiri, *In Other Words*, trans. Ann Goldstein (New York: Alfred A. Knopf, 2016), xiii, 207.

34 Ibid., 37, 83.

35 Ibid., 43.

36 Ibid., 95.

37 Ibid., 37, 213.

38 Ibid., 65.

39 Ibid., 117.

40 Mark Greif, *Against Everything* (New York: Vintage Books, 2016), 163.

41 Ibid, 137.

42 Lahiri, *In Other Words*, 183.

43 Greif, *Against*, 139, 136.

44 Ibid., 54.

45 Ibid., xi.

46 Ibid., 141.

47 Ibid., 139.

48 Brian Blanchfield, *Proxies: Essays Near Knowing* (New York: Nightboat Books, 2016), viii.

49 Ibid., viii.

50 The story about Auerbach is recounted in Majumdar, 21.
51 Blanchfield, *Proxies*, vii.
52 Ibid., vii.
53 Ibid., 127.
54 Ibid., 20, 22.
55 Ibid., 177.
56 Lahiri, *In Other Words*, 29.
57 Greif, *Against*, 299.
58 Blanchfield, *Proxies*, 97.
59 Gilroy, *The Black Atlantic*, xi.
60 Eric Hayot, "The Sky Is Falling," *Profession*, May 21, 2018. Available online: https://profession.mla.hcommons.org/2018/05/ (accessed July 18, 2018).

## Bibliography

Ahmed, Sara. *Living a Feminist Life*. Durham: Duke University Press, 2017.

Blanchfield, Brian. *Proxies: Essays Near Knowing*. New York: Nightboat Books, 2016.

Chiang, Mark. *The Cultural Capital of Asian American Studies: Autonomy and Representation in the University*. New York: New York University Press, 2009.

Gilroy, Paul. *The Black Atlantic: Modernity and Double Consciousness*. Cambridge: Harvard University Press, 1993.

Greif, Mark. *Against Everything*. New York: Vintage Books, 2016.

Gumbs, Alexis Pauline. *Spill: Scenes of Black Feminist Fugitivity*. Durham: Duke University Press, 2016.

Gumbs, Alexis Pauline. *M Archive: After the End of the World*. Durham: Duke University Press, 2018.

Hayot, Eric. "The Sky Is Falling." *Profession*, May 21, 2018. Available online: https://profession.mla.hcommons.org/2018/05/ (accessed July 18, 2018).

Kindley, Evan. "Growing Up in Public: Academia, Journalism, and the New Public Intellectual." *PMLA* 130, no. 2 (2015): 467–473.

Lahiri, Jhumpa. *In Other Words*, trans. Ann Goldstein. New York: Alfred A. Knopf, 2016.

Lévi-Strauss, Claude. *The Savage Mind*, trans. George Weidenfeld and Nicolson, Ltd. Chicago: University of Chicago Press, 1966 (1962).

Loofbourow, Lili and Phillip Maciak. "Introduction: The Time of the Semipublic Intellectual." *PMLA* 130, no. 2 (2015): 439–445.

Majumdar, Saikat. "The Critic as Amateur." *New Literary History* 48, no. 1 (2017): 1–25.

Marcus, Sharon. "How to Talk about Books You *Have* Read." *PMLA* 130, no. 2 (2015): 474–480.

Rancière, Jacques. "The Emancipated Spectator." *ArtForum* 45, no. 7 (2007).

Ryan, Kay. "Great Thoughts," *Say Uncle: Poems*. New York: Grove Press, 2000.

Sasidharan, Keerthik. "In Praise of Amateurs in an Age of Professionals." *The Hindu*. January 14, 2018. Available online: http://www.thehindu.com/opinion/columns/in-praise-of-amateurs-in-an-age-of-professionals/article22437509.ece (accessed May 21, 2018).

Talley, Heather Laine. "Brilliance Remastered: An Interview with Alexis Pauline Gumbs." *Feminist Teacher* 22, no. 2 (2012): 165–167.

Trinh T. Minh-Ha. *Woman, Native, Other: Writing Postcoloniality and Feminism*. Bloomington: Indiana University Press, 1989.

Wiegman, Robyn. *Object Lessons*. Durham: Duke University Press, 2012.

Woolf, Virginia. *A Room of One's Own*. New York: Harvest, 1989 (1929).

Yaffe, David. "The Department that Fell to Earth: The Deflation of Duke English." *Lingua Franca* 9, no. 1 (1999): 24–31.

# 4

# Beyond Professionalism: The Pasts and Futures of Creative Criticism

*Peter D. McDonald*

Trigger warning: *the following does not contain a definition of "creative criticism" which is not a determinate or determinable critical method and can never be a school. Using Rabindranath Tagore and Maurice Blanchot as guides, the essay takes an alternative, anti-scholastic route through the labyrinth of a multilingual intellectual history in order to explore the promise of creative criticism as a practice, particularly in today's corporatized university, and to reaffirm the public value of innovative literary writing in all its unpredictable, generative and experiential dimensions.*

*for Mike Holland*

"Can the criticism of literature and culture really be professionalized? With such objects of study, does criticism retain an amateur impulse even as it evolves into a highly specialized activity enshrined in the university?" These are the central questions this collection seeks to address. In my view, we cannot approach them today without first considering two pairs of awkwardly juxtaposed quotations. Here is the first pair:

> Professionalism is a means not an end. Less is more. Professors are better off when they professionalize less and risk extinction when professionalization is primary.[1]

> An academic can get on a treadmill where the task is just to keep on churning out papers for the peer-reviewed journals without looking up and asking oneself that most challenging of questions—what is it all for?[2]

And here is the second pair:

> Any attempt at serious thought, be it mathematical, scientific, metaphysical or formal, in the widest creative-poetic vein, is a vocation. It comes to possess one like an unbidden, often unwelcome summons.[3]

> This talk will argue for a transformative vision of the university that positions it not as a separate enclosed space but as a busy informational crossroads in which the university clearly identifies the "value added" it provides and takes an active role not only in creating and disseminating knowledge but also in directing it toward better and more productive practices that contribute to human and planetary flourishing.[4]

If I was giving this as a talk, I would pause at this point to allow you to reread each statement without being distracted by any thought of its provenance. But since this is a piece of writing, I will have to move swiftly on to the who, the when, and the where.

The first is thesis no. 1 of the "95 Theses" the poet-academic Charles Bernstein published on the MLA *Profession* website in October 2016. Part mock-Lutheran pronouncement, part "swan song" or "duck soup," as he prefaces them, the theses are both a preretirement speech-manifesto, drawing on his experience of the American university system as a salaried academic and a playfully aphoristic warning about the perils of over-professionalization, given in his guise as a leading L=A=N=G=U=A=G=E poet. Having made his literary debut in the mid-1970s, Bernstein took his first academic job at SUNY Buffalo in 1989. He retires as Professor of English and Comparative Literature at the University of Pennsylvania in 2019. The second quotation comes from *A University Education* (2017), a memoir-cum-PR exercise by the British Conservative politician David Willetts who, as Minister for Universities and Science from 2010 to 2014, led the latest phase in the marketization of higher education in England. He makes his own observation about solipsistic (Sisyphean?) professionalism in a passage justifying the introduction of impact assessments in the 2008–2014 Research Excellence Framework (REF), a state audit of research in UK universities the Thatcher government initiated in 1986. While researchers allegedly feared the new requirement "brought the barbarians even closer to the gates of academe," Willetts insists it was meant simply to encourage them "to think about the potential contribution their research can make to economy and society."[5]

The second pairing is less extreme but perhaps no less consequential. Rather than putting a poet-academic alongside a politician, it juxtaposes two academics with apparently very different interests, sensibilities, and much else besides. The first comes from *Errata* (1997), George Steiner's memoirs of an academic career begun in the late 1940s. Though primarily concerned with the fate of "high culture" in "mass-consumption and egalitarian democracies," a preoccupation that reflects his indebtedness to the Frankfurt School of the 1920s and 1930s, Steiner does not restrict the "vocation" of "serious thought" to major artists and thinkers alone: "Even the teacher, the expositor, the critic who lacks creative genius but who devotes his existence to the presentment and perpetuation of the real thing, is a being infected (*krank an Gott*)."[6] This idea of the critic in turn reflects his understanding of the university as a place where "the student is brought into personal contact with, is made vulnerable to, the aura and the threat of the first class."[7] In the second quotation, the critic N. Katherine Hayles, who made her name with *How We Became Posthuman: Virtual Bodies in Cybernetics, Literature and Informatics* (1999), sets out her stall for a lecture she gave in March 2018 entitled "Universities at the Crossroads." Various forms of online learning, she believes, "pose significant challenges to traditional ideas of the university as a cloistered space where students came and learned about subjects they could not access otherwise," making it incumbent on academics to develop "robust modes of discourse that reach beyond scholarly communities to the general public."[8] In fact, as the lecture itself reveals, Hayles is wary of this brave new world and has far more in common with Steiner than her overly provocative billing suggests.

So, looking across the pairings, we have, on the one hand, an unlikely trio—an avant-garde poet, a scholar of new technologies, and a Thatcherite politician—articulating a consensus of sorts about the hazards of academic professionalism. I say "of sorts" because this is the only point on which they agree. Among other things neither Hayles nor Bernstein shares Willetts's enthusiasm for a particular brand of economics Mark Fisher aptly calls "capitalist realism."[9] Adopting its characteristic idiom, Willetts repeatedly represents his marketizing interventions as a challenge to the "producer power" of universities in the interests of the student-consumer—this is the language of "realism," the only language its proponents take seriously.[10] Despite her appeals to a readily definable "value added" and her call for academic knowledge to be directed toward "more productive practices," other favorite phrases in the "realists" lexicon, Hayles spends a significant portion of her lecture pointing out the damaging effects of corporatization in the United States, echoing the sentiments of Bernstein's mordant thesis no. 42: "The poetry and poetics I read and write are not a product of the world financial system but of the world semantic system."[11]

On the other hand, again looking across the pairings, we have in contrast to this oddly discordant trio Steiner's lofty tenor coruscating in a self-consciously antiquated if semi-secularized theological language of vocation. True, he does not talk about the "gates of academe" or celebrate the university as "a cloistered space"—he is too interested in the disruptive effects of being "exposed to the virus of the absolute"—but he is in no doubt that his untimely minoritarian meditations on culture, criticism, and the university "will strike the vast majority of 'normal' citizens as absurd and even offensive."[12] Having outlined his credo, he comments: "I think of myself as a Platonic anarchist. Not, I realise, a winning ticket."[13] Part of the challenge, then, is how to think the "amateur impulse"—a phrase to which I shall return—when the pressures, if not the attacks, on professionalism both from within and beyond the university are so various and acute and when it often appears as if the only way forward involves either a capitulation to the "business ontology" of "capitalist realism" or a knowingly defeatist return to a theology of vocation.[14]

The awkwardness of these various conjunctions, no less than the extremity of the disjunctions, may be peculiar to our times. The quarrels about professionalism within the university are not: they have shadowed and often shaped the history of literary studies since at least the 1920s. Just as I. A. Richards was seeking "to habilitate the critic" as an "expert in matters of taste"—in the face not just of a commercialized mass culture but as a counter to censorious, inexpert moralists and to an older generation of critics wedded to a bankrupt version of 1890s aestheticism—Rabindranath Tagore was provocatively comparing academic professionalism with all its disciplinary disputes over boundaries to the "Cult of the Nation," describing it as "the region where men specialise their knowledge and organize their power, mercilessly elbowing each other in the struggle to come to the front."[15] This reflected Tagore's life-long unease about expert critics who have, as he put it in an essay of 1894, "worked out a fixed weight and number of set formulations for literature."[16]

These early tensions persisted, morphing over time and resurfacing at various charged moments, notably with the rise of cultural studies in the 1980s. For Bruce Robbins, a proponent of and commentator on that particular turn, the expansion of "academic literature departments" in the "decades immediately before and (especially) after the Second World War" helped institutionalize the idea of "culture, art, the aesthetic" as marking "a distance from the sordidness of the material, utilitarian, power-ridden world where livings are earned."[17] This idea then fostered, and was in turn fostered by, the emergence of a "professional anti-professionalism" in which the academic critic figured at best as a "self-appointed conscience of society," at worst as a "free-floating *Luftmensh*."[18] Rejecting this particular brand of professional bad faith, Robbins defended cultural studies as a "secular vocation," though not in Steiner's sense.[19] If his new-style cultural critics of the 1980s did not disavow professionalism like the old-style literary critics of the 1950s, neither did they claim a Steineresque "unaccountable authority."[20] According to Robbins, the only professionalism that mattered for them was one that "appeals to (and helps refashion) public values in its efforts to justify (and refashion) professional practice."[21]

Not everyone shared his enthusiasm for this new development. Echoing Harold Bloom's *The Western Canon* (1994), the academic critic Rónán McDonald blamed cultural studies for precipitating a fatal "turn from evaluative and aesthetic concerns in university humanities' departments."[22] Admittedly, other factors, some internal to the profession, others external to it, played a part as well. He highlights "the tendency of academic criticism to become increasingly inward-looking"—in this case as a consequence of "Theory"—and, following the rise of the internet and the blogosphere, "the momentum for journalistic and popular criticism to become a much more democratic, dispersive affair, no longer left in the hands of the experts."[23] Yet since it was cultural studies that really "led to the death of the critic" as an "arbiter of public taste," these developments were only secondary.[24] By forsaking "evaluation," apparently in the interests of democratic engagement, cultural studies cut academic critics off from "a wider public," relegating them to the specialist journal and the seminar room.[25]

McDonald's is not a counsel of ironized despair like Steiner's, however. "Perhaps the critic is not dead," he comments cautiously in his conclusion, "but simply sidelined and slumbering" like a fairy-tale princess.[26] He pins his hopes of a revival on a new Prince Richards bearing "the idea of artistic merit."[27] Not that he believes Richards can simply come back from the dead. For one thing, any pretender to his eminence would have to relinquish his claims to scientific authority because "the discipline of English literary studies needs to make room for impressionistic, subjective response."[28] No pretensions to scientific objectivity, then, nor, indeed, any old-style anti-professionalism—he insists "it will take years to master the art of criticism"—but an accredited, and presumably publically recognized, expertise based on firm convictions about literary value (recall Steiner's "real thing") leavened or checked by subjectivist impressionism.[29] For university-based critics concerned about the future of the profession and committed to understanding and promoting the public value of literature, McDonald, in my view, offers neither a viable way forward nor a plausible means of coming to terms with the various historical and contemporary entanglements I have sketched so far. Yet, if we also discount Steiner's more baroque retro-vision, then what other possibilities are there? As ever, some lie in the obscure recesses of the past or, as I shall argue in this case, in a series of unlikely affinities between two writer-philosophers of the long twentieth century: Maurice Blanchot (1907–2003) and Rabindranath Tagore (1861–1941).

* * *

I start with Blanchot's short essay originally published in French as "Qu'en est-il de la critique?" (What about Criticism?) in 1959. For my purposes it is important that Blanchot begins by briefly situating his own question in the context of a wider debate about institutions of knowledge creation in postwar France. As he saw it, literary criticism at that moment occupied an uneasy, even "compromised" position—"a half-way house" in Hill's translation—between "two weighty institutions": journalism and the university, the one producing "day-to-day knowledge, which is rushed, inquiring and ephemeral," the other "scholarly knowledge, which is established and permanent."[30] Blanchot's own essay originally appeared in *Arguments*, which was also neither one thing nor the other. A short-lived little magazine produced by a dissident group of Marxists and fellow travelers who broke with the strongly Stalinist French Communist party following Khrushchev's denunciation of Stalin in 1956, it included a range of political, cultural, and literary essays—that is, neither ephemeral newspaper reviews nor solid scholarly articles. Blanchot's own contribution appeared alongside others by Jean Starobinski (on psychoanalysis) and Lucien Goldmann (on Marxism) under the general heading "Ou en est la critique aurjourd'hui?" (Where Is Criticism Today?)—hence his interest in its institutional locations.[31]

Rehearsing Blanchot's answers to this question would be impossible today. Under pressure from the digital revolution and a collapse in advertising revenues, contemporary newspapers devote less and less space to literary reviews whether in print or online, though, for Katharine Viner, editor of the UK *Guardian*, this is the least of their problems. Their very raison d'être as a primary source of "day-to-day knowledge," not to mention their "weighty" institutional standing, is itself threatened as the likes of Google and Facebook replace "editors with algorithms—shattering the public square into millions of personalized newsfeeds, shifting entire societies away from the open terrain of genuine debate and argument."[32] The same cannot be said of the university, which has, for better or worse, become criticism's principal host, some might say, at the expense of "scholarly knowledge" in Blanchot's sense. Yet its prestige is no less precarious than journalism's and for similar reasons. While various forms of corporatization have steadily hollowed out universities in the UK, the United States, and beyond over the past three decades, other forces have proved as corrosive elsewhere in more recent years. Speaking as president of the Central European University in Hungary, Michael Ignatieff, for instance, argues that a combination of factors—the digital revolution coupled with the rise of populism and the turn toward authoritarianism—have made institutions like his own as vulnerable as the "free press" in many parts of the world.[33] Echoing Hayles's defense of university autonomy, albeit without embracing her enthusiasm for its potential as a "busy informational crossroads," he calls on fellow academics to defend its traditional mission in terms Blanchot may well have recognized, reaffirming its responsibility to "winnow the hard facts of knowledge from the chaff of opinion, rumour, fantasy, paranoia, tweets, blogs and the whole deluge of false information which makes it almost impossible for societies to deliberate freely on a basis that we actually know to be true."[34]

This is of course not the whole story. Criticism's uneasy liaison with journalism may have weakened as much as its compromise with the university has gained strength, but alternative venues, like that represented by *Arguments* itself, have survived and continue to emerge. *Arguments* may have run for only six years (1956–1962) but it served as a model for the British *New Left Review* (1960–), which still appears bimonthly, and new forums, like the print and digital magazine *n+1* (2004–), and the online journal *Prac Crit* (2014–), still create space for a kind of criticism self-consciously positioned outside the mainstream media and the university. Also worth noting in this regard is the writer Amit Chaudhuri's "literary activism" initiative, which has been running since 2014. Responding in part to the rise of cultural studies in terms McDonald would recognize, this initiative is directed primarily against the "market activism" characteristic of the corporatized publishing world that emerged in the mid-1990s, which, Chaudhuri argues, deformed the Anglophone cultural landscape of the new millennium by reconfiguring literary value in exclusively commercial terms.[35]

In his brief survey of the very different landscape of late 1950s France, Blanchot was less concerned about criticism's institutional compromises than he was about their consequences for literature. "Literature is what criticism is applied to," he notes, identifying the key challenge, "but criticism does not manifest literature."[36] Instead, given its dependency on two institutions each "having a firm direction and organization of its own," it simply shows "how journalism and the academy assert themselves."[37] In effect, caught between the journalistic and the scholarly, criticism at that point revealed little or nothing about literature as such and rather a lot about the interests, forms of knowledge, and discourses of the two powerful institutions on which it depended for its very existence. This claim sounds exaggerated, perhaps even anachronistic given the many changes both have undergone since the 1960s, but only if we discount the testimony of some contemporary writers. Consider, as one example among many, the Nigerian novelist Chimamanda Ngozi Adichie's response to a question about postcolonial theory: "Postcolonial theory? I don't know what it means. I think it is something that professors made up because they needed to get jobs."[38] Given that the university is now criticism's main host, it is unsurprising that this offhand, not to say knowingly deflationary, comment caused a stir, especially among academics.

Yet do criticism's entanglements with journalism and the university mean it has no serious function even in these terms? On this question Blanchot keeps an open mind but only just: "It may be, of course, that the conclusion to draw from this is that criticism plays a fairly important role, which is to establish a relationship between literature and such realities, which are indeed significant ones. The role of criticism, it could be said, is to mediate, and that of the literary critic to act as honest broker."[39] Think of McDonald's "public critic," perhaps, or the idea of criticism James Wood advocates in books like *The Nearest Thing to Life* (2015) and the space he has made for himself in the *Guardian*, *New York Times*, *London Review of Books*, and *New Yorker*, among others, since the early 1990s—though he has been Professor of the Practice of Literary Criticism at Harvard since 2014.[40] Any more institutionalized university critics doubtful about the mediating aspirations underpinning this kind of writing could do well to reflect on the latest publishing figures for academic monographs. A major British report of 2017 shows that while the number of titles in the "Literature" category produced annually between 2005 and 2014 rose by 37 percent (from just under 8,000 to just under 11,000), the average sales per title fell from 88 to 34. Literary criticism is the largest sub-category, accounting for 70 percent of titles published in 2014, but it garnered only 38 percent of sales. Literary biography, by contrast, made up 12 percent of the titles and 30 percent of the sales; whereas literary theory represented 4 percent and 6 percent respectively.[41] As these figures suggest, UK-based academic critics do not need state-imposed impact assessments to remind them to ask, what is it all for? No doubt the answer has rather a lot to do with career advancement within the university as well as recognition within increasingly disparate academic micro-communities (guilds? cliques? cults?), linked via hyper-specialized conferences and journals, and almost nothing to do with mediating between scholarly and journalistic forms of knowledge. Recall Bernstein on the risks of extinction.

Not that Blanchot thought much of the prospects for critics willing to play any such mediatory role in postwar France. As his own syntax implies, he does not give the public critic much credence. All this rather hapless figure requires, he observes sardonically, is "a degree of competence, a talent for writing, a willingness to please and a measure of good will"—and "this hardly amounts to much; it could even be said to amount to nothing at all."[42] Rather than call for this kind of critic to be revived, as McDonald did in 2007, he embarked on a "quest" to characterize an alternative, non-mediatory mode of writing that might do justice to literature as such or to echo his reflexive French formulation, through which it might affirm *itself* rather than the interests of journalism and the university.[43]

What to call this other kind of writing? "Creative criticism" is one label Blanchot suggests though this downplays the emphasis he puts on "the movement of self-effacement" essential to its operations.[44] "Precisely because, modestly, obstinately" this kind of critical writing "ceases to distinguish itself from its object," he notes, it "takes on the mantle of creative language," willingly "fading as to nothing" itself.[45] Shifting into a more philosophical register, and returning to his preoccupation with *forms* of knowledge, he elaborates:

> "Criticism," in the sense intended here, might be said to be closer (though the comparison is misleading) to *critique* in the Kantian sense: in the same way that critical reason in Kant is a questioning of the conditions of possibility of scientific experiment, so criticism, or *critique* in the sense I am using it here, is inseparable from an exploration of the possibility of literary experience; exploration here is however not purely theoretical, it is the way in which literary experience is constituted, and constituted in the act of challenging and testing out its own possibility in the process of creation itself.[46]

This passage is not just philosophically intricate. It includes some knotty problems of translation because Blanchot uses one word (*critique* and *l'expérience*) where Hill, quite understandably, uses two (*criticism/critique* and *experiment/experience*). Keeping all the semantic possibilities in play, we could parse it as follows: the creative critic who engages experientially with innovative forms of literary writing is obliged to rediscover the amateur within on each occasion. By temporally suspending the acquired learning, established forms of disciplinary knowledge, and specific interests that constitute her professionalism, she allows herself to emerge from the experience with a transformed critical language attuned to, as well as expressive of, the new ways of writing, reading, thinking, and knowing the work opens up. The interdependency is key: on the one hand, the innovative work obliges the critic to unlearn her previously acquired expertise; on the other, the work's generative capacities become manifest only through her exploration of literature's "conditions of possibility" in all their theoretical and experiential dimensions.

Just what creative criticism in this exacting sense might entail becomes a little clearer when Blanchot turns to the question of value. Anticipating McDonald's objections to cultural studies, he notes that "the complaint is sometimes made that criticism is no longer capable of judging."[47] Yet, for Blanchot, "it is not criticism which lazily [or, according to McDonald, culpably] resists evaluation, it is the novel or poem that withdraws from evaluation because it seeks to affirm itself in isolation from all value."[48] Returning to the idea of interdependency, he adds:

> Criticism is no longer a form of external judgement, which confers value on a literary work and, after the event, pronounces on its value. It has become inseparable from the inner workings of the text, it belongs to the movement by which the work comes to itself, searches for itself, and experiences its own possibility.[49]

Importantly, when talking of value, Blanchot does not have in mind McDonald's aestheticist criterion of "artistic merit," let alone Steiner's Neoplatonist "real thing." He pointedly refers to "all value," that is, something closer to Robbins's concept of "public values," in the context of describing the contribution innovative literary writing and creative criticism, working in concert, can make to the refashioning or Nietzschean transvaluation of all collective or communal values, whether literary, philosophical, political, religious, economic, legal, or something else. In his conclusion, he calls this larger project "one of the most difficult, but most important tasks of our time," characterizing it as "the task of preserving and of releasing thought from the notion of value, and consequently opening history up to that which, within history, is already moving beyond all forms of value and is preparing for a wholly different—and still unpredictable—kind of affirmation."[50] The relevant "notion of value" here is absolutist both in Steiner's philosophical sense and in the political, specifically nationalist, sense Blanchot championed in the 1930s as an apostle of the extreme French right. I shall return to his volte-face later. For now, I simply note that while his non-mediatory, perpetually renovating amateur-professional *practice* of creative criticism might in some respects be akin to Kantian critique, it is the obverse of the professionalized "ethos" of "critique," which Rita Felski argues has dominated and deformed the Anglo-American academy for the last forty years or more.[51]

* * *

Blanchot was well aware that he was thinking about criticism "in Western cultures like our own."[52] Yet, somewhat uncannily, given their very different backgrounds, not to say political positions in the 1930s, Tagore anticipated many of the later Blanchot's central tenets—that is, the Blanchot of the 1950s and 1960s who shifted allegiance to the radical French left—while developing his own practice of creative criticism in the world of Bengali letters over half a century earlier. As I have already intimated, Tagore had his own reservations about academic professionalism and critical expertise, which he justified in equally uncompromising, anti-scholastic terms. Prefiguring Blanchot's later insistence that "the essence of literature is precisely to evade any essential characterization," for instance, he begins an essay of 1889 noting that "the essence of literature does not allow itself to be trapped within a definition."[53] In part, this reflects his indebtedness to the Buddhist traditions that cast doubt on all rationalistic and reifying forms of thought, but when it came to literature his anti-scholasticism had as much to do with his own lived experience of the writing process. "I have myself experienced, over and over," he remarks in the same essay, "what is probably familiar to everyone: when immersed in literary composition, one seems to achieve a kind of superconscious state, as though an inner self separate from my own has run off with the greater part of my consciousness, and is carrying out its task half unknown to me."[54] He then goes on to distinguish "construction," which "consciously exercises the authority of the self" from "creation," which, being partly involuntary, involves a degree of self-extinction.[55] Though well aware that this sounds implausibly "mystic," he insists "one cannot put the matter more clearly" because the creative process blurs boundaries between "the witting and unwitting experience I have gathered, the *Real* and the *Ideal* within me, my everyday self and my potential self."[56] The idiom may be peculiarly Tagore's but many writers across the twentieth century from Woolf to Coetzee attest to the underlying sentiment, Blanchot among them.[57] Though he would have been wary of Tagore's idea of the "*super*conscious," given his debts to Mallarmé's more negatively construed poetics of impersonality, he too understood writing as a process of self-extinction. "If to write is to surrender to the interminable," he notes in *The Space of Literature* (1955), "the writer who consents to sustain writing's essence loses the power to say 'I'."[58]

For Tagore, as for Blanchot, this way of thinking about the generative process of writing has direct consequences for criticism, beginning with the question of value. This is why he objects to the "worthy critics" with their "set formulations for literature" who rely on "a pair of scales," weighing each work as if it is a commodity with a set market value, effectively seeing criticism as "a form of external judgement." "Whatever composition is placed before them," he comments wryly in the essay of 1894, "they can confidently stamp it on the back with the appropriate number and seal."[59] Yet, since literary creativity for Tagore opposes all forms of reification, his doubts apply not just to the question of value but to any of academic criticism's "set formulations." "We do not properly understand literature," he comments in an essay of 1907, "if we reduce it to place-time-pot (*desh-kal-patra*)," which translates roughly as "context," but equally we cannot see the innovative work merely as a "constructed artefact" because it constitutes "a world," the generative potential of which is always "ongoing" and "incomplete."[60] This puts pay simultaneously to the historicist's curatorial object and to the formalist's well-wrought urn. The reason? Innovative literary writing is an expression of creative "ananda" ("joy" or "delight"), a cognitive-affective experience, which, for Tagore, sets it apart from all rationalistic forms of thought, whether political, economic (e.g., "capitalist realism"), or, indeed, literary-critical, and links it to an array of other seemingly gratuitous or superfluous human activities, ranging from the elaborate rituals of a wedding ceremony to the needless theatricality of warfare, which are also manifestations of "man's excess, his wealth, that which overflows all his need."[61]

Like Blanchot, Tagore recognizes that any critical writing equal to the challenge of engaging with this "vital power" has to be just as creative.[62] This is partly why he preferred to describe himself as an "amateur," particularly when addressing scholars in an academic setting.[63] Eschewing "the professor's rostrum" in a talk simply entitled "Literature," which he gave at the University of Calcutta in 1924, he insists, "I have gleaned the answers to my queries from the experience of joy out in the world and within my own heart."[64] Earlier, and in a similar spirit, he applauds the amateur critic who abandons the professional's "set of weights" and strategies of "argument and classification, wishing to gift his readers only with the state of mind induced in him on reading the poem."[65] This sounds like McDonald's subjectivist impressionism but, given Tagore's wider ambitions, it is more plausible to see it as a forerunner of Blanchot's creative criticism, which is at once immersed in the uncertain, often disorienting but always potentially generative flow of "literary experience" and part of a larger project to do with the transvaluation of public values. For Blanchot, as we have seen, this was "the task of preserving and of releasing thought from the notion of value"; for Tagore, it concerned the no less demanding challenge of thinking interculturally in ways that are at once anti-absolutist, radically situated and open.

"Falling between the push and pull of two sides," he wrote in 1912, "we will realise that it is by knowing other peoples that we truly know ourselves and by knowing ourselves that we know all others; we simply must understand that just as to sacrifice one's self in the desire for the other is useless beggary, so too, to diminish one's own self by forsaking the other is the ultimate impoverishment."[66] The "we" in this case refers to India's diverse communities and the "two sides" to the rivalrous but, for Tagore, equally absolutist forces of British imperialism and Indian anti-colonial nationalism.

Rejecting both, and, contrary to the standard "Western" idea of him as an otherworldly "Eastern" mystic, embracing what he called in a poem of 1910 the "grand concourse of humankind," he dedicated the last three decades of his life to "opening history up to that which, within history, is already moving beyond all forms of value" and to "preparing for a wholly different—and still unpredictable—kind of affirmation" centered on a decolonized, intercultural future yet to come.[67] Here too the connections with the later Blanchot are suggestive. Responding to the insurrectionary spirit of May 1968 and summarizing his own by then strongly anti-nationalist and anti-imperialist convictions, Blanchot wrote:

> Everything that allows men to become rooted, through values or sentiments, in *one* time, in *one* history, in *one* language, is the principle of alienation which constitutes man as privileged in so far as he is what he is (French, of precious French blood), imprisoning him in contentment with this own reality and encouraging him to offer it as an example or impose it as a conquering assertion.[68]

For Blanchot, it was Marx who first recognized this, declaring "with calm forcefulness: *the end of alienation can only begin if man agrees to go out of himself* (from everything that constitutes him as an interiority): *out from religion, the family and the State*."[69] Marx may have been the first to recognize alienation in these terms but it was Tagore who first understood how innovative literary writing and creative criticism might work to overcome its effects, anticipating Blanchot's own postwar commitment to an anti-absolutist, open-ended relationality and to an idea of writing that "will never be confined by us in a book, for a book, even when open, tends towards closure, which is a refined form of repression"—for "book" in this sense we could just as well substitute Tagore's "place-time-pot."[70]

* * *

So much for the cunning passages of history. What of the future? Can creative criticism in the Tagore-Blanchot sense even be said to have one, particularly when its fate now seems tied to the embattled, increasingly corporatized, and over-professionalized university of today? Here, for all the ongoing resonance of their thinking, Blanchot and Tagore are less useful or even plausible as guides. Like many leading French intellectuals of his generation, Blanchot never returned to the university after studying philosophy in Strasbourg in the 1920s, making a career as a political journalist in the 1930s—the period in which he associated with the extreme French right—and then as a literary reviewer and essayist in the postwar period. Despite his principled aversion to publicity—he practiced what he preached about the disappearance of the author—he became a particularly influential figure during his radical left phase in the 1950s and 1960s when he wrote regular reviews for the revived *Nouvelle Revue Française*, then one of France's most eminent literary magazines.

By contrast, having escaped the strictures of formal education and the pressures of having to earn a living from his writing largely because of his wealthy family background, Tagore went on to found the counter-university he called Visva-Bharati in Bengal in 1921. As he wrote in *The Centre of Indian Culture* (1919), this gave institutional expression to two of his guiding principles: first, that the "shock" of the "foreign" was "necessary for the vitality of our intellectual nature"; and second, that the imposition of "European culture" via the colonial education system not only turns the colonized into "hewers of texts and drawers of book-learning," it "kills, or hampers, the great opportunity for the creation of new thought power by a new combination of truths."[71] In essence, he founded Visva-Bharati—the name can translate as "World-Learning"—as a pioneering center of Indian intercultural studies, dedicated to a Tagorean transvaluation of values conducted in a spirit of creative *ananda*.[72] Unsurprisingly, the professionalized scholars of his day did not look favorably on the experiment. As Jadunath Sarkar, then India's leading academic historian, crisply commented in a letter of 1922, a proper university education has to be about "intellectual discipline and exact knowledge."[73]

Making a career, let alone a living, as a creative critic writing for literary magazines as Blanchot did is clearly not a realistic prospect in today's media environment, though it is encouraging that ventures like *n+1* are able to survive. There is also the increasingly affordable, albeit unremunerative, blogosphere, which has created other openings for writing outside the constraints of journalism and the university. Equally, not having Tagore's vision or resources, there are no doubt few who would be willing or able to found an alternative Institute for Creative Criticism and Intercultural Studies—less encouragingly, Visva-Bharati still exists but in a form now very far from its founder's ideals; more encouragingly, Columbia University's new Paris-based Institute for Ideas and Imagination, launched in 2018, may provide an opportunity for their revival. Realistically, then, it looks like the most workable option might be to make space for creative criticism within the contemporary university itself. At a time when various forms of "post-critique" in Felski's sense appear to be on the ascendency, when the category of "World Literature" is being resuscitated, and when a forum like the Columbia Institute is opening up the debate about how knowledge is defined, created, and taught, this may not be as utopian as it sounds. But what would this kind of creative criticism, at once inside and outside the university, within and beyond the profession, look like?

Taking bearings from Tagore and Blanchot, I would single out three broad aspirations. First, it should locate literature not only within the formal academic discipline of literary studies, or, for that matter, only within literary history, but in the spaces between disciplines—extra- rather than interdisciplinary—and within the history of thought in all its manifestations. Second, creative criticism should make alliances with world literary studies, although taking its cue from Tagore, rather than David Damrosch, in part because, for the former, worldliness is inseparable from the larger project of decolonizing and desectarianizing knowledge. Anticipating the forms of alienation Blanchot highlighted in 1968—being imprisoned in one time, one history, one language, one culture, one religion, and one state—Tagore conceives of the "world" in his landmark essay "World Literature" (1907) neither as a globalized circulatory system nor as a determinate set of universal values but as an effort toward an ever greater understanding of interconnectedness, outside rationalistic, absolutist, colonial, and sectarian forms of knowledge, always in the making and never complete. Finally, it should recognize that when it comes to writing about literature amateurism can never be optional, or understood as an impulse (or a virtue), since it constitutes one of creative criticism's conditions of possibility, reflecting its dependency on innovative literary writing and vice versa. This same interdependency, which entails a perpetual process of learning and unlearning, as well as a constant unmaking and remaking of critical language, means that any particular method of "post-critique," say Best and Marcus's "surface reading" or even Sontag's earlier "erotics of art," can have only provisional or polemical value.[74]

If this still sounds implausibly utopian, especially given the pressures universities currently face, it is at least a utopia with prospects. For one thing, despite the vagaries of the publishing industry, the rise of alternative media, and the many threats to intellectual literary culture and the freedom of expression more generally, innovative literary writing shows no sign of dying out, and, for another, the task of freeing thought from absolutisms of all kinds remains as difficult and important today as it was for Tagore in the 1920s and Blanchot in the 1960s. True, there are no easy ways of measuring the impact creative criticism understood in these terms might have on journalism and the university, let alone society and the economy, but at least its practitioners will never find themselves at a loss when they or anyone else asks David Willetts's "most challenging of questions—what is it all for?"[75]

## Notes

1 Charles Bernstein, "95 Theses," *Profession*, October 4, 2016.
2 David Willetts, *A University Education* (Oxford: Oxford University Press, 2017), 106.
3 George Steiner, *Errata* (London: Weidenfeld & Nicholson, 1997), 118.
4 N. Katherine Hayles, "Universities at the Crossroads: Directing Cultural Transformations," March 7, 2018.
5 Willetts, *University Education*, 106.
6 Steiner, *Errata*, 118.
7 Ibid., 42.
8 Hayles, "Crossroads."
9 Mark Fisher, *Capitalist Realism* (London: Zero Books, 2009).
10 Willetts, *University Education*, 3 and *passim*.
11 Hayles, "Crossroads" and Bernstein, "Theses."
12 Steiner, *Errata*, 44, 117.
13 Ibid., 121.
14 Fisher, *Capitalist*, 17.
15 I. A. Richards, 1924. *Principles of Literary Criticism* (London: Routledge, 1995), 26; Rabindranath Tagore, *Creative Unity* (London: Macmillan, 1922), 145–146.

16 Rabindranath Tagore, "Children's Rhymes" (1894), in *Selected Writings on Literature and Language*, ed. S. K. Das and S. Chaudhuri (New Delhi: Oxford University Press, 2001), 100.
17 Bruce Robbins, *Secular Vocations* (London: Verso, 1993), 14 and 64.
18 Robbins, *Secular*, 60 and 110.
19 Ibid., 25.
20 Ibid.
21 Ibid.
22 Rónán McDonald, *The Death of the Critic* (London: Continuum, 2007), ix.
23 McDonald, *Death*, ix.
24 Ibid., vii.
25 Ibid., 134.
26 Ibid., 149.
27 Ibid.
28 Ibid., 148.
29 Ibid.
30 Maurice Blanchot, "The Task of Criticism Today," trans. L. Hill, *Oxford Literary Review* 22, no. 1 (2000): 19. I have slightly modified some of Hill's translations. All subsequent references in the text.
31 Maurice Blanchot, "Qu'en est-il de la critique?" *Arguments* 3, nos. 12–13 (1959): 34.
32 Katharine Viner, "A mission for journalism in a time of crisis," *Guardian*, November 18, 2017: 32.
33 Michael Ignatieff, "The role of universities in an era of authoritarianism," *University World News Global Edition*, April 13, 2018.
34 Ignatieff, "Universities."
35 See Amit Chaudhuri, ed., *Literary Activism: A Symposium* (Norwich: Boiler House Press, 2016), 11.
36 Blanchot, "Task," 19.
37 Ibid.
38 Wandia Njoya, "French racism, anxiety and love for postcolonialism," *Aljazeera*, February 7, 2018.
39 McDonald, *Death*, ix.
40 Blanchot, "Task," 19.
41 Michael Jubb, *Academic Books and Their Futures: A Report to the AHRC and the British Library* (London: 2017), 143–145.
42 Blanchot, "Task," 19.
43 Ibid., 23.
44 Ibid., 22–23.
45 Ibid., 21–22.
46 Ibid., 23.
47 Ibid.

48 Ibid.
49 Ibid.
50 Ibid., 24.
51 Rita Felski, *The Limits of Critique* (Chicago: University of Chicago Press, 2015), 4 and *passim*.
52 Blanchot, "Task," 19.
53 Maurice Blanchot, "The Disappearance of Literature" (1953), in *The Blanchot Reader*, ed. Michael Holland (Oxford: Blackwell, 1995), 141; Tagore, "Literature" (1889), in *Selected Writings*, 49.
54 Tagore, *Selected Writings*, 50.
55 Ibid., 49.
56 Ibid., 50.
57 See, for instance, Woolf's "Professions for Women" (1931), in *The Crowded Dance of Modern Life* (Harmondsworth: Penguin, 1993), 104–105; and Coetzee's "A Note on Writing" (1984), in *Doubling the Point*, ed. David Attwell (Cambridge, MA: Harvard University Press, 1992), 94–95.
58 Maurice Blanchot, *The Space of Literature*, trans. Ann Smock (Lincoln: University of Nebraska Press, 1982), 27.
59 Tagore, *Selected Writings*, 100.
60 Rabindranath Tagore, "Bishwasahitya" (1907, "World Literature"), *Rabindra Rachanabali*, 13 (Calcutta: Government of West Bengal, 1961), 771. I am grateful to Rosinka Chaudhuri for translating the parts of the original essay I have quoted. For an earlier translation, see Tagore, *Selected Writings*.
61 Tagore, "Bishwasahitya," 769.
62 Tagore, *Selected Writings*, 49.
63 Tagore, "Literature" (1924), in *Selected Writings*, 264.
64 Tagore, *Selected Writings*, 264.
65 Ibid., 101.
66 Rabindranath Tagore, "Bharatbarshe Itihaser Dhara" (1912, "The Flow of History in India"), *Rabindra Rachanabali*, 13 (Calcutta: Government of West Bengal, 1961), 165. I am grateful to Rosinka Chaudhuri for translating the parts of the original essay I have quoted. For an earlier translation, see Rabindranath Tagore, "My Interpretation of Indian History," trans. Jadunath Sarkar, *The Modern Review*, August–September 1913.
67 Rabindranath Tagore, *I Won't Let You Go: Selected Poems*, trans. K. Kushari Dyson (Tarset: Bloodaxe Books, 2010), 150.
68 Blanchot, "Disorderly Words" (1968), in *Blanchot Reader*, 202.
69 Blanchot, "Disorderly Words," 202.
70 Ibid., 204.
71 Rabindranath Tagore, *The Centre of Indian Culture* (Calcutta: Visva-Bharati Bookshop, 1951), 33–34.

72 For more on Visva-Bharati, see Peter D. McDonald, *Artefacts of Writing: Ideas of the State and Communities of Letters from Matthew Arnold to Xu Bing* (Oxford: Oxford University Press, 2017), 16–26, 72–74 and *passim*; also www.artefactsofwriting.com, especially webnote b.

73 Rosinka Chaudhuri, "'Only what does not fit in can be true': Deprofessionalization and Academia in relation to Adorno and Tagore," *Economic and Political Weekly* 51, no. 43 (October 22, 2016): 51.

74 Stephen Best and Sharon Marcus, "Surface Reading: An Introduction," *Representations* 109, no. 1 (2009): 1–21; Susan Sontag, *Against Interpretation* (London: Vintage, 1994), 14. The title essay, from which the quotation comes, first appeared in 1964.

75 Willetts, *University Education*, 106.

# Bibliography

Bernstein, Charles. "95 Theses." *Profession*. October 4, 2016. Available online: https://profession.mla.hcommons.org/2016/10/04/95-theses/ (accessed May 14, 2018).

Best, Stephen and Sharon Marcus. "Surface Reading: An Introduction." *Representations* 109, no. 1 (2009): 1–21.

Blanchot, Maurice. 1955. *The Space of Literature*, trans. Ann Smock. Lincoln: University of Nebraska Press, 1982.

Blanchot, Maurice. "Qu'en est-il de la critique?" *Arguments* 3, nos. 12–13 (1959): 34–37.

Blanchot, Maurice. *The Blanchot Reader*, ed. M. Holland. Oxford: Blackwell, 1995.

Blanchot, Maurice. "The Task of Criticism Today," trans. L. Hill, *Oxford Literary Review* 22, no. 1 (2000): 19–24.

Coetzee, J. M. *Doubling the Point*, ed. David Attwell. Cambridge, MA: Harvard University Press, 1992.

Chaudhuri, Rosinka. "'Only what does not fit in can be true': Deprofessionalization and Academia in relation to Adorno and Tagore." *Economic and Political Weekly* 51, no. 43 (October 22, 2016): 46–52.

Felski, Rita. *The Limits of Critique*. Chicago: University of Chicago Press, 2015.

Fisher, Mark. *Capitalist Realism*. London: Zero Books, 2009.

Hayles, N. Katherine. "Universities at the Crossroads: Directing Cultural Transformations." March 7, 2018. Available online: https://www.dur.ac.uk/university.college/events/?eventno=38049; for the full lecture see https://www.youtube.com/watch?v=ufHCN9a0xY4 (accessed May 15, 2018).

Ignatieff, Michael. "The role of universities in an era of authoritarianism." *University World News Global Edition*, April 13, 2018. Available online: http://www.universityworldnews.com/article.php?story=20180413093717351 (accessed May 15, 2018).

Jubb, Michael. *Academic Books and Their Futures: A Report to the AHRC and the British Library*. London: 2017. Available online: https://academicbookfuture.files.wordpress.com/2017/06/academic-books-and-their-futures_jubb1.pdf (accessed May 15, 2018).

McDonald, Peter D. *Artefacts of Writing: Ideas of the State and Communities of Letters from Matthew Arnold to Xu Bing*. Oxford: Oxford University Press, 2017.

McDonald, Rónán. *The Death of the Critic*. London: Continuum, 2007.

Njoya, Wandia. "French racism, anxiety and love for postcolonialism." *Aljazeera*. February 7, 2018. Available online: https://www.aljazeera.com/indepth/opinion/french-racism-anxiety-love-postcolonialism-180207061506901.html (accessed May 15, 2018).

Richards, I. A. 1924. *Principles of Literary Criticism*. London: Routledge, 1995.

Robbins, Bruce. *Secular Vocations*. London: Verso, 1993.

Sontag, Susan. *Against Interpretation*. London: Vintage, 1994.

Steiner, George. *Errata*. London: Weidenfeld & Nicholson, 1997.

Tagore, Rabindranath. 1919. *The Centre of Indian Culture*. Calcutta: Visva-Bharati Bookshop, 1951.

Tagore, Rabindranath. *Creative Unity*. London: Macmillan, 1922.

Tagore, Rabindranath. *Rabindra Rachanabali*, 13. Calcutta: Government of West Bengal, 1961.

Tagore, Rabindranath. *Selected Writings on Literature and Language*, ed. S. K. Das and S. Chaudhuri. New Delhi: Oxford University Press, 2001.

Tagore, Rabindranath. *I Won't Let You Go: Selected Poems*, trans. K. Kushari Dyson. Tarset: Bloodaxe Books, 2010.

Viner, Katharine. "A mission for journalism in a time of crisis." *Guardian*, November 18, 2017: 30–32.

Willetts, David. *A University Education*. Oxford: Oxford University Press, 2017.

Woolf, Virginia. *The Crowded Dance of Modern Life*. Harmondsworth: Penguin, 1993.

# PART TWO

# The Amateur in the Age of Professionalization

# 5

# Leavis, Richards, and the Duplicators

*Christopher Hilliard*

The professionalization of criticism meant more amateurs doing it. As literary criticism became institutionalized in universities and schools, critical procedures were taught to thousands of people for whom criticism would never become a profession. The most important figure in this process as it played out in Britain was the Cambridge critic F. R. Leavis. To mention this name is to suggest further ironies or cruxes in the relationship between the amateur and the professional, authority and democracy, exclusivity and inclusivity.

Leavis is famous for narrowing the canon and pronouncing that many conventionally esteemed books were not worth a reader's time.[1] Leavis's position was more complex, and more playful, than is usually recognized, but no one could describe him as egalitarian or pluralist.[2] Similarly, Leavis's idea of "minority culture" was not straightforward snobbery, but as a considered elitism it did not allow much room for positive cultural contributions from those without the most rigorous training in criticism. "In any period," Leavis wrote in his pamphlet *Mass Civilisation and Minority Culture* (1930), "it is upon a very small minority that the discerning appreciation of art and literature depends: it is ... only a few who are capable of unprompted, first-hand judgment. They are still a small minority, though a larger one, who are capable of endorsing such first-hand judgment by genuine personal response."[3] Beyond that, there was (in the 1930s) the "public" that sought guidance from reviews in the Sunday newspapers, and so on radiating outward.[4] In a healthy culture, each of these larger publics would be connected, at some remove, to the "critically adult public." In this way, the judgments of a "very small minority" would be transmuted into "standards" governing a wider community of taste. Leavis invoked Samuel Johnson's "common reader," who was not an "ordinary" reader but an unusually "competent" and "cultivated" one.[5]

By the early twentieth century, according to Leavis and his wife Q. D. Leavis, whose book *Fiction and the Reading Public* provided most of the empirical support for her husband's historical claims, the minority was embattled, and communications between it and a mass readership had been blocked. Twentieth-century reviewers pandered to anti-intellectualism and book-of-the-month clubs played on readers' fears that they might not be smart enough to enjoy Virginia Woolf or other "highbrows," a word that became common in the 1920s and whose currency was, the Leavises believed, a sign of the further fragmentation of the reading public.[6]

In F. R. Leavis's just-so history, eighteenth-century culture was sufficiently unified, its various publics sufficiently articulated, that an elite figure could also represent and shape the collective, the "common." Here he was seeking to mark out a cultural authority that was neither professional nor amateur: professional in the sense of scholastic and pedantic, like the Anglo-Saxonists he wanted to wrench dominance of university English from; and "amateur" with the upper-class associations that term had in Britain in the first half of the twentieth century—a belletristic knowledge of literature and art as a cultural attainment akin to knowing about wine. Amateurs in another sense, interested but not strenuously "trained" readers, barely registered in Leavis's model of cultural standards and influencers. Those other "amateurs" were several atmospheric layers further out beyond the Sunday newspaper public. Yet Leavis's practice directly and indirectly set the agendas of many English teachers in universities, high schools, and adult education between the 1930s and the 1960s. A criticism whose rationale rested on a small "minority" was brokered to a great many.

The central pedagogical instrument was "practical criticism." Leavis quickly became its most energetic proponent, but its progenitor was his sometime senior colleague I. A. Richards. In his practical criticism course at Cambridge in the 1920s, Richards distributed anonymized copies of poems and asked the students, colleagues, and hangers-on to write critical evaluations of them. Richards would then evaluate the evaluations: the lectures were an examination of readers' responses and the practice of criticism more than a direct modeling of literary analysis. In time, the phrase "practical criticism" came to refer to close reading generally. My focus here is on practical criticism in this original sense as a pedagogical technique for learning to read difficult texts and improving the reader's capacity to discriminate. Later evangelists for practical criticism as a teaching method took their cues from Leavis rather than Richards himself. Through Leavis and his followers, practical criticism became embedded, and appropriated, in high schools, adult education, and a writers' workshop between the 1930s and the 1960s. A poetics and a set of criteria for literary value were disseminated as well as a critical procedure.

* * *

I. A. Richards was not so much a votary of literature as someone interested in the psychological and semiotic questions that reading entailed. *Principles of Literary Criticism* (1924) was an attempt to establish the psychological basis of responses to literary texts and to clarify the nature of aesthetic value. Despite the title, the book was more an exploration of the underlying bases of literary judgment than a set of principles to be applied in interpretation. Criticism was "the endeavour to discriminate between experiences and to evaluate them." That endeavor was not possible "without some understanding of the nature of experience, or without theories of valuation and communication."[7] Richards suggested that literature was a kind of language use that synthesized differing, opposing responses. His conception of the text as a force field of impulses enabled him to read for patterns and movement in poetry that was still new and difficult: "the central process in Mr Eliot's best poems is the same; the conjunction of feelings, which, though superficially opposed,—as squalor, for example, is opposed to grandeur,—yet tend as they develop to change places and even to unite." For Richards, the extent to which a text reconciled its conflicting impulses was an index of its quality, or "efficiency," as he put it.[8]

In the mid-1930s, Leavis would break with Richards as a "Benthamite" who was not really committed to literature.[9] Nevertheless, the idea of literary texts as efficiently reconciling impulses had some affinity with Leavis's approving emphasis on "fully realized" works of literature. In his early programmatic essays, which had a greater impact on the practice of criticism than some of the better-known pieces dating from when he was an eminence but less involved in college teaching, Leavis would sometimes describe literary effects and literary accomplishments in terms akin to Richards's. Leavis's prose has none of Richards's scientific bearings nor the playful mathematics of William Empson's reference to the permutations of the different senses of each element in a poem: but like theirs, Leavis's interpretations of poetry focus on relational networks of meanings and sensations. Thus in 1932's *How to Teach Reading*, which riffs on Ezra Pound's *How to Read*, Leavis discusses a short exchange between Banquo and Duncan early in *Macbeth* ("This castle hath a pleasant seat; the air | Nimbly and sweetly recommends itself | Unto our gentle senses") as an example of "Shakespeare's marvellous power of using words to compel on the reader or listener a precise complex response, to evoke the combination of emotions and associations appropriate to the context." An adjective "co-operates with" two nouns to "evoke" "associations." An adverb represents a "set of associations." Banquo points out a martlet on the wing, and the bird's vitality and delicacy "represents a combination analogous to 'nimbly and sweetly'." "All these suggestions, uniting again with those of 'temple' and 'heaven,' evoke the contrast to 'foul murder.'" Combine, evoke, cooperate with, unite, precise: for all Leavis's rejection of utilitarianism, his attention to textual patterns and their effects was indebted to Richards's conception of the mechanics of poems.[10] Concentrating on short poems and excerpts in a classroom could introduce students to these kinds of patterns and effects.

In Leavis's teaching, the analysis of the poems and prose passages in the handouts was not self-contained in the way it had been in Richards's lectures, and it did not assume an autonomous work of art the context of which was immaterial. Leavis's classroom performance of close reading was directed toward an encompassing understanding of literature and culture. One of his students recalled: "He talked us through, in effect, a chronological history of English poetic styles based on 'dating' poems on ... roneo'd sheets ... and through literary history both social and critical."[11] "History" would emerge from literary texts. Leavis was never very impressed by academic historians and didn't revise his early position even after social and cultural history increased the discipline's ambit and brought it closer to literary studies. In the mid-1960s, when he was teaching in semi-retirement at the new University of York, he prepared a seminar series on "'*Judgment and Analysis*' (Criticism in Practice)" based on "Passages for assignment to period (etc), and for intelligent comment." He explained to the chair of department: "This is Literary History, Cultural History, Background, as much as it is 'Practical Criticism.'"[12]

* * *

As a kind of disciplined sight-reading, practical criticism proved a model that could be deployed in high school English teaching and adult education classes. Both were pedagogical settings where the default expectations tended toward passive appreciation and rote contextualization in which "background" about the author's times or philosophy and "message" threatened to marginalize the workings of texts. Being forced to read a text without the crutches of context or conventional valuations opened up opportunities for genuine critical analysis and serious personal engagement with poetry or prose.

Adult education tutors in the late 1940s and the 1950s—the heyday of literature courses in adult education, now catering to middle-class people, especially women, as well as the working class—were sometimes explicit about this. Raymond Williams, who at this time was strongly influenced by Leavis's pedagogy, remarked in an adult education journal that people who collected "marginal facts" about literary works were often "unable to read intelligently an unnamed piece of verse or prose that might be set before them."[13] Those who signed on for multiyear "tutorial classes" in English literature seldom came without preconceptions or prior self-directed learning. Practical criticism was a means of jolting them out of what they thought they knew and directing them to the words on the page. In that respect it was a kind of intellectual empowerment that was directed *against* the greatest manifestation of the amateur principle in British intellectual life: the autodidact tradition.[14]

In 1950 Williams published a book, *Reading and Criticism*, that brokered Leavisian criticism to adult education tutors. Like Leavis, Williams insisted on the importance of value judgments and deplored lazy reviewing. Among the exercises included in the book were comparisons of passages from good novels paired with bad best sellers. Reviewing Williams's book in the journal *Adult Education*, T. W. Thomas remarked that *Reading and Criticism* reflected several decades of critical efforts "to discourage us talking 'about' literature and to get us to read the text as our sole source and authority." This might now be a commonplace in university English departments, Thomas wrote, but "one can still find in the adult education movement surprising reluctance to approach literature through the critical reading of texts": Williams's book was an attempt to overcome that reluctance, "a case for practical criticism in the extra-mural class."

Thomas professed enthusiasm for Williams's argument, but his praise was vague while his reservations were specific. "We all know how easy it is to dissect a poem and leave it a heap of dismembered parts." The method was especially weak for making sense of novels. Williams was aware of the problem and moved on from juxtaposition exercises to incorporating textual analysis into the reading of set texts. Given the time constraints of the tutorial class, sessions would be based on one or two short poems, for instance, or "one crucial chapter, or two or three crucial paragraphs, from a novel." Thomas wondered whether this was so different from sight-reading paired passages on duplicated sheets. "Reading extracts, however intensively, is not reading the novel," said Thomas, "and as a method of class study I have not found it satisfactory since it obliges the student to rely on the tutor's interpretation which determined the selection."[15]

Another adult education tutor—and another progenitor of cultural studies—remained an adherent of impromptu evaluations of contrasting poems and excerpts, especially as a way of learning how advertising and other mass-cultural forms worked to manipulate readers. Richard Hoggart, unlike Williams, had never been in a classroom with Leavis: he had learned from Leavis's books and from the journal he edited, *Scrutiny*.[16] Hoggart's classroom practice is better documented than that of most adult education tutors because he had his students keep a class log. Each week a different student would act as secretary, summarizing the discussion. The log for his evening class in Scarborough in 1948 shows Hoggart introducing the students to practical criticism through a homework assignment comparing Shakespeare's sonnet 71 ("No longer mourn for me when I am dead") with Christina Rossetti's sonnet "Remember me when I am gone away."[17] (One of the sessions in Richards's practical criticism course had used another poem by Rossetti as the bad poem in a pair.)[18] After returning their work, Hoggart gave his students some general feedback. "[We] were interested," wrote the secretary, "in the point that the difference between these sonnets is that of one age opposed to another": an example of practical criticism as "Literary History," the necessary cultural context already there in the text. With some prodding from Hoggart, the students were now able to produce Leavisian valuations of the two sonnets. Rosetti stood for "Victorian sentiment" and the Shakespeare of the sonnets for "Elizabethan robustness." "Robustness" was a favored Leavisian term for the products of Elizabethan English; it was the main thing Thomas Nash had going for him. Some of the younger women in the class had fallen for Rossetti's Victorian sentimentalism because they were not equipped to resist "her gentle, conventionally poetic euphemisms and her narcotic rhythms."[19] The "narcotic" power of second-rate literature was a recurrent theme of the interwar critiques of mass culture to which Hoggart was indebted.[20]

Hoggart then introduced the class to "a new scheme in criticism, writing down our considered opinions on two passages of prose which dealt with the liberty of the individual. Mr Hoggart summarised for us, after which we tried to look pleased or silently crumpled our pages."[21] One passage in the first pair came from D. H. Lawrence's letters, which F. R. Leavis regarded as exemplary instances of the spontaneous, receptive intelligence he prized.[22] The phrases Hoggart or his students or both used to praise Lawrence's letters could have come from Leavis himself ("taut and nervous in its style").[23] The evening concluded with a comparison of two descriptions of gardens—a match-up between L. H. Myers and John Galsworthy. Myers was a novelist championed by some in Leavis's circle; Galsworthy's reputation was among the collateral damage from Woolf's "Mr Bennett and Mrs Brown." The students duly pronounced the Galsworthy passage "a crude and blatant 'build up' for a love scene, using sickening alliteration—e.g. 'tiny tremors,' foolish adjectives, e.g. 'warm, sweet night' and the pathetic fallacy that a flower can look wistfully at a human being." With

Myers, by contrast, "we knew well enough that this writer was not anticipating a reader with a dulled critical faculty."[24]

Though "Leavisites" had a lot invested in distinguishing great literature from the second-rate, a developed concept of the literary was not fundamental to their critical practice. They were confident that reading skills honed on Donne or Eliot could reveal the workings of other kinds of language use, including mass culture. As he taught adult education classes in the late 1940s and early 1950s, Hoggart was beginning to think about the questions of culture and agency that he would explore in *The Uses of Literacy* (1957). (The book's subtitle was: "Aspects of Working-class Life, with Special References to Publications and Entertainments.") He assigned his students texts of mass culture (advertisements, pep talks) as well as "bad" poems and novels so that they could grapple with the culture industry. Like a number of early *Scrutiny* contributors, Hoggart was interested in the ways the culture industry sought to manipulate emotion and saw practical criticism as consciousness raising. One evening Hoggart's Scarborough class read an advertisement "appealing to the emotion of mother-love. It was written in a style reminiscent of a sensational Hollywood film, flashing from scene to scene in a dynamic fashion. We concluded that this style of psychological advertisement meets with the desired response as shown by the enormous sums charged for newspaper and magazine space." Hoggart then delivered a firmly Leavisian case against the corrupting tendencies of mass culture. His class analyzed a lurid newspaper report of a crime. It was

> a badly-written, crude piece of work. Such a writer could have no real values in life or he would not misuse images to gain his effect. It was evidently written to stir up crude emotions ... Mr Hoggart stressed the point that the reading of crude and sensational literature, as published by some of the press, may make people incapable of appreciating real literature.[25]

These ideas about writing and emotional well-being were part of the currency of "left-Leavisism." In *Reading and Criticism*, Williams had quoted Eliot's dictum that "every vital development of language is also a development of feeling" and said that the converse also seemed true: "The crude or vague language, the pompous and mechanical rhythms, which we have discerned in these extracts, subsist—there is no other explanation—on crudity and imprecision of *feeling*."[26] Hoggart was perhaps at his most Leavisian in the final comment recorded by the student on duty that night: if people become habituated to the manipulations of the press and unable to appreciate real literature, "the management of their own lives might be affected."[27] Hoggart was succeeding in getting his students to respond of their own volition in the way he wanted. The layperson, or the amateur, was learning to wield the cultural judgments of the professional but was not being encouraged to evolve new and potentially heterodox ones of their own. Leavisian criticism's record in high schools was less reliably directive.

* * *

No one did more to bring F. R. Leavis's approach to literature into British high schools—especially the academically selective grammar schools—than Denys Thompson. One of Leavis's earliest undergraduate supervisees, Thompson was *Scrutiny*'s main writer on mass culture, especially advertising.[28] He became a schoolteacher and prominent educationalist. Thompson was, in Leavis's phrase, a "magnificent propagandist."[29] He was capable of translating Leavis's methods—and his urgent sense of mission—into forms that teachers who had not "been there" could apply in their classrooms. Thompson wrote an instruction manual in evaluative practical criticism, *Reading and Discrimination*, that did for schoolteachers what Williams's *Reading and Criticism* did for adult education tutors. Thompson's book sold in large numbers in the 1940s and 1950s.[30] Thompson also edited the teachers' journal *English in Schools* and its successor *Use of English*.

For most of the 1950s, *Use of English* served as the hub of a program of practical criticism for high school students. The journal issued sheets with prose passages and whole poems for class use. The accompanying section of each issue of the journal bore the title "Criticism in Practice," the phrase Leavis had come to prefer to "practical criticism" (perhaps to indicate the difference between his training program and Richards's more diagnostic one, or perhaps to stress that he dealt in *activity*). The section was curated at first by Thompson and Raymond O'Malley, another of Leavis's earliest students and now a teacher at a conspicuously progressive school. The format of the exercises—two thematically or superficially similar texts juxtaposed for evaluation—was familiar from

Richards's *Practical Criticism*, from Thompson's *Reading and Discrimination*, and Leavis's own teaching materials, notably the entrance examinations he set for prospective students at his college. Students in the final years of high school, the lower and upper sixth forms, would be asked to compare anonymized lines by Donne with lines by Shelley or a passage from the English nature writer Richard Jefferies (a favorite of Thompson and O'Malley, both of them proto-environmentalists) with an advertisement for cornflakes.[31]

It was taken as a given that this was an exercise with right and wrong answers, though these could be happy or unhappy in their own ways. The strengths and weaknesses of the passages presented were not treated as self-evident, and the framers of the exercise provided pointers and suggestions for teachers. Moreover, teachers were encouraged to report on their experiences using the exercises in the classroom, and *Use of English* commented on the various reports. In this way the "Criticism in Practice" section became an educational and critical collaboration. Readers were reminded that the series' ongoing success "depend[ed] to a great extent upon the continuance of a 'two-way traffic' in ideas and classroom experience."[32] The responses that teachers reported back to the journal offer a glimpse of this pedagogy in action.

When asked to compare Donne's "A Valediction: Forbidding Mourning" with Lord Lytton's "Absent Yet Present," identified only as poem A and poem B, grammar school sixth-formers provided evidence of "genuine and discerning appreciation of the Donne ... but, on the whole, unfavourable reactions to the Victorian poem found more coherent and quotable expression." A number of pupils commented on the Lytton poem's emotional shallowness and "unchanging rhythm." Others faulted it for stringing images together without a "unifying principle." One student wrote: "There is no development of the main idea; the poet simply meanders round the main subject. The ideas have no connexion with each other and when the ideas are taken together the poem does not make sense."[33] Another offered a contrasting assessment in the Victorian-romantic tradition of Francis Turner Palgrave's *Golden Treasury* anthology: "The first poem [Donne] is much too calculated and clever ... The flow of ideas and images in B [Lytton] is typical of the rush of emotions in young people."[34] Such responses, said Frank Whitehead, the coordinator of "Criticism in Practice" for that issue, should be allowed to run free in classroom discussion, "since for many adolescents they represent a necessary phase of growth." If it was gratifying that a number of the respondents were receptive to Donne's poetics, their responses also revealed the limitations of their understanding of imagery—that its function was illustrative or mimetic. Whitehead's assignment for the next month was designed to prompt them to consider a poem in which the imagery did not depend altogether upon "the resemblance of the things compared."[35]

The goal of "Criticism in Practice" was thus not simply to promote particular kinds of poetry at the expense of others but to foster an understanding of the poetics on which those valuations rested. That tastes tended to align themselves with implicit theories of poetry was suggested by a teacher reporting on his pupils' comparison of Donne's description of the whale in *The Progress of the Soul* and Shelley's "To a Skylark": in the responses of two "able pupils" who preferred the Shelley he saw in references to "caesuras and other technical preoccupations the effect of old-type academic-conventional training; he says that discussion left them unconvinced, though uncomfortable that cherished unconscious prejudices had been challenged."[36]

Worth quoting at length is the response of a young woman in her final year of school to a pair of poems that bore on the Leavisian concern with unity—with the demanding relationship between formal order and the open exploration of experience:

> Has the writer of B(i) [Donne], by his apparent complete preoccupation with the whale, in any way limited the range of his interests and the subtler possibilities of poetry? Has the poet of B(ii) [Shelley], by allowing his imagination to wander without control, succeeded in giving a more complex impression of the experience which he wishes to encompass? ... [Donne's poem] incorporates in the verse structure a series of images which are extremely well adapted to show the nature of the whale, especially its size and the nature of its power.
>
> At every stroke his brazen fins do take,
> More circles in the broken sea they make
> Than cannons' voices when the air they tear.
>
> It is important to notice the verse movement here: the heavy rhythm which is accentuated by both the sound and the meaning

> of the metallic images: "brazen" and "cannon," which suggest not only the colour and strength of the whale but also something of its unnaturalness—it is outside living nature in the remote, insensitive, inanimate world of metal.

Here we can see a high school student learning the ropes of modern literary criticism. The passage from imagery to "verse movement" as the locus of a poem's more profound operations was a characteristically Leavisian move. Like Richards, and the early Leavis, this sixth-former saw poetry as working through coordination, by drawing in and orchestrating different effects: "The shifting of metaphor in these first lines is remarkable—a large number of separate sensuous effects are called into play: movement, colour and substance, definition of the movement ... Now two elements are called into the metaphor."[37]

Leavis expected contradictory things from practical criticism. It was supposed to elicit authentic, vital responses, as an alternative to the passive learning of conventional valuations, but Leavis's standards were uncompromising and the range of acceptable judgments correspondingly narrow. In his own teaching, a "wrong" answer from a student derailed a discussion, and a monologue from the teacher would begin.[38] The people he taught as undergraduates who then became schoolteachers had, by virtue of their situation, to be more accepting of inferior readings as part of the process of becoming educated. Whitehead later described his approach to teaching as an effort to combine "a concern with those standards of discrimination which *Scrutiny* had upheld so valiantly in the face of the vulgarity of the modern publishing and entertainment industry" with a "fostering of the young person's innate creativity."[39] Whitehead faulted Leavis for never "put[ting] on record any concern for the education of the less able and less privileged pupils in our school system." This was not out of callousness, Whitehead thought, but because Leavis's priorities lay elsewhere—with those "publics" more able to enforce standards on contemporary writers.[40] One of Leavis's students, David Holbrook, devoted his teaching career to those less privileged and less "academic" students, pioneering creative writing in British high schools.[41] Holbrook thought of this work as extending Leavis's project of renewing culture in the machine age. Leavis did not recognize his own values and ambitions in Holbrook's initiatives, but the tension between empowerment and conformity in Leavis's critical and educational program was such that it tended to split and transform as it was appropriated by others.

* * *

Practical criticism was often an exercise in salutary destruction: learning not to be able to enjoy Victorian poems or be taken in by copywriters' sentimentality. It is thus more surprising that Leavisian classroom practice was an inspiration for a writers' workshop, a setting where the identification of the bad and the not-fully-realized could not be the final step in the process. Leavis himself was not an active sponsor of new writing after the early 1930s, and the conduct of his lieutenant Harold Mason at a college literary society meeting in the mid-1950s provides an illustration of the inhibiting effects that this concern with "standards" could have. With the editor of the Cambridge literary magazine *Delta* present, Mason "asked whether an editor should include weaker poems in order to make the magazine sufficiently large. Mr Mason further proposed that the meeting vote on the motion, that it was not worth the editor's going into print if he had not a better collection than that in the present number of 'Delta.'"[42]

Despite encouragement like this, *Delta* was edited by a succession of undergraduates reading English under Leavis at Downing College. The editor on the receiving end of Mason's disapproval was Philip Hobsbaum, who went on to adapt practical criticism for use in a writers' group. Together with Peter Redgrove, Peter Porter, Martin Bell, and Edward Lucie-Smith, Hobsbaum was a core member of the Group in London in the 1950s. Hobsbaum took over the stewardship of a London poetry group that had met at G. S. Fraser's flat until Fraser moved to Leicester University. The gatherings at Fraser's had been boisterous. Under Hobsbaum, another member recalled, alcohol was replaced by coffee and the circle became "the sort of concerned critical group which he had had at Downing College, Cambridge, and the evenings were much more formally organized."[43]

Hobsbaum thought of his Group as "an experiment in practical criticism," "an activity derived ultimately from the practical criticism classes of Richards and Leavis." The poems, stories, and chapters to be read were stenciled and duplicated and circulated to participants a week before the meeting. "The provision of scripts meant that there was a built in aid towards relevance in discussion. Divergent opinions could always be referred back to the words on the page, and this prevented discussion from straying into the realms of metaphysics and conjecture."[44] Lucie-Smith quipped that the Group's biggest debts were to Cambridge English and the duplicating machine: the approaches of the former could not have been put to work without the provision for making multiple copies.[45] Lucie-Smith elaborated in an unpublished memoir:

> Philip's plan was very simple. He planned to base himself on Dr Leavis's teaching methods, but to apply these to the work of his own contemporaries. A text would be put in front of us, and we would be asked to react to it, and to discuss it as candidly as we liked. In addition to the fact that the work would be new, with nothing known about it from previous report or experience, there would be another significant deviation from university practice. The discussion would be a complete democracy. The moderator would undertake a purely technical function—that of keeping the discussion going on reasonably coherent lines—but there would be no question of him putting himself above the rest.[46]

This was Leavisian in procedure, but unlike Williams's or Hoggart's adult education classes, it does not seem to have enforced Leavisian notions of good poetry, insofar as one can tell from the few surviving duplicated sheets with annotations by multiple participants in an evening's meeting. The several comments on a poem by Anne Dyke read: "collapses into adjectivalism"; "KEY"; "Good detail but not quite fitting with the right tone of the poem"; and "Crude": none of them distinctively Leavisian.[47] Of course, Lucie-Smith was wrong when he said that responding to poems about which one had no "previous report or experience" was a deviation from university practice: depriving readers of contextual cues had always been part of the exercise, a guarantor of its rigor. That experience could not be replicated in a writers' group: not only was anonymity out of the question, the poems discussed were the work of acquaintances if not friends, and the group heard the author read them as well as having access to the duplicated "song sheets." Nevertheless, Hobsbaum's insistence on the words on the page went some way toward estranging the poems on the duplicated sheets from the author in the room. His conduct of the meetings compounded the emphasis the Group poets placed on "clarity of intention as well as clarity of expression."[48]

There was another limit on the capacity of practical criticism to force disinterested and disciplined scrutiny of the text. "After some years of regular meetings," Lucie-Smith recalled, "it was possible to anticipate nearly all the arguments which would be produced for or against a particular poem, and sometimes, even, the very phrases which would be uttered in the course of the discussion."[49] The duplicating machine could distance you from the text, but you could get to know your fellow readers too well.

* * *

Lucie-Smith described the Group's discussion practice as "a complete democracy." Another member of the Group in the 1950s, Peter Redgrove, recalled that individual personalities became sublimated in "the general concern for what we were all interested in—the possibility of accurate expression that could be shared between all of us."[50] This Rousseauian democracy of the general will recalls Leavis's idea of a small "critically adult public" able to agree on standards. Yet in Leavis's own teaching, the teacher was an authority, and in practice there was a tension between the independent judgment Leavis valued and the standards he insisted upon, as we have seen in Hoggart's initiation of his adult students into Leavisian ideas and high school teachers' acceptance, with varying degrees of happiness, that young people's "innate creativity" would not always yield critical valuations of the sort their teachers subscribed to. The Group's replacement of the authoritative teacher with a moderator went further in defusing the tensions in the mission of Leavis's criticism.

If the Group empowered amateurs, or, more accurately, aspirants, by importing Leavisian protocols of criticism into a creative writers' workshop, the Group was also a step toward a professionalization of a different sort. When the Group began, university-based creative writing courses were unknown in Britain, and there were no ready-made models for writers' groups of comparable focus and discipline.[51] As members of the Group became established, they took up visiting positions teaching creative writing at American universities. Redgrove taught at Buffalo and at Colgate and in the early 1970s submitted a report to the Arts Council of Great Britain that led to the funding of writer-in-residence slots at British universities. At the time Redgrove himself was teaching in a further-education college in Cornwall. He told an acquaintance he had been able to

> swing this [course] towards creative writing ... with the result that we have had two very fine young writers brought along to their degrees ... This having been accomplished in one art school, others are now following suit ... Far from being "death for poets" at least in our situation we promise fair to get a better deal for young writers (for why should young painters and sculptors get three years on grant-aid and not young writers, so that they can do their work with helpful instruction from practitioners and such freedom as they require) and a better deal for older writers also, who ought to be employed, if they wish it, in teaching the "use of the imagination."[52]

## Notes

1 F. R. Leavis, *The Great Tradition: George Eliot, Henry James, Joseph Conrad* (1948; London, 1960), 1–3.
2 Christopher Hilliard, *English as a Vocation: The "Scrutiny" Movement* (Oxford, 2012), 252.
3 F. R. Leavis, "Mass Civilisation and Minority Culture" (1930) in Leavis, *For Continuity* (Cambridge, 1933), 14.
4 F. R. Leavis, "'This Poetical Renascence,'" *Scrutiny* 2, no. 1 (June 1933): 65–76, 69.
5 F. R. Leavis, *How to Teach Reading: A Primer for Ezra Pound* (Cambridge, 1932), 3–4; Leavis, "What's Wrong with Criticism?" *Scrutiny* 1, no. 2 (September 1932): 132–146, 145–146.
6 Q. D. Leavis, *Fiction and the Reading Public* (London, 1932), 22–26, 158–159; Leavis, "Mass Civilisation and Minority Culture," 38. On the language of "brows" in the interwar decades, see Stefan Collini, *Absent Minds: Intellectuals in Britain* (Oxford, 2006), 110–119; John Baxendale, "Popular Fiction and the Critique of Mass Culture," in Patrick Parrinder, gen. ed., *The Oxford History of the Novel, vol. 4, The Reinvention of the British Novel, 1880–1940*, ed. Parrinder and Andrzej Gasiorek (Oxford, 2011), 555–570.

7 I. A. Richards, *Principles of Literary Criticism* (1924; repr., London, 1926), 2.
8 Ibid., 194–195.
9 F. R. Leavis, "Dr Richards, Bentham, and Coleridge," *Scrutiny* 3, no. 4 (March 1935): 382–402, 388–389, 400, 402.
10 Leavis, *How to Teach Reading*, 30–31. While he lectured, Richards would turn to the blackboard to draw "cross-sections of a reader's mind, full of springs, pulleys, and arrows indicating emotions, images and incipient impulses to act." Basil Willey, *Cambridge and Other Memories, 1920–1953* (London, 1970), 21.
11 Tony Inglis, Untitled Essay, *Cambridge Quarterly* 25, no. 4 (1996): 353.
12 Leavis to Philip Brockbank, May 12, 1965, F. R. Leavis Papers, University of York Library.
13 Raymond Williams, "Some Experiments in Literature Teaching (1948–1949)," in *Border Country: Raymond Williams in Adult Education*, ed. John McIlroy and Sallie Westwood (Leicester, 1993), 148.
14 On which see Jonathan Rose, *The Intellectual Life of the British Working Classes* (New Haven, 2001); David Vincent, *Bread, Knowledge and Freedom: A Study of Nineteenth-century Working Class Autobiography* (London, 1981).
15 T. W. Thomas, "Practical Criticism and the Literature Class," *Adult Education* 24, no. 2 (1951): 20, 23–24, 25.
16 Richard Hoggart to F. R. Leavis, May 4, 1953, Richard Hoggart Papers, 3/9/10, University of Sheffield Library.
17 "Scarborough W.E.A.: Literature Class Log" (notes for January 29, 1948 and February 26, 1948), Hoggart Papers, 4/1/3, University of Sheffield Library (hereafter "Scarborough log").
18 I. A. Richards, *Practical Criticism: A Study of Literary Judgment* (London, 1929), 32–41.
19 Scarborough log, February 26, 1948.
20 See Christopher Hilliard, "Popular Reading and Social Investigation in Britain, 1850s–1940s," *Historical Journal* 57, no. 1 (March 2014): 247–271, 269, 270–271.
21 Scarborough log, February 26, 1948.
22 Ian MacKillop, *F. R. Leavis: A Life in Criticism* (London, 1995), 183–184; F. R. Leavis, "D. H. Lawrence and Professor Irving Babbitt," *Scrutiny* 1, no. 3 (December 1932): 273–279.
23 Scarborough log, February 26, 1948.
24 Ibid., January 29, 1948, and February 26, 1948.
25 Ibid., January 29, 1948.
26 Williams, *Reading and Criticism*, 17.

27 Scarborough log, January 29, 1948.
28 Denys Thompson, "Advertising God," *Scrutiny* 1, no. 3 (December 1932): 241–246.
29 Leavis to Ian Parsons, November 5, 1932, Chatto & Windus Archive, CW 53/2, University of Reading Library.
30 Chatto & Windus ledgers, 9/634, 10/268, 10/712, 11/148, 11/382, 11/578, 12/247, University of Reading Library.
31 "Criticism in Practice: II … Report by Raymond O'Malley," *Use of English* 1, no. 2 (1949): 93; "Criticism in Practice: XIII … Further Work by Denys Thompson," *Use of English* 4, no. 1 (1952): 48–49; "Criticism in Practice: II … Further Work Set by Denys Thompson," *Use of English* 1, no. 2 (1949): 97.
32 "Criticism in Practice: V: Part 'A' by Frank Whitehead," *Use of English* 2, no. 1 (1950): 29.
33 Ibid., 29–30 (ellipsis in original).
34 For Palgrave's poetic, see Stefan Collini, *Public Moralists: Political Thought and Intellectual Life in England, 1850–1930* (Oxford, 1991), 357; Christopher Clausen, "The Palgrave Version," *Georgia Review* 34 (1980): 273–289.
35 "Criticism in Practice: V: Part 'A' by Frank Whitehead," 30, 32.
36 "Criticism in Practice: II: Report by Raymond O'Malley," 95.
37 Ibid., 95–96.
38 Frank Whitehead, "F. R. Leavis and the Schools," in *The Leavises: Recollections and Impressions*, ed. Denys Thompson (Cambridge, 1984), 144.
39 Ibid., 145.
40 Ibid., 148–149.
41 David Holbrook, *English for the Rejected: Training Literacy in the Lower Streams of the Secondary School* (1964; repr., Cambridge, 1968).
42 Doughty Society Minute Book, November 23, 1954, DCCS/4/4/1/1, Downing College, Cambridge.
43 Alan Brownjohn, untitled typescript, n.d., Group Papers, MS 4557/1360, University of Reading Library.
44 Philip Hobsbaum, untitled typescript, n.d., Group Papers, MS 4557/1358, University of Reading Library.
45 Edward Lucie-Smith, "Uses and Abuses of the Literary Group," *Critical Survey* 1, no. 2 (Spring 1963): 78.
46 Edward Lucie-Smith, "Abridged from a forthcoming book," n.d., Group Papers, MS4557/1359, University of Reading Library.
47 Group Papers, MS 4457/2026, University of Reading Library.
48 Lucie-Smith, "Abridged from a forthcoming book."
49 Ibid.

50 Redgrove to Fletcher, March 28, 1974, Group Papers, box 2, University of Reading Library.
51 See Christopher Hilliard, *To Exercise Our Talents: The Democratization of Writing in Britain* (Cambridge, MA, 2006), esp. chapter 8.
52 Peter Redgrove to Ian Fletcher, March 28, 1974, Group Papers, box 2, University of Reading Library.

# Bibliography

## Unpublished Manuscripts

Chatto & Windus Archive. University of Reading Library.
Doughty Society. Minute Book. Downing College, Cambridge.
Group, The. Papers. University of Reading Library.
Hoggart, Richard. Papers. University of Sheffield Library.
Leavis, F. R. Papers. University of York Library.

## Published Works

Baxendale, John. "Popular Fiction and the Critique of Mass Culture." In Patrick Parrinder, gen. ed., *The Oxford History of the Novel, vol. 4, The Reinvention of the British Novel, 1880–1940*, edited by Parrinder and Andrzej Gasiorek, 555–570. Oxford, 2011.

Clausen, Christopher. "The Palgrave Version." *Georgia Review* 34 (1980): 273–289.

Collini, Stefan. *Public Moralists: Political Thought and Intellectual Life in England, 1850–1930*. Oxford, 1991.

Collini, Stefan. *Absent Minds: Intellectuals in* Britain. Oxford, 2006.

Hilliard, Christopher. *To Exercise Our Talents: The Democratization of Writing in Britain*. Cambridge, MA, 2006.

Hilliard, Christopher. *English as a Vocation: The "Scrutiny" Movement*. Oxford, 2012.

Hilliard, Christopher. "Popular Reading and Social Investigation in Britain, 1850s–1940s." *Historical Journal* 57, no. 1 (March 2014): 247–271.

Holbrook, David. *English for the Rejected: Training Literacy in the Lower Streams of the Secondary School*. 1964; repr., Cambridge, 1968.

Hoggart, Richard. *The Uses of Literacy: Aspects of Working-class Life, with Special References to Publications and Entertainments*. London, 1957.

Inglis, Tony. Untitled Essay. *Cambridge Quarterly* 25, no. 4 (1996): 353.
Leavis, F. R. "D. H. Lawrence and Professor Irving Babbitt." *Scrutiny* 1, no. 3 (December 1932): 273–279.
Leavis, F. R. *How to Teach Reading: A Primer for Ezra Pound.* Cambridge, 1932.
Leavis, F. R. "What's Wrong with Criticism?" *Scrutiny* 1, no. 2 (September 1932): 132–146.
Leavis, F. R. *For Continuity*. Cambridge, 1933.
Leavis, F. R. "This Poetical Renascence." *Scrutiny* 2, no. 1 (June 1933): 65–76.
Leavis, F. R. "Dr Richards, Bentham, and Coleridge." *Scrutiny* 3, no. 4 (March 1935): 382–402.
Leavis, F. R. *The Great Tradition: George Eliot, Henry James, Joseph Conrad*. 1948; London, 1960.
Leavis, Q. D. *Fiction and the Reading Public*. London, 1932.
McIlroy, John, and Sallie Westwood, eds. *Border Country: Raymond Williams in Adult Education*. Leicester, 1993.
MacKillop, Ian. *F. R. Leavis: A Life in Criticism*. London, 1995.
O'Malley, Raymond. "Criticism in Practice: II … Report by Raymond O'Malley." *Use of English* 1, no. 2 (1949): 93.
Richards, I. A. *Principles of Literary Criticism*. London, 1926 (first pub. 1924).
Richards, I. A. *Practical Criticism: A Study of Literary Judgment*. London, 1929.
Rose, Jonathan. *The Intellectual Life of the British Working-Classes*. New Haven, 2001.
Thomas, T. W. "Practical Criticism and the Literature Class." *Adult Education* 24, no. 2 (1951): 20, 23–24, 25.
Thompson, Denys. "Advertising God." *Scrutiny* 1, no. 3 (December 1932): 241–246.
Thompson, Denys. *Reading and Discrimination*. London, 1934.
Thompson, Denys. "Criticism in Practice: II … Further Work Set by Denys Thompson." *Use of English* 1, no. 2 (1949): 97.
Thompson, Denys. "Criticism in Practice: XIII … Further Work by Denys Thompson." *Use of English* 4, no. 1 (1952): 48–49.
Thompson, Denys, ed. *The Leavises: Recollections and Impressions*. Cambridge, 1984.
Vincent, David. *Bread, Knowledge and Freedom: A Study of Nineteenth-century Working Class Autobiography*. London, 1981.
Whitehead, Frank. "Criticism in Practice: V: Part 'A' by Frank Whitehead." *Use of English* 2, no. 1 (1950): 29.
Willey, Basil. *Cambridge and Other Memories, 1920–1953*. London, 1970.
Williams, Raymond. *Reading and Criticism*. London, 1950.

# 6

# The Critic as *Rasik*: Pramatha Chaudhuri, Tagore, and the New Language of Literary Writing

*Rosinka Chaudhuri*

Writing in 1948, a year after the declaration of Indian independence, the Bengali writer Buddhadeva Bose (the most important critic of his generation) described the most eminent surviving Bengali critic of the previous generation in an essay titled "A Review of Modern Bengali Literature" written in the English language—not the language of his primary works—in a memorable passage:

> Pramatha Chaudhuri, in his seventies, said goodbye to Mayfair and all that, and a visitor to Santiniketan, while straying in the Uttarayan grounds, could have caught a glimpse of him in one of the lovely little houses designed and built for Rabindranath. If the visitor was intrepid, or curious, or a lover of literature, he would perhaps have walked in and for a few moments sat face to face with one of the master artificers of Bengali prose. Sharp eyes, a dagger-like nose, a clean-shaven handsome face wreathed with wrinkles, a splendid body of a man shattered by illness, looking for all the world like a great mountain eagle, wounded

> in combat, wings broken, alone. As the long trembling fingers reached out for the golden cigarette-case lying on a little table amid books and cups and things, the bright eyes, pouncing on the visitor, lingering, questioning, would so unnerve him that he would forget to strike a light for the cigarette and begin to think of taking his leave. If he was lucky, however, Indira Devi Chaudhurani would appear at the right moment and immediately start the right sort of conversation. A niece of Rabindranath's, herself gifted in music and *belles-lettres*, tall, ivory-complexioned, splendid in an old-world way, she was the lesser known half, and is now the only half, of Bengal's most distinguished couple. The eagle, if alone in his last days, was not companionless.[1]

Several details in this descriptive account may need an explanation for the uninformed reader. When Bose writes, right at the start, that Pramatha Chaudhuri, in his seventies, said goodbye "to Mayfair and all that," he means the street in Calcutta named Mayfair Road in the Ballygunge area in the southern part of the city where some of the city's prominent families and the professional classes had increasingly settled from the early twentieth century onward. Meanwhile, the visitor to Santiniketan would obviously have been there because it was where the Bengali poet Rabindranath Tagore, awarded the Nobel Prize for Literature in 1913, had established first his school and then the university he named Visva-Bharati. An insufficiently acknowledged innovator of architectural forms and interior design, Tagore built a number of interesting homes within the space of a small compound housed in the university and school premises, the chief among which was named Uttarayan by him.[2] Tagore died in 1941, so "the visitor" would have seen Pramatha Chaudhuri in this house at any time between 1941 and 1948. His wife, Indira Devi, very much the Q. D. to his F. R. (Leavis), was an equal partner and contributor to their life-long enterprise of an intense engagement with literature and with life. Rabindranath's favorite niece, to whom, as a young man, he wrote (addressing her as "Bob") a series of letters that were later immortalized in a publication called the *Chinnapatrabali* in Bengali, Indira Devi was an intelligent and astute commentator, scholar, and writer in her own right.[3] But perhaps the most important part of the description is contained in the words: "one of the master artificers of Bengali prose." For Pramatha Chaudhuri was acknowledged not just as a critic and a writer and an intellectual, but as an essentially *urban* and *urbane* man of sharp wit and "courtly" prose—a word used deliberately and repeatedly by many after him to gesture at the sophistication and excellence of the craft he practiced.

Unlike Professor Leavis, though, the figure of Pramatha Chaudhuri (1868–1946) was as far removed from a professional career or a professorial position in an established university campus as humanly possible. Incontestably enacting the primary role of the critic as amateur in the field of Bengali letters, Chaudhuri was an independent spirit with independent means and never actually became a professional in any of the possible careers he might have taken up. It may be worth recalling here the notion of de-professionalization and its implications in relation to the critic as amateur. De-professionalization, interpreted as the experience of a person finding that both temperamentally as well as practically—that is, on the level of personal impulse as well as with regard to professional/academic requirements, one doesn't fit into the demands of the profession—seems to reside at two levels in this context.[4] The first is the inability to find a place for your subject matter within the straitjackets of current academic or writerly publishing imperatives that have been put in place by these professions. The second is a relatively rare condition: to find that that inability may be a direct consequence not just of content but of the form and style in which the text is written, which makes it unfit for inclusion or wider dissemination within the parameters that the profession demands. In the case of Adorno's *Aesthetic Theory*, what Hullot-Kentor calls his "paratactical style" makes his writing there "difficult" or "obscure"; the result was that this work seemed "obliquely remote," at the time, to the national literary spheres of both Germany and the United States, where it was not "received" well. "And this remoteness," the translator says, "is requisite to any plausible value it may have. For as Adorno wrote in constantly varied formulations, only what does not fit in can be true."[5]

De-professionalization, for Adorno, was of course the norm: even a rudimentary acquaintance with his life's work reveals he wrote on subjects ranging from musicology to metaphysics and that his writing span included such things as philosophical analyses of Hegelian metaphysics, a critical study of the astrology column of the *Los Angeles Times*, and the music of, among others, Beethoven and Schoenberg, not to mention jazz. "In terms of both style and content, Adorno's writings defy convention" seems to be the leitmotif of commentators on his work. In this refusal to fit into any one sphere of specialization, of course, he embodies the notion of the "amateur" as a de-professionalized intellectual—"the urge, as a creative practitioner, or, indeed, a practitioner of any kind, *not* to be identified with one genre or activity," but rather than say he was "in general, a critic of specialisation and a champion of dabbling," it might be more accurate to acknowledge that he may have demanded specialization in dabbling instead.[6]

Pramatha Chaudhuri's writing style could be called paratactical as well; "obliquely remote," it was perceived to be the creation of a "master artificer"—he was a writer's writer and did not sell well, something Buddhadeva Bose lauded in the essay he wrote on him. His skill at his craft and assortment of interests seem no less vertiginous than Adorno's, ranging from classical and modern literature in India and the world to philosophy, science, linguistics, sociology, economics, history, archaeology, and world and Indian politics. He was passionate about music and wrote *Hindu Music* on the indigenous traditions of song, *Prachin Hindustan* on ancient India, and *Rāyater Kathā* (The Peasant's Story), published a year after the infamous Bengal Famine of 1943.[7] These were slim books, more in the nature of extended essays, as he was, in the end, always first and foremost an essayist. His essays spanned political subjects, as in *Tel-Nun-Lakri* (Oil-Salt-Wood) (1905), to essays on translation, on the crisis in our language, on education, on Hindu–Muslim relations, on Marx's dialectics, on book covers, wine, and what the rains said. But as a critic he made the deepest impact in his analysis of literature and literary writing, writing on early modern poets such as Jayadeva, Sri Chaitanya, and Bharatchandra, on the sonnet form ("*Sonnet Keno*" [Why the Sonnet?]), the new age in Bengali literature ("*Banga Sahitye Nabajug*"), the real in realism ("*Bastutantrata Bastu Ki*"), Buddhism and literature, reading, contemporary Bengali prose, children's literature, literature and politics, new fairy tales, translation, as well as several articles on Sanskrit, French, and English literature including individual essays on Maupassant and *Salomé*. He also wrote on Rabindranath—eighteen essays in all—from an enviable vantage point of intimacy and evaluation, though with most of these essays being written after Rabindranath's death in 1941.[8]

What, after all, is an amateur? An amateur is not a professional, first of all, by which is meant that his/hers is not a paid job but a vocation followed. The origins of the word are traced to the late eighteenth century: from the French, from the Italian *amore* "to love," from the Latin *amator/amatoris* meaning enthusiastic admirer or pursuer, friend, devotee, lover. The word "amateur," today, generally denotes inexperience or insufficiency; an amateur golfer is one not good enough for the professional circuit; an amateur physicist or economist is unheard of. Nonetheless, around the late nineteenth and early twentieth centuries, the sense in which the word was used, curiously, was the inverse of its current usage, when applied, for instance, to the term detective. An amateur detective is not part of the police force but gifted with knowledge, curiosity, and a desire for justice—in this sense, both Miss Marple and Sherlock Holmes, as amateurs, actually excel and exceed the job requirement. This excellence resides in the love ("amore") he or she brings to the work but also, crucially, in the distance from the professional field—in the world of the amateur, location is all—not to be part of a group, not to be a colleague or a co-worker, but to work brilliantly in isolation. The amateur detective, therefore, is in essence alone, talented, aloof, and creative, full of passion but remote. Above all, the amateur, ironically, is in this case the opposite of inexpert; rather he or she *is* the expert, more skilled, more talented, and more of a virtuoso than the paid employee. Strangely all of this is true not just of the amateur detective but also of the critic as amateur.

The critic, in fact, is an amateur by definition—there is no profession labeled "Critic" in any college, university, or print and publication department—and more often than not, those designated as such are those whose skills go beyond the occasional book review or classroom pedagogy. If you are an academic who reviews books or publishes essays in journals, you remain primarily an academic—it is only after a certain reputation has been made and consolidated by critical books that you may be called a critic as Frank Kermode or Terry Eagleton are in the present day. On the other hand, if you are on the staff of the *New York Times* or the *New Yorker*, you will, once again, attain the status of a critic only if you are Michiko Kakutani or James Wood and have built up a reputation over time for incisive literary analysis. Writers too, sometimes, attain the status of critics, but only if they have published critical essays in some form or the other. A certain aura seems to be demanded before the label "critic" may be applied even in this age of post-mechanical reproduction. Otherwise you are simply a reviewer or professor or author; interestingly, in no instance is any critic designated an amateur when engaged in the task of criticism itself.

The crucial factor in the attainment of the status of critic seems to be the essay form. Critics inhabit the essay format in relation to the literary field, and the essayist is one who practices "the highest level of prose," as Buddhadeva Bose said in an essay titled "Modern Bengali Prose"—paragraph by paragraph the writings of a great critic and essayist weave a spell dependent not on content but upon the thought process:

> It is advisable to go to the essayists (sometimes they are poets or poet-novelists at the same time) for the highest levels of prose ... In other words, to those who write not primarily to impart instruction or convey information, but as practitioners of an art whose validity, apart from the value of the content, they recognize.[9]

Barthes says in *Criticism and Truth*, "The critic separates meanings, he causes a second language—that is to say, a coherence of signs—to float above the first language of the work ... what controls the critic is not the meaning of the work, it is the meaning of what he says about it."[10] In this sense, all critics are essayists, and in their being essayists—in that instant of the inhabitation of the essay form—they occupy, whatever their actual profession, the status of the amateur (in the sense of an amateur detective/expert analyst of the literary).

It makes sense then that the word "amateur" originated in the late eighteenth century at a time when institutions had begun to dominate social life—once institutions had filled all empty spaces in social and political life, a demand for distance from institutions seemed preordained. There is no equivalent for the word in Bengali—the word *apeśādār* simply means one outside of a regular business or job—here the implication of distance from money inherent in the term "amateur" comes more sharply into focus. If the word was used of an amateur detective such that Bengali literature abounds and revels in, from Kiriti to Byomkesh to Feluda, it would necessarily imply a man (always a man) without a regular income who relies for his livelihood instead on skill, expert knowledge, and formidable talent. Pramatha Chaudhuri encapsulated every one of the qualities, as evidenced in the individual style of his prose, which was rare and bright and lean, militating against sentimentality, generality, exaggeration, and standardization. Appreciated by a few for these qualities, he was not a popular writer and did not sell well, yet his criticism has endured. Like Michael Madhusudan Datta half a century before him, he too could have chosen as an epigraph for his career the line Michael used from Horace for his first book of verse: "*Neque te ut turba miretur, labores, / Contentus paucis lectoribus.*"[11]

Scion of landed gentry rooted in the Pabna district of East Bengal (later Bangladesh), Chaudhuri's father was Deputy Magistrate of Jessore district when he was born, traveling to West Bengal when he was five. Remarkably, he never identified himself as a Calcutta man despite spending much of his life in that city. He graduated from Hare school and then Presidency College and was a resident at a succession of genteel middle-class locations almost all his life, yet he maintained: "*Kintu tāi bale āmi Kolkātāi haye uthini.*" ("But I didn't become a Calcuttan as a result of that.")[12] He left for England in 1893, spending a year in Oxford before moving to London (although, typically of him, not as a student at the university), and though he returned to India as a barrister, he did not practice at the Calcutta High Court for very long. Never at home within the constraints of professional life, he taught Roman law at Calcutta University for a while and then also managed the Tagore estates for some time. Fluent in English and French and conversant with Italian literature, he was a great aficionado of both music and writing, spending the rest of his life established first and foremost as a critic and *rasik* in the true Indian sense of a word that denotes one who delights in and appreciates art from the premises of real knowledge of the art form. Without going into the semantics and nuances of Sanskrit terminology, and treating the word as it is ordinarily understood by Indians to this day, one could maintain that *the critic is always a rasik*—like amateurism, demonstrable appreciation and real knowledge are foundational characteristics of any true critic.

Nirad C. Chaudhuri (no relative) had referred to Pramatha Chaudhuri as a *rasik* in an essay, also quoting him as having said of himself: "As a writer I have been identified as a *rasik*; as a result I have had to let go of many subjects."[13] By this he might have meant the identification of his métier by the literary and general reading public as belonging to the realm of aesthetics—consequently, a sharp interest in politics and society, as expressed in some exceptional publications, seems to have taken a back seat in the course of his career as critic. Although the reference here was not made in praise, as the two belonged to opposing camps of writers (as I explain below), the tension inherent in the comment points toward the identification of the *rasik* with the aesthete, as the core element of the ancient Indian term lay in an informed appreciation of the arts. In no instance was the *rasik* ever understood as an amateur in the sense of someone not fully trained but rather as always the opposite, as critic and connoisseur in times when professionalization never pertained to the world of letters or arts in the sense it does now.

Critics, of course, never function in isolation. To read and reevaluate an important critic such as Pramatha Chaudhuri should also involve an appreciation of the galaxy of other writers, critics, and poets surrounding him, without whom the critical enterprise would not have been what it was at the time. The circle surrounding him and his famous Bengali journal, *Sabujpatra* (Green Leaves), which he started in 1914 primarily to inaugurate a new unstuffy, youthful, and modern Bengali prose, was of a legendary character, though such groups were not anomalous in early twentieth-century Calcutta. Calling themselves the *sabujsabhā* (the green gathering), this amorphous group were like a *mandala* with Chaudhuri as its center point—an intricate diagram of connections and networks arranged around a central locus. They would meet at Pramatha Chaudhuri's residence, then at 1 Bright Street, Calcutta, and among the constituents of this group were Atulchandra Gupta, Dhurjatiprasad Mukhopadhyay, Bimalaprasad Mukhopadhyay, Baradacharan Gupta, Sunitikumar Chattopadhyay, Satyendranath Bose and others, including, of course, above all and as often as his schedule would permit, Rabindranath himself. Not unlike the situation in French literary history, argument and visceral disagreement animated the Bengali public sphere then and now. The opposing side—that is, those opposed to all that *Sabujpatra* stood for—published a journal titled *Sanibārer Cithi* (Saturday Letter), which made fun of, satirized, and mocked the endeavors of the other group relentlessly, edited, among others, most famously by Sajanikanta Das and Nirad C Chaudhuri.

If Chaudhuri resembled Adorno in some aspects, then a parallel may also be found with Barthes—both resisted the academy and functioned creatively outside of it for most of their careers, and both were embroiled in some of the bitterest literary quarrels of their time. The roots of *Criticism and Truth*, as we know, were in a dispute between the French critic Raymond Picard and Barthes over interpreting Racine—here, Barthes replied to Picard's objections by writing a book on what he thought criticism ought to be, arguing about the language of criticism, attempting to change the style in which artistic and literary issues could be discussed. Going against accepted convention regarding the language to be used for literary writing was also Pramatha Chaudhuri's mission, in and outside the journal *Sabujpatra*, and he was advocating a language for literary composition that would have seemed just as strange to the Bengali public sphere as Barthes's, for Barthes's reply in *Critique et vérité* is accompanied by a cultural as well as an intellectual and linguistic challenge. For both, the argument was between university critics or pundits and themselves on the outside, about critical idiom as much as about institutional/cultural locations. This is what amateurism entailed for both writers—a location outside of institutional positions, creating an independent space to forge an independent idiom with little recognition and almost no remuneration at the time.

*Sabujpatra*'s first issue carried an editorial by Pramatha Chaudhuri under the heading "*Om Prāṇāy Swāhā*"—the Sanskrit translating roughly to mean the infusion of new life. It began by quoting Dwijendralal Ray's advice to the Bengalis: "Do something new!" followed by a disclaimer that they were not trying to follow that advice entirely. In its critical stance, it had an ally in another famous progressive writers' journal, *Kallol* (1923), of which Buddhadeva Bose was an integral part while still a young man in Dhaka. While the modernist *Kallol* exhibited some impatience with what they perceived to be Rabindranath's transcendentalism, *Sabujpatra* was of the opinion that Rabindranath was essentially modern, always at the vanguard of the new, and the very emblem of renewal—someone who reinvented himself again and again in response to the call of innovation, never succumbing to the forces of conservatism or traditionalism, never looking backward at any time. While the *Kallol* group—joined later by others of this generation in periodical publications such as *Kalikalam* (1926), *Pragati* (1927), *Parichay* (1931), and *Kavita* (1935)—rebelled openly against the long shadow cast by Rabindranath's great presence in their midst, they nevertheless remained indebted to his writing in a myriad ways. Dipesh Chakrabarty cites Buddhadeva Bose, who wrote of his own initial hostility to Rabindranath: "I know at least of one young man who every night in bed recited [the poems of] 'Purabi' like crazy, and spent the daytime denouncing Tagore in writing."[14] Pramatha Chaudhuri, on the other hand, perhaps due to his personal relationship with Rabindranath, or perhaps because he was astute enough as a critic to see through the immaturity of most of these attacks, never wasted any time trying to disavow his own and his generation's involvement with and investment in Rabindranath. He summed up his own career's indebtedness to various impetuses by saying: "If my writing is obdurate, that is because I am from East Bengal; if it is clever with words that is because I am a citizen of Krishnanagar; and if it has life then that is because I have been animated by the touch of Rabindranath's great life from my youth onward."[15]

Pramatha Chaudhuri will be best remembered in Bengali letters for his unflagging and successful advocacy of the use of everyday language in the writing of Bengali literature, winning the war for *calit bhāshā* or the spoken tongue against those who would rather have *sādhu bhāshā* or the elevated style in writing. He shaped not just Bengali literary history but the future of Bengali writing as the publisher of *Sabujpatra* by publishing Rabindranath Tagore's new writings regularly and serially in this journal in this period. Following the Nobel Prize in 1913 Rabindranath is recorded as having expressed the desire to stop writing altogether to his two companions—Manilal Gangopadhyay and Pramatha Chaudhuri—on the houseboat on the river Padma from which he managed his family's estates in East Bengal; he felt he had said all that he had to say and had no more to give. In the argument that followed—the two had, expectedly, protested furiously—he is said to have smiled and made a concession: "All right—if you publish a periodical I will write for it, but I will not write anywhere else."[16] Pramatha Chaudhuri named the resultant journal *Sabujpatra*—and Rabindranath's next novel, *Ghare Baire* (The Home and the World), next play, *Phalguni* (Of Spring), and his next, most radical, book of poetry, *Balaka* (Wild Geese) all appeared within its pages incrementally, portion by portion, over the next two or three years. Following the editor's proclamation that this new venture was in the service of literature alone and would have no truck with business—thus it carried no advertisements or images—the periodical folded up within four years of its inception, having achieved a great measure of success in that brief period. Above all else, it was responsible for Rabindranath adopting a new literary language and style, validating the enormous importance of Pramatha Chaudhuri's role of critic as facilitator, interlocutor, and shaper of the future of Bengali writing—the better craftsman (*il miglior fabrio*) helping to birth a seminal change in the language of literature by nudging a master poet toward innovation and change.

The argument for or against the use of everyday Bengali for literary pursuits was an old one. The first novel in the language, published in 1854, was written in colloquial speech, but the most famous poet of the time is repeatedly quoted arguing against it. This was a time when Bengali was still in the process of being self-consciously fashioned into a modern and usable thing, and Peary Chand Mittra, whose novel, *Ālāler Ghare Dulāl*, was being serially published under the name of Tekchand Thakur, had embarked on a mission to initiate the practice of using spoken Bengali for literary composition. An argument between Michael Madhusudan Datta and Peary Chand ensued when, referring to his efforts, Madhusudan had suddenly exclaimed:

> What on earth are you trying to write?—People wear everyday clothes at home and mingle with their close relatives; but you cannot go outside in that apparel. For that you need formal wear. It appears that you seem to be advocating the disuse of formal clothes and the use of informal attire in the house and outside it, in society and at functions, in short, everywhere. How can that be possible?

In response, Pearychand had retorted, "What do you know about the Bengali language? But mark my words, it is my style of composition that the Bengali language will adopt and this will become permanent." In reply, Madhusudan, in his usual easy humorous way remarked: "*It is the language of Fishermen, unless you import largely from Sanskrit*. You call that a language! You will see it is the language I create that will be permanent."[17] The discussion about what an authentic literary Bengali would or should be continued in the latter half of the century in a more polemical and vigorous manner through the works of Vidyasagar and the contestations between Rabindranath and Bankimchandra; it is an argument, which was then decisively settled at the intervention of Pramatha Chaudhuri, who, as we have seen above, turned Rabindranath Tagore toward one of the most important decisions of his life, ensuring that Tagore never went back, subsequent to the *Sabujpatra* years, to the elevated literary style of convention.

Pramatha Chaudhuri was also instrumental in shaping the future of Bengali prose through his own writings, critical and otherwise. He was an inspired writer of essays—political, sociological, historical, but most of all, satirical. This last type was written pseudonymously as Birbal, the legendary Hindu minister in the court of the Mughal emperor Akbar, around whose fabled presence accrues a series of tales of wit and wisdom popular in India to this day. Acknowledged as one of the most successful satirist essay writers in Bengali, he was famous for the refinement of his language and the sharpness of his intellect, the wide range of his reading no less than the uses to which he put that reading in his writings. Critic and essayist above all, he also wrote poetry and stories, his first book of poetry being *Sonnet Pancāśat* (Fifty Sonnets) in 1913, the second *Padacāraṇ* (To Walk/To Recite) appearing in 1919. In the latter book, he set down his philosophy of life, love, and poetry in a short poem addressed to Manilal Gangopadhyay, "*Premer Kheyāl*" (Love Song) in which he said the scent of flowers is not found in language the poet artificially arranges, and the gift from the heart is not there in the poet's premeditated move of the pawn, but if you drink deep of the wine of the flowering sky, of the never-ending mistake, only then will you sing the song that is the origin of life, the song of *rasa*. "*Thāke nā kabir sājāno bhāshāy / Phuler ghrāṇ / Paṛe nā kabir sājāno pāśāy maner dān / Kara jadi tumi ākāś-phuler / kara jadi tumi ananta bhuler / madirā pān / Tāhole gāhibe prāṇer mūler / raser gān*"[18]

It is not as a poet, however, that Pramatha Chaudhuri is remembered—his verse was occasional at best—but as a critic, lover of literature, and essayist on a diverse range of topics. Commenting on the publication of a collection of Pramatha Chaudhuri's essays on contemporary social and political life at home and abroad in a collection whose title replicated Rabindranath Tagore's famous novel of the same name, *Ghare Baire* (Home and the World), another well-known intellectual and critic at large, Dhurjatiprasad Mukhopadhyay, said: "It is a real feat to have been able to transform independent paragraphs into the larger structure of the essay form. In this sense, the entire book is like a Chinese scroll, continuous and full of movement."[19] Dhurjatiprasad's understanding of "the independent paragraphs" having an existence of their own (apart from the "structure of the essay form") gestures here at the craft of prose, while the comparison with a Chinese scroll is fortuitous: one is reminded of David Hockney's interpretation in *Day on the Grand Canal with the Emperor of China (or Surface Is Illusion but so Is Depth)*, where a 70-foot seventeenth-century Chinese scroll is unrolled continuously in a fluid movement while the camera focuses on moments captured individually—independent paragraphs—full of detail and craft.

As I have said elsewhere, almost exactly at the same time as developments in the Western hemisphere, at around the same time that Barthes said (in *Writing Degree Zero*) that literature with a capital L was coming into place in French letters in 1850, two adjacent developments—literary criticism and literary history—were inaugurated in their modern form in colonial India.[20] Literary criticism, written in English or the regional languages, was quite often produced by writers themselves but also by men in the literary sphere (rarely women, although exceptions like Toru Dutt sparkled in the early 1870s), taking the form of book reviews and extended articles in the periodical press.[21] From the late nineteenth century onward, there developed the hugely important domain of the creative writer turned literary critic engaging with the contemporary and traditional production of literature in the varied languages of India. In the Bengali literary sphere, Bankimchandra Chatterjee's essays on the "*uttar ramcharit*" or "*giti kabya*" or Rabindranath Tagore's "*sahitye swarup*" or "*chhele bhulano chhora*" were radical reassessments, quickly becoming essential reading for an understanding of the various positions that defined the literary past. Thus, many eminent writer-critics in Bengali have consistently defined the literary culture of their time and of their pasts, through essays that mean less and less in a culture little concerned today with its literary heritage and its relationship to history.

At the start, literary criticism and literary history in Bengali were often conflated, wherein Macherey's distinction, in *A Theory of Literary Production*, of literary criticism as an "art" and literary history as a "science" had not yet become operational. Located as he is within the domain of the French public sphere, Macherey acknowledges, of course, right at the start while talking of "the meanings and usages of the word 'criticism'—which has been used ever more exclusively since the seventeenth century to denote the study of literary works"—that "it was soon felt necessary to distinguish between literary history and literary criticism."[22] The career of criticism in India in the context of the classical languages is different from its career in the context of modern Bengali. Sanskrit poetics goes back thousands of years—and many provinces in India used Sanskrit or Persian as a literary language right up to the modern period, including in Bengal. The career and characteristics of literary criticism in the classical languages need not concern us here; if we look at the modern Bengali literary sphere, which comes into existence around 1852, we see that the state of criticism in the so-called West developed at the same time and in quite similar ways in Bengal as well. Barthes realized, for example, that:

> in the bourgeois periods (classical and romantic), literary form could not be divided because consciousness was not; whereas, as soon as the writer ceased to be a witness to the universal, to become the incarnation of a tragic awareness (around 1850), his first gesture was to choose the commitment of his form, either by adopting or rejecting the writing of his past. Classical writing therefore disintegrated, and the whole of Literature, from Flaubert to the present day, became the problematics of language.
>
> This was precisely the time when Literature (the word having come into being shortly before) was finally established as an object.[23]

The word "*sahitya*"—used in many Indian languages to denote "Literature"—too had assumed its modern form in India a little before the time around 1860 when it is "finally established as an object." A comparison here with the situation in Bengal is intriguing, all the more so because the process of "adopting or rejecting the writing of his past" had been contaminated, in the context of the Indian writer, by the advent of colonialism. Moving away from the language of "impact" and "influence," it is time now to read the efflorescence of modern Bengali literature as existing in relation to colonialism in some instances quite directly, when it concerned a cultural or nationalist or reactionary or nativist stance taken by particular critics and writers, but also, in many other instances, working its own path quite independently of colonial rule in practitioners who took from the best of world literature much as Borges did in Argentina or, indeed, Pound did for English poetry.

It was with the publication of Rangalal Bandyopadhyay's literary manifestos in 1852 and 1858 that this movement toward the establishment of Bengali "Literature" as craft, as an object, and as a process of history was tentatively inaugurated. After this, Bengali Literature was then set spectacularly on its modern path by his peer, Michael Madhusudan Datta. The "West" was not more advanced or more professionalized in this respect than Bengal—in book production alone Calcutta was second only to London in the nineteenth century—with literary journals, literary editors, book reviews, and criticism flourishing here in both the English and Bengali languages parallel to similar developments in the Western hemisphere. The tradition of writing about Bengali literature in English, for instance, had been inaugurated by a poet in the English language, Kasiprasad Ghosh, in the pages of the *India Gazette* in 1831 in a piece called "On Bengali Writers"; roughly forty years later, Bankimchandra Chatterjee's two influential English essays ("A Popular Literature for Bengal," 1870; "Bengali Literature," 1871) were landmarks of this particular convention.

This is the lineage to which Pramatha Chaudhuri belongs—of writers writing in either the English or the Bengali language while taking from the French (Toru Dutt), the Italian (Michael Madhusudan Datta), the Greek (Rangalal Bandyopadhyay), and the Latin (Michael, the Dutt family), with Sanskrit and sometimes Persian mediating always in the practice of each of these writers in significant ways.[24] The career of English and the other cosmopolitan European languages in the early literary modernity of Bengal provides material for an exploration of the new notion of the individual as it emerged, not in the sense of post-Enlightenment rationality being replicated in various provincial outposts but as evidence of the new symbolic and ideological constructs that made up distinct evolving modernities in the non-Western world. The discourse of literary writing in the nineteenth and twentieth centuries in Bengal is not seamless and internally consistent but rather suffers from various tensions, disjunctions, and contradictions that opened up creative possibilities and fashioned new syntheses from constituent elements of this discourse.

Reading the history of Bengali modernity as a type of epistemological "bricolage," it is possible to see in an English essay such as Pramatha Chaudhuri's "The Story of Bengali Literature" (written in 1917 at the request of Rabindranath) an embodiment of the search for a new idiom with which to articulate both modernity and experience. An appreciation of the achievement of a critic such as Chaudhuri should then lead, it is hoped, to an understanding of how the literary acted upon the cultural formulation of the modern in India. Written in English, "The Story of Bengali Literature" brings to us a reading of the past in relation to the moment of its writing if we can read that moment not in the content of the discussion but in its voice—in the tone, tenor, language, and élan of the critic's interpretation of the literary turn of modernity. Commenting here on the fact that "the whole of our poetic literature was intimately connected with religion" in the premodern period and therefore assumed "almost a sectarian character," Pramatha Chaudhuri wrote of the eighteenth-century poet Bharatchandra:

> But there is one striking exception to this rule. There is a unique book, the Vidya Sundar of Bharat Chandra—unique both in its merits and faults—which marks the birth of secular spirit in our literature ... The Vidya Sundar is a love story, a novel in verse. And the love he treats of has nothing spiritual or ideal about it, but is of the common mundane passion which lends itself to humorous and even indelicate treatment. ... In his hands the sacred drama of the Hindu pantheon degenerates into secular comedy ... Gay and frivolous, cultured and cynical, witty and perverse, Bharat Chandra represents the utterly secular spirit of 18th century poetry ...
>
> Bharat Chandra's reputation is under a cloud now ... A subtle and persistent odour of decaying morals and dying faith pervades the whole poem, which makes the modern reader feel uncomfortably squeamish. I have no hesitation in admitting that Bharat Chandra's masterpiece is a *fleur de mal*, but it is a flower all the same, many petalled and of perfect form.[25]

Pramatha Chaudhuri was writing a few years in advance of Benjamin's reclamation of Baudelaire for the modern world, but with this reappraisal of Bharatchandra for what he calls the "modern mind," Chaudhuri locates him as a formative influence in a period of flux that was subsequently to witness the first phase of British imperialism in India.[26] Bharatchandra, the preeminent poet of premodern Bengal, was, and still is, read as emblematic of the indigenous inheritance of traditional poetic practices, a strain of which came to be stigmatized by charges of immorality and licentiousness made chiefly in Bengal's Victorian age, which categorized him as unworthy of inclusion in the national project of a modern literature for Bengal. Such a reading as Pramatha Chaudhuri's challenges accepted convention and creates a changed signification in the already available conventional practices of reading Bengali literature, practices that had created a binary understanding of native and foreign, moral and immoral, and leads to a realization instead that the production of modernity involved various members of a historical situation acting together and upon each other in unexpected ways. If we are to find, in the constitutive arenas of the Indian modern, some notion of creativity and specificity independently of the argument of Western influences, then this cross-sectional reading by Pramatha Chaudhuri becomes significant for the self-created identity of Indian modernity. It attempts to fashion a vocabulary that encompasses the significance of the "rude" in Bengali literature, its creative foundations, and its slippery relationship to nationalism.

Pramatha Chaudhuri's practice of criticism offers fresh avenues of thought for crafting a new geography of modernism for India and the world. The circuits of reciprocal influence and transformation that take place within his range of references and creative use of sources from every direction—apart from his formal innovativeness—show up in the shape of an amateurism that involves the recognition that this modernity was, in essence, a world modernity as understood in Rabindranath's conceptualization of world literature or *visva sahitya* in 1907. Rabindranath had memorably maintained there that literature (which, in Tagorean terminology, sometimes seems a metaphor for, and interchangeable with, play) needs to exist in a domain "without self-interest" (*swartha sekhan hoite dure*) and of the superfluous (*prayajan chhara*).[27] The notion of excess is returned to more than once: he points out that "beauty is extravagance, it is excessive and wasteful expenditure" (*behishabi baje kharach*), that literature "exceeds need"; it expresses man's excess (*prachurya*) and his wealth (*aisharya*). This preoccupation with all that is not born of necessity in the practical sense and with pleasure in the sense of *amore* takes us back then to the domain of the amateur, of the critic as amateur, as both the world of literature and the distance from professionalization are crystallized here in a viewpoint that belonged to both Rabindranath and Pramatha Chaudhuri in their respective outlooks.

The predominant endeavor nowadays in relation to literature—to understand the place of literature in history, largely through an analysis of the textual production of cultural meanings and the sociopolitical conditions of creating texts—takes us very far from this early twentieth-century understanding of the pleasure in excess that exists outside of necessity, with professional expertise and professorial preoccupations turning literary criticism and history today largely into a branch of the social sciences. To rediscover a lost dimension of literature by returning to the act of literary criticism cannot of course be done by jettisoning the challenging and important aspects of both field and text but by making allowance for a timely change in the perspective with which we view both. Pramatha Chaudhuri's career as critic and amateur might be well worth revisiting in that context.

## Notes

1 Buddhadeva Bose, *An Acre of Green Grass* (first published 1948) in Rosinka Chaudhuri, ed. *An Acre of Green Grass and Other English Writings of Buddhadeva Bose* (Delhi: Oxford University Press, 2018), 15.

2 For Tagore's impact on modern Indian décor, see Rosinka Chaudhuri, "Modernity at Home: A Genealogy of the Indian Drawing Room," in *Freedom and Beef Steaks: Colonial Calcutta Culture* (Delhi: Orient Blackswan, 2012).

3 See Rabindranath Tagore, *Letters from a Young Poet (1887–1895)*, trans. Rosinka Chaudhuri (Delhi: Penguin Modern Classics, 2014).

4 See Rosinka Chaudhuri, "'Only What Does Not Fit in Can Be True': De-professionalization and Academia in Adorno and Tagore," *Economic & Political Weekly*, October 22, 2016.

5 Theodor W. Adorno, *Aesthetic Theory*, Newly translated and edited with a translator's introduction by Robert Hullot-Kentor (London: Bloomsbury, 2014), xix. All subsequent citations are from this volume.

6 Amit Chaudhuri, Concept note for symposium on "De-professionalization" organized by the University of East Anglia at India International Centre, Delhi, January 7–8, 2016.

7 Pramatha Chaudhuri, *Hindu Sangīt* (with Indiradebi Chaudhurani) (Calcutta: Visva-Bharati Library, 1945); *Prāchīn Hindustān* (Calcutta: Visva-Bharati Library, 1941); *Rāyater Kathā* (Calcutta: Visva-Bharati Library, 1944).

8 It is Bengali literary convention to refer to a writer by his first name, which is the convention followed here too in most instances.

9 Buddhadeva Bose, "Modern Bengali Prose," in *An Acre of Green Grass*, xix.

10 Roland Barthes, *Criticism and Truth*, trans. Katrine Pilcher Keuneman (London: Continuum, 2007), 32–33.

11 Horace, *Satires* (1.10.73f) as it appeared misprinted on the title page of Michael Madhusudan Datta's *Tilottamāsambhab kābya* (Calcutta, 1860). Horace wrote: *Neque te ut turba labores, / Contentus paucis lectoribus*: labor not for the admiration of the crowd but be content with a few choice readers.

12 Pramatha Chaudhuri, *Bīrbaler Ātma-paricay* in Sajanikanta Das, ed. *Śanibārer Cithi* (*Agrahāyan* 1348BE [November–December 1941]), 177–182.

13 See Nirad C. Chaudhuri, *Nirbācita Prabandha* (Selected Essays) (Calcutta: Ananda Publishers, 1997), 130.

14 Cited in Dipesh Chakrabarty, *Provincializing Europe* (Delhi: Oxford University Press, 2001), 162.

15 Cited in Aryakumar Sen, *Bīrbaler Ātma-paricay* (Birbal's Life) first published in Sajanikanta Das, ed. *Śanibārer Cithi* (*Agrahāyan 1348* BE/ November–December 1941) reprinted in Sandipan Mitra, ed. *Ekuśer Caryā* (Year 2, Vol. II) (Kolkata, 2013).

16 Ibid.

17 Nagendranath Som, *Madhū-smriti* (Memories of Madhu / Sweet Memories), 1st ed. 1921 (Calcutta: Vidyodaya, 1989), 97–98. My translation; italicized portions are originally in English. For an extended discussion, see Rosinka Chaudhuri, *The Literary Thing: History, Poetry, and the Making of the Modern Cultural Sphere* (Delhi: Oxford University Press, 2013). It is worth remarking here, though, that Madhusudan was not speaking literally, as he also declared: "It is my intention to throw off the fetters forged for us by a servile admiration of everything Sanskrit."

18 Pramatha Chauduri, *Padacāraṇ* (Calcutta: Sri Gauranga Press, 1919).

19 Dhurjatiprasad Mukhopadhyay, *Ghare Bāire: Pustak ālocanā* (*Home and the World: Book Review*) in *Paricay, Fālgun 1343* (February–March 1936).

20 See *The Literary Thing*, ibid.

21 Toru Dutt's "An Eurasian Poet" (1874) about Leconte de Lisle, a Mauritian Creole poet who wrote in French, is one such outstanding piece of criticism from the pen of a woman in nineteenth-century

Bengal, though largely forgotten and unread in later years. Dutt published regularly in the *Bengal Magazine.*

22 Ibid., 3.

23 Roland Barthes, *Writing Degree Zero*, trans. Annette Lavers and Colin Smith (New York: Hill and Wang, 1968), 3.

24 "For a century now, every mode of writing has thus been an exercise in reconciliation with, or aversion from, that objectified Form inevitably met by the writer on his way, and which he must scrutinize, challenge and accept with all its consequences .... Form hovers before his gaze like an object; whatever he does, it is a scandal." Barthes, *Writing Degree Zero*, 4.

25 Cited in Shankari Prasad Basu, *Kabi Bhāratchandra* (Calcutta: Dey's Publishing, 2001), 94–95.

26 Bhāratchandra Ray (1712–1760) was court poet of Raja Krishnachandra of Nadia in an age when the English were already a troublesome presence in Bengal; his best-known work, the *Annadāmangal*, was written five years before the fateful Battle at Palashi that Sirajuddaula lost to Clive in 1757, thereby losing Bengal, and so India.

27 *Visva-Sāhitya* or "World Literature" was presented at the National Council of Education, Bengal, on February 9, 1907, and published immediately in the January–February 1907 number of the revived journal *Bangadarsan* that Rabindranath was editing at the time with Srishchandra Majumdar. It appeared again in the collection of five essays titled "*Sāhitya*" (Literature) published by Visva-Bharati Press on October 11, 1907. A translation by Swapan Chakravorty is available in the Oxford Tagore Translations series, and it has been collected by David Damrosch for his 2014 anthology, *World Literature in Theory*.

# Bibliography

Adorno, Theodor W. *Aesthetic Theory*. Translated with a new introduction by Robert Hullot-Kentor. London: Bloomsbury, 2014.

Barthes, Roland. *Criticism and Truth*, trans. Katrine Pilcher Keuneman. London: Continuum, 2007.

Barthes, Roland. *Writing Degree Zero*, trans. Annette Lavers and Colin Smith. New York: Hill and Wang, 1968.

Basu, Shankari Prasad. *Kabi Bhāratchandra* (The Poet Bharatchandra). Calcutta: Dey's Publishing, 2001.

Bose, Buddhadeva. "An Acre of Green Grass and 'Comparative Literature in India.'" In *An Acre of Green Grass and Other English Writings of Buddhadeva Bose*, edited by Rosinka Chaudhuri. New Delhi: Oxford University Press, 2018.

Chakrabarty, Dipesh. *Provincializing Europe: Postcolonial Thought and Historical Difference*. Delhi: Oxford University Press, 2001.

Chaudhuri, Nirad C. *Nirbācita Prabandha* (Selected Essays). Calcutta: Ananda Publishers, 1997.

Chaudhuri, Pramatha. *Bīrbaler Ātma-paricay* (Birbal's Life Story). *Śanibārer Cithi* (*Agrahāyan* 1348BE [November–December 1941]).

Chaudhuri, Pramatha. *Rāyater Kathā* (The Peasant's Story). Calcutta: Visva-Bhārati Library, 1944.

Chaudhuri, Pramatha. *Tel-Nun-Lakri* (Oil-Salt-Wood). *Bharati* (1905).

Chaudhuri, Pramatha. *Padacāraṇ* (To Walk/To Recite). Calcutta: Sri Gauranga Press, 1919.

Chaudhuri, Rosinka. "'Only What Does Not Fit in Can Be True': De-professionalization and Academia in Adorno and Tagore." *Economic & Political Weekly*, October 22, 2016.

Chaudhuri, Rosinka. *The Literary Thing: History, Poetry, and the Making of the Modern Cultural Sphere*. Delhi: Oxford University Press, 2013.

Datta, Michael Madhusudan. *Tilottamāsambhav kābya* (The Story of Tilottama). Calcutta: 1860.

Macherey, Pierre. *A Theory of Literary Production*. Oxon: Routledge Classics, 2006.

Mukhopadhyay, Dhurjatiprasad. "*Ghare Bāire: Pustak ālocanā* (Home and the World: Book Review)." *Paricay* (*Fālgun 1343* [February–March 1936]).

Sen, Aryakumar. "*Bīrbaler Ātma-paricay* (Birbal's Life)." *Ekuśer Caryā*, no. 2 (2013): 41–48.

Som, Nagendranath. *Madhū-smriti* (Memories of Madhu). Calcutta: Vidyodaya, 1989.

Tagore, Rabindranath. *Letters from a Young Poet, 1887–1895*, trans. Rosinka Chaudhuri. Delhi: Penguin Modern Classics, 2014.

Tagore, Rabindranath. "*Visva Sāhitya* (World Literature)." In *Sāhitya* (Literature). Calcutta: Visva-Bharati Press, 1907.

# 7

# The Sophisticated Amateur: Vernon Lee versus the Vital Liars

*Mimi Winick*

The first decade of the twentieth century in Britain saw the rise of the professional academic scholar and his foil, the amateur scholar; with this oppositional pairing came the longing to synthesize their qualities into some superior form, generally conceived of as the critic or the intellectual.[1] Professional scholars aimed especially to co-opt supposedly amateur qualities to vitalize their work. Vernon Lee (b. Violet Paget, 1856–1935) saw peril in this ambition. She particularly feared a willingness among professional scholars to treat whatever was most emotionally satisfying as "truth" and saw this ersatz amateur standard as shaping a range of popular scholarly writing on religion and politics that she called "Vital Lies."[2] Lee regarded this writing as sophistical, antidemocratic, and as a contributing factor in the Great War, wherein "countries [are] at present destroying each other on behalf of their various Vital Lies."[3]

Rather than merely denouncing these early twentieth-century "Vital Lies," Lee offered an alternative to them and, more broadly, to the modes of authority she saw taking shape around her. She practiced this alternative across a wide-ranging career as a writer of novels, short stories, essays, and "studies," cultivating a responsible and methodologically self-aware approach that would compete with the appeal of vital lies, while avoiding their perilous political effects. Across her varied oeuvre, I argue, Lee models a style of authority that reconciles practices of affection with detachment, standards of objective truth with emotional honesty, and literary style with the specialist vocabularies of scholarship. I call this model of scholarly authority, latent within Lee's long, diverse career, the "sophisticated amateur." Its sophistication consists in its knowing play with conventions: while amateurism is generally associated with naïveté, Lee depicts an amateurism emphatically informed regarding the conventions of professional and amateur scholarship. The sophisticated amateur knows not only the conventions of amateur practice and the criticisms of them by professionals but is master too of the purportedly superior professional practices. By turning to amateurism despite "knowing better," the sophisticated amateur enacts the kind of "sophisticated naiveté" Joseph Litvak describes as invested in "prov[ing] the interpretative advantages of dilatory, anachronistic attachment over" a more linear professionalism.[4] In this way, Litvak's sophisticated naïveté —which he finds not only in novelists such as Proust but also in critics such as Adorno and Barthes—manifests a similar queer temporality to what Carolyn Dinshaw finds in amateur scholars of medievalism who flourished in the same years as Lee.[5] Litvak's sophisticated naïveté and Dinshaw's queer amateur scholarship are both characterized by the backwardness associated, in the wake of nineteenth-century evolutionary sexology, with women and homosexual men.

Lee embodied and embraced many of the queer practices illuminated in these studies of sophistication and amateur scholarship. More broadly, as a woman who had love affairs with other women, an Englishwoman living in Italy, and a woman scholar, Lee wrote aslant mainstream British literary culture at a queer, cosmopolitan angle. As a writer, she was prolific and promiscuous, publishing across prose genres, from essays to dramas to novels, her works circulating in England and in Europe from the 1880s to her death in 1935. Today, Lee has been recovered as an aesthete who promoted a socially responsible "art for life's sake" and as a writer of ghost stories.[6] To a lesser degree, she is gaining recognition as a literary critic who anticipated various major twentieth-century critical methods.[7] Outside of literary studies, historians of other disciplines including art history and psychology have begun to identify Lee as a foundational figure.[8] While she is increasingly acknowledged as a shaper of modern disciplines, Lee is not easily recognizable in familiar roles in intellectual history. From the beginning of her career, she had a fraught relationship to categorical identifications such as the amateur scholar, the academic specialist, and the public intellectual.

The sophisticated amateur constitutes Lee's alternative to these roles. It differs not only from professional scholars but also from old-fashioned amateurs (whether the Victorian man of letters or the female enthusiast) who were understood to lack the discipline and specialist expertise that were coming to define modern knowledge practices. Sophisticated amateurism celebrates artificiality, idiosyncrasy, and emotional attachment, and its style features purposefully rough edges. It partakes of some of the markers of Victorian sophistication, such as self-awareness of codes and conventions and "the ability to cope with—indeed, revel in—paradox and contradiction," as well as of twentieth-century sophistication, such as connoting an "advanced" and "cutting-edge" relation to the mainstream.[9] This latter quality manifests in Lee's writing in an aesthetic of "edginess": despite its reputation for a certain kind of urbane smoothness, sophistication, in exceeding and commenting on what it marks as less sophisticated, also pushes out into unfinished edges. For Lee, her writing's roughness was not only a sign of scholarly sophistication but what John Kucich calls "moral sophistication."[10] Participating in what Kucich refers to as a struggle "among competing middle class elites" over who can claim "an 'exceptional' moral authority, whose flexibility and freedom signifies its anti-bourgeois moral progressiveness," Lee asserted the superiority of her work over the scholarship she called "Vital Lies," which, she argued, signaled their sophistry in their smoothness.[11]

This chapter traces Lee's sophisticated amateur as it emerges as an authorial position in her nonfiction and as a character in her fiction, from the 1890s through the early twentieth century. In close readings of Lee's texts, I show how her sophisticated amateurism played not only with conventions of writing from fin de siècle aestheticism to university scholarship but with the Victorian conventions of gender with which these literary conventions were closely intertwined.

I conclude by considering the implications of Lee's sophisticated amateur scholarship for addressing sophistry in public discourse around the academy today. In accusing "vital liars" of using the style of modern science to construct coherent but false arguments, which they present as bravely unconventional, Lee furnishes strategies for contending with twenty-first-century sophists who claim to be speaking truth to power. Readers today will recognize a new generation of vital lies in contemporary discourses that use the style of modern science to legitimate conspiracy and the language of liberalism to advocate free speech from illiberal positions.

## Lady amateurs, academics, aesthetes, and "Man-of-Letters-Kind"

In late Victorian Britain, as Bonnie G. Smith has shown, conventions of amateur and professional scholarship emerged in distinctly gendered terms.[12] By the 1870s, professional scholarship had become identified with the so-called scientific method pursued in the almost exclusively male faculties of the emerging research university, while amateur scholarship was increasingly associated with the nonscientific writing practices of women. *Amor*, the Latin root of "amateur," looms over these distinctions: effeminate amateur scholarship featured passionate attachments to the objects of study, while masculine academic scholarship was defined by detachment in allegiance to the increasingly prominent standard of objectivity. Women's passion was seen as a sign of their mental and physical inferiority. Arbiters of scholarly practice regarded women as mentally weak and thus incapable of objectivity; they similarly regarded women as physically weak and thus unfit for rigorous scholarly work because it would be dangerous to their health, risking physical as well as mental breakdown. Such judges of scholarly standards found not only the impassioned but also the sometimes ornate style of women's amateur scholarship morally suspect. As Smith notes, stylish writing was associated with prostitution, as in the criticism of the "'tawdry trappings' of more literary works" of history.[13] By contrast, professional academic scholarship, differentiating itself from *belles lettres*, laid claim to objectivity, models of experimental science, careful documentary citation, and a plain style. While most late Victorians regarded women as necessarily amateurs, some granted them a supplementary, second-rate role in professional scholarship as a sort of helpmeet doing clerical tasks in support of original work by men.[14]

At the same time as women were seen as less capable of original work in scholarship, their scholarly efforts were associated with apparently subordinate imaginative work: they were known for writing poetry and fiction on the same topics as their scholarly writing. The woman amateur scholar could thus be seen as akin to both the mid-Victorian man of letters, who wrote fiction or poetry as well as history or criticism of art and society, and the late Victorian aesthete, who combined fiction, history, and criticism in new genres such as "aesthetic criticism."[15] Tellingly, both the man of letters and the aesthete became increasingly feminized and associated with amateurism in the late nineteenth century.

Aestheticism offered a model for Lee's sophisticated amateurism as a practice that both embraced feminized qualities of scholarship and claimed superiority over the professional scholar. For Lee (as for other women) aestheticism provided access to expertise in support of her desire to "write serious works on literature and art."[16] By focusing on deeply felt observations of art objects, rather than philological or archival expertise, aestheticism not only embraced amateur practices but also claimed superiority to academic scholarship of which it was alternately appreciative and critical. It presented itself not as preprofessional but rather as something more than professional scholarship. Out of these repertoires of the effeminate amateur, the masculine academic, the second-rate professional woman scholar, and the aesthete, Lee created a new scholarly authority.

By reworking the scholarly practices and gendered behaviors associated with amateurs and academics, Lee took advantage of a remarkable paradox inherent in the increasing prominence of and access to scholarly institutions in Britain. As Smith has argued, while gendered ideas of scholarship had become more rigid in discourse, they had also become more fluid in practice: women, working-class men, colonial subjects, and other feminized subjects of the British Empire were entering colleges, taking university extension courses, and even publishing in university presses and teaching in universities. The new standards of "scientific" academic scholarship appeared in particular to offer a way to change stereotypes of gender. Science was seen as both unnatural for women and non-Westerners but also "as universal, as available to all, as unmarked, and ungendered; scholarship was thus the conduit away from a degraded femininity toward the higher universal."[17] If women and non-Westerners could practice science, then they could access a universal humanity. At the same time, women's and non-Westerners' identities as marked subjects undermined the idea of an exclusively masculine and Western universal. Thus, while some saw scholarship as an identifiable route to transform themselves and achieve a privileged Western, masculine status, others instead aimed to transform the standards of scholarship and with them conventional standards of masculinity and femininity, even to the point of imagining a "third sex."[18] Lee's sophisticated amateurism effects such double-edged change: with it, Lee introduced an authority grounded in stereotypes of feminine emotion and embodiment, while at the same time valorizing such feminine attributes as essential to the future of scholarship. Ultimately, she depicted these qualities in an androgynous scholarly ideal.

## An androgynous "intellectual prestige"

Lee's sophisticated amateur first emerges as an authorial position in her early fiction and develops into a character in her last novel *Louis Norbert* (1914). Lee's story collection *Hauntings* (1890) is the best-known site of her play with conventions of masculine professional scholarship and effeminate, naive amateurism, and helps us see how her sophisticated amateur differs from these categories. Here, professionalism is linked with academic training and amateurism with the preprofessional aims and practices of those who have not experienced such training—the naïve. While most critics see *Hauntings* as critiquing professionalism in favor of such naive amateurism, such a critique is not the end but the starting point of the book. Ultimately, the stories suggest how both models of inquiry are fatally flawed—either deadly dull or murderously thrilling. The male scholars of *Hauntings* begin with a sense of the inadequacies of their professional practices and seek a more satisfying encounter with the past than their professional practices offer. The desire for an emotionally rewarding encounter with the past was itself a sign of naive amateurism: as Smith notes, "pre-professional scholarship" was less directed at knowing the past as it was than encountering it and making a bridge between the past and future.[19] Dinshaw too argues that desires "for connections" with the past have long been specifically marked as amateur.[20]

In *Hauntings*, Lee's scholars ultimately eschew their professional methods in favor of naïve practices associated with amateur scholars who have not been taught better skills. Ultimately, each story provides the protagonist with the encounter he desires through an uncanny femme fatale (or in one case, an effeminate young man). We see this most vividly in *Haunting*'s "Amour Dure" in which the male scholar-narrator, straying from his usual dry historical practices, passionately summons a historical figure from the Renaissance through composing a poem that "call[s] on her"—only to be stabbed in the heart by her.[21] His amateur desire for direct connection with the past and the amateur means through which he pursues it lead to his violent death. These stories move beyond showing the limits of professional scholarship to show not only the thrills but also the dangers of naïve amateur desires and methods in pursuit of a more intimate encounter with history than professional practice allows.

In contrast to these flawed approaches of professionalism and naive amateurism, Lee models a sophisticated amateurism in the preface to *Hauntings*. There, Lee claims she knows better than either the professionals or amateurs whose misadventures the stories chronicle. She dismisses male professional scholars by associating them with female enthusiasts, mocking the authorities of the Society for Psychical Research (SPR), who included prominent university professors such as William James, for their flawed thinking and dull ghosts. According to Lee, those "highly reasoning men of semi-science" share a reductive view of ghosts with the same deluded Spiritualists that the SPR sometimes investigated for fraud.[22] For Lee, the investigators and the Spiritualists are equally fraudulent: both claim scientific authority and operate in a scientific style marked by an apparently legitimizing dullness, while in actuality they make unprovable claims grounded in wishful thinking. In their embrace of scientific style and unscientific substance, the objects of Lee's criticism claim the authority of science to bolster unprovable or even disproven ideas. Such strategies are far from unfamiliar today: think of Jordan Peterson's use of evolutionary psychology to support Jungian concepts of transhistorical human characteristics or Flat-Earthers' celebration of empirical observation as providing proof for their discredited theory.[23]

Rejecting the fin de siècle version of sophistical science and its putatively real but unimaginative spirits, Lee offers instead "spurious" but superior ghosts, grounded in a literary rather than a professional scientific or an enthusiastic Spiritualist tradition.[24] Invoking Shakespeare, she sets herself firmly in a lineage of first-rate literary treatments of the supernatural. Importantly, by positioning herself both in relation to literary writers and to the professional scholars of the SPR, Lee has literary and scientific authority contest the same ground. And by criticizing the scientific position on its own terms—for being merely "semi-science"—she suggests not that her literary approach is categorically better than their scientific approach but that her literary approach is sound while their science is flawed. Lee thus embraces the authority of good literature, while disavowing bad science on its own terms.

At this point in her career, Lee had a recognizable literary authority but could not yet claim the newer, specialized authority of the scientist. In this 1890 preface, she was leaning on the nearly outmoded Victorian novelist's authority to proclaim broadly about knowledge and morality; more specifically, she was writing in an aesthetic tradition of skepticism regarding the totalizing claims of the scientific method.[25] While in the 1880s she had begun reading and engaging with modern psychology and the science of aesthetics, it was only in the decade following the publication of *Hauntings* that she became a proven, if controversial, authority in these fields, publishing review articles and even her own unusual experiments. Lee drew on both literary and scientific authority in her later writings, especially her novel, *Louis Norbert* (1914), to more fully formulate the sophisticated amateur as a first-rate literary writer who is also a judge of scientific scholarship.

*Louis Norbert* is an epistolary double romance anticipating A. S. Byatt's 1990 novel, *Possession*, chronicling two contemporary researchers investigating two historical figures. The researchers are the "Young Archeologist," a male academic, and a woman amateur, Lady Venetia Hammond. The Archaeologist and Lady Venetia reconstruct the marvelous history of the eighteenth-century figure Louis Norbert and his contemporary Artemesia through letters and transcribed documents, while playfully but earnestly debating various methods of historiography. Most critics regard the novel as an allegory in which the characters stand in for their initial methods. In this view, Lady Venetia represents feminine amateur practices, marked by emotion and enthusiasm, and the Archaeologist the masculine practices of the academic specialist. Some readers have found an "ideal balance" in their combined methods; others, "an impasse."[26] I argue that the novel offers neither such synthesis nor abdication; rather, it depicts the triumph of Lady Venetia over the Archaeologist by virtue of the sophisticated amateurism I have begun tracing in *Hauntings*.

Lady Venetia, while introduced initially as the typical woman amateur historian, comes to embody this new sophisticated amateur—the amateur who knows the conventions of amateurism and of academic, scientific scholarship. Indeed, both she and the Archaeologist complicate the apparent allegory of the novel by acknowledging and exceeding the familiar categories of academic and old-fashioned amateur. Lady Venetia and the Archaeologist (who is called only by his roles—e.g., "Professor"—and never by a personal name) reflect on their roles and tease each other about them. The Archaeologist aligns himself with "us professional critics" and identifies as a "poor plodding historian," only to have the narrator reveal early on that he "after all, was secretly a poet."[27] Lady Venetia, in turn, manifests all the signs of the amateur, from being susceptible to historical "impressions" to penning exclamation-ridden historical narratives to having "visions" that the Archaeologist associates with "occultism."[28] But she turns out also to be a diligent archival researcher.

The novel emphatically mocks the gendered roles of amateur and professional scholar. The Archaeologist's male gaze is prominent from the first page, when he displays erotic delight in Lady Venetia's attention to his account of archaeological sites and then "chill" disappointment when she turns her attention elsewhere.[29] Later, Lady Venetia explicitly connects amateur historians and femininity when she accuses the Archaeologist of seeing her only "as a foolish woman with a hopeless tendency to romancing about everything, what you call a *born poet or novelist*."[30] The novel even mocks the idea that a better method comes from the union of these gendered methods by setting up a romance plot between the protagonists only to have it fail. The flirtation fizzles out when Lady Venetia writes to the Archaeologist of her impending marriage to an older man.

At a crucial juncture, the novel offers a sharp comment on the constructed nature of these gendered roles and introduces a role gendered in new ways. Late in the novel, Lady Venetia accuses the Archaeologist of creating a fictional version of herself. She writes to him that he has been corresponding not with her but with an imaginary character: "And all the time it is *you*, my dear young learned friend, who have been inventing, *inventing a me* utterly unlike the reality."[31] The Archaeologist agrees: "He became aware that he had made her up during the past seven or eight months."[32] Lady Venetia turns the tables and shows the professional scholar that his critical acumen is subject to incursions of fantasy, suggesting more broadly how the figure of the amateur might be a fantasy of the professional.

The specifically erotic character of that fantasy is highlighted in its collapse. When the researchers meet again after this exchange, the Archaeologist perceives a different version of Lady Venetia, one who embodies both a different form of femininity and of intellect. Importantly, in both cases, these forms are superior to his former delusions: she is at once "much more beautiful" than his invented version and possesses "an *intellectual prestige* he had never before guessed."[33] In a departure from *Hauntings*, where the male professional's desire leads to death or disappointment via a femme fatale, in *Louis Norbert* the male expert's ideal female creation simply evanesces when a real woman points out the fantasy. While she is even "more beautiful," this version of Lady Venetia manifests a more complicated femininity than the Archaeologist's imagined version. Her appearance now has androgynous qualities: the Archaeologist notices her masculine hands, which appear "almost like very exquisite man's hands."[34] There is also a shift from the former erotic desire the Archaeologist had felt regarding Lady Venetia, which initially framed their relationship narrowly in sexualized and gendered terms. By contrast, in the moment when the Archaeologist believed himself to be encountering the real Lady Venetia rather than his earlier construction of her, he experiences their interaction as emotionally but not erotically charged. In this later encounter, he perceives Lady Venetia to have "smiled … so simply, humorously, maternally, divinely, friendly."[35]

This Lady Venetia is unrecognizable as the typical woman amateur scholar or even the typical female protagonist of a novel. She is neither love interest nor comic spinster; she is neither erotically desirable nor laughably undesirable or undesiring. Rather, she recalls the alternative femininity of Jane Harrison's archaic goddesses, who are maternal, divine, and companionate, in contrast to the narrowly sexualized roles of the later Olympian goddesses. In this way, Lee draws on the work of a contemporary woman scholar (and acquaintance) who herself had famously mastered the conventions of professional and amateur scholarship. Harrison (1850–1928), a classicist at Newnham College, Cambridge, introduced a new feminine archetype in her account of Greek myth: the independent mother goddess. Harrison argued that religion originated in a matriarchal stage of society in which women were "dominant and central."[36] Goddesses might have consorts, but male deities were not their husbands or masters. Thus, for instance, Harrison argues, the Olympian Hera bears traces of an earlier "matrilinear system" in which she "reigned alone" until she was "coerced, but never really subdued, by an alien conqueror."[37] Harrison had thus introduced in a prestigious scholarly context a model for a femininity marked by independence, even singleness, and compatible with a maternal and companionate but not a connubial role. Arguably, this is the role of Lady Venetia at the end of *Louis Norbert*: she has been revised, in the perspective of the Archaeologist, from an eroticized love interest to someone "maternal ..., divine ..., friendly."[38]

With this shift, *Louis Norbert* participates in two discourses with roots in the nineteenth century: the depiction of scholars—especially amateur scholars—as having queer relations to gender and sexuality,[39] and the valorization of friendship as a queer relationship that enables, in Heather Love's words, "think[ing] intimacy beyond the family and the couple."[40] Dinshaw has shown how amateur scholarship, as it had been practiced since the nineteenth century, is aligned with "some form of sexual or gender queerness" through shared temporalities: both amateurism and homosexuality "are 'belated' or 'underdeveloped' in relation not only to the professional but also to the reproductive family."[41] In *Louis Norbert*, Lady Venetia exemplifies a gender queerness that is analogically connected to her status as a scholar. Her androgyny as well as her sophisticated amateur practice both exceed the conventions of the binaries that inform them and, in exceeding them, appear to supersede them. In this, they depart from a queer temporality in favor of a squarely evolutionary timeline in which types evolve and advance. Specifically, the depiction of Lady

Venetia as androgynous invokes a fin de siècle idea that androgynes (a category that included homosexuals) were "a possible species of the future" and were more highly evolved than conventionally heterosexual men and women.[42] Similarly, Lady Venetia's newly apparent "*intellectual prestige*" exceeds the Archaeologist's own academic prestige, not to mention the naïve amateurism he had originally ascribed to her, suggesting a similarly advanced state.

As the more advanced androgyne and scholar, Lady Venetia formulates a practice of sophisticated amateur scholarship constituted around "friendly" love. Arguing that the Archaeologist's earlier fantasy of her is symptomatic of his misunderstanding of how to do historical research, Lady Venetia presents her superior approach to historical inquiry. The Archaeologist had suggested Lady Venetia ought to "*invent*" Louis Norbert, since "what is loving except making [the beloved] up to please one's heart's desire?"[43] But Lady Venetia is appalled at this conflation of love and "making up."[44] She insists that scholars ought to encounter historical figures as "friends" who "know and love each other when they meet."[45] In this latter model, the scholar recognizes the subject of her research; he does not invent it to please himself.

As part of this superior scholarly practice grounded in love between friends, Lady Venetia shows the Archaeologist the value of historical work based in affective authority more broadly. She refers the Archaeologist to her childhood encounter with a portrait of Louis Norbert, during which she had a specific emotional reaction; and to her encounter, as an adult, with a letter attributed to Louis Norbert, during which she felt the same unique feeling. In this clinching episode, Lady Venetia combines authority grounded in the feminized realm of emotion with a systemization—pattern finding across time—that asserts an objectivity characteristic of academic scholarship. This combination informs her new "*intellectual prestige*."

Lady Venetia's focus on emotional responses to historical objects illuminates affinities between the protagonist and her author, and the centrality of queer love to both their practices. In Lee's own amateur scholarship, queer, friendly love fueled her conversational writing, as in *Belcaro* (1887), dedicated to her lover A. Mary F. Robinson, and her gallery experiments in the 1890s with another lover, Clementina (Kit) Anstruther-Thomson.[46] Further, Lee's scholarly practices feature love not only between herself and her collaborator but love and even collaboration between scholars and objects. Lee's scholarship focuses on the effect aesthetic and historical objects have on perceiving subjects—the viewer in a gallery, the reader before a book, the listener at a concert. This effect is not passive; rather, the viewer, reader, or listener responds to the object, even in a sense co-creates it. In this active engagement with the object, the viewer, reader, or listener is necessarily acting the amateur, forgoing critical distance in favor of intimacy. Importantly, this intimacy is a means to accurate knowledge: it is the queer love of "friends" who "know and love each other when they meet" and not the delusive, heterosexual love of "making [the beloved] up to please one's heart's desire." Crucially, this knowing through feeling does not define truth by what feels true, or what one desires to be true, without reference to further proofs beyond one's own subjectivity; rather, it assumes a truth "out there," beyond individual subjectivity that can be recognized through engagement with others' feelings and with the reality of other subjectivities. Thus, in Lee's sophisticated amateur scholarship, knowledge is not threatened by feminized categories such as love or emotional response but is constituted through them—or, rather, is constituted through the proper versions of them, which are not only feminized but emphatically queer.

## "Towards a rough philosophy"

Lee's sophisticated amateur scholarship is exemplified in the nonfiction she published around the same time as *Louis Norbert*. There is meaningful continuity between the most pressing concerns expressed by Lady Venetia and by Lee. Lady Venetia's outrage over the Archaeologist's "making-up" is apparent in Lee's own long project—pursued with particular energy just before and during the Great War—of exploring the interrelations of fiction and history and the proper definition of truth. In this project, Lee expanded her critique of *Hauntings*' "highly reasoning men of semi-science" into *Vital Lies* (1912). That book of essays focuses on a variety of men writing with scholarly authority on religion, including psychologists, anthropologists, and Catholic modernists. Prominent among them is William James, author of what Lee pejoratively calls

"'Will to Believe' Pragmatism."[47] Lee categorizes these writers as "obscurantists," "myth-mongers," "professional prophets," and "Man-of-Letters-kind" and accuses them of conflating history and romance, truth and pleasure, in pernicious ways.[48] Like Lee herself in her earlier work, as she later admitted, they do not "distinguish ... between novelist's plausibility and historic probability."[49]

As a writer and, since the 1890s, as a researcher in the overlapping fields of aesthetics, psychology, and religion, Lee finds fault with the methods and standards of these putatively scientific writings on religion and truth. Specifically, Lee objected to what she regarded as James's and his peers' redefinition of "truth." According to Lee, James and his fellow travelers asserted that truth can never be definitely known, and so should be redefined as what is most useful, easy, or pleasant to believe. By contrast, Lee believed truth could in theory be definitively established; indeed, she accepted another account of pragmatism, which claims that truth, though it may only emerge as a consensus after long investigation, is ultimately discoverable and reflects reality. This, for Lee, is the proper "formula for scientific thinking."[50] Essentially, she faults the "vital liars" for embracing sophistry over science. In criticism that seems to locate a "post-truth" era already in the 1910s, Lee accused the "vital liars" of taking truth to be what works best rhetorically—what persuades the most people.

Lee regarded the aesthetics of such writing as symptomatic of its methodological flaws: featuring "the pleasant cogency of all symmetrical things," the writings that constitute "Vital Lies" are too systematic, coherent, and aesthetically pleasing.[51] Their investment in persuasion makes them too smooth. This smooth sophistry, moreover, had mystical qualities. Lee criticized the vital liars for staking their authority not on conventional logic but on mysticism: accepting their arguments involves not logical assent but a feeling akin to "mystical revelation," constituting an "overwhelming satisfactory emotion."[52]

As in *Hauntings* and *Louis Norbert*, Lee links the flawed scholarly practices of the vital liars to gendered knowledge practices. On the one hand, the vital liars exhibit a kind of macho vanity, while on the other they are susceptible to the delusions of Spiritualism usually attributed to women. In the first case, tough-guy "professional prophets ... like Nietzsche and Tolstoi" think that "they are manfully facing the whole truth because they are pinning their attention to some aspect of Reality which inflicts pain on themselves, and through them, on their neighbors."[53] But, according to Lee, they are seduced by this heroic suffering into self-aggrandizement at the expense of accuracy. In the second case, Lee links "Vital Lies" to feminized delusions, especially what she regarded as the wish-fulfilling fad of Spiritualism. When writing of pragmatism in *Vital Lies*, Lee repeatedly uses similes and metaphors of Spiritualism, noting its "Sludge-the-Medium gesture[s]" and its methodological "sleight of hand."[54]

Lee further points out that "Vital Lies" are not merely Spiritualist in form but in content: she accuses James's "'Will-to-Believe' pragmatism" of concerning itself with "the tenets of optimistic theism and the hypotheses of mediumistic spiritualism" but not with chemistry, physics, or biology.[55] That is, vital liars only seem to be interested in truth when it is "the *truth* of some variety of theology; or ... of some mediumistic kind of 'spiritualism.'"[56] Thus such pragmatism dishonestly presents itself as a universal method, while concerning itself only with certain subjects, for example, religion. In this way, vital liars both delude themselves and others.

Ultimately, Lee connects this sophistical writing to elitist political forms such as monarchism and fascism. She finds affinities between "Vital Lies" and antidemocratic politics, decrying modern anti-rationalism as "an intellectual tendency parallel to the neo-monarchic and neo-aristocratic arraignments of the shams and drawbacks of democracy."[57] She regards these vital liars as engaged in a form of priestcraft, misleading the populace for the sake of an elite, spectacular vision. In later notebooks, she asserts her aim to provide, in her writing, "an example of avoiding the modern forms" of such deluding practices, which she has come to link explicitly with fascism.[58]

Lee's answer to the flawed and pernicious practices of both amateurish "Man-of-Letters-kind" and their equally mistaken specialist colleagues is her sophisticated amateurism. A major fault of the writers she discusses in *Vital Lies* is their conflation of art and religion, and of novelistic and historical aesthetics. These errors involve writing religiously about religion—writing to convert, to foster unprovable belief, even to encourage mystical experiences. Lee corrects this with what she calls a "spiritual" approach. For her, the spiritual is linked to art and to art's superiority to religion. According to Lee, art is, or should be, proud of its artificiality. It should embrace its "spurious" ghosts. For Lee, art seems more sacred than religion itself: "I ask myself for the hundredth time whether art is not itself a more wonder-working, nay, a more spiritual, divinity than [religion]."[59] By suggesting that art is "more spiritual" than religion, Lee refers to its power to foster contemplation. For Lee, contemplation is a "spiritual" activity, "as distinguished from the utilitarian or merely personally emotional, essence of all high religions," and "does not imply belief."[60] Contemplation allows for a sense of artificiality, whereas belief does not. While Lee mostly applies this idea of the spiritual-as-contemplative to religion and art, it also applies to her treatment of new ideas in science.

Lee's "spiritual" realm maps onto what sociologist Mark A. Schneider calls the "edifying" register in which claims are made for heuristic but not ontological knowledge.[61] Where scientific "naturalism" aims to describe the world as it is, and deals in observations, "edification" aims to describe the world as it might be and deals in concepts.[62] Edificatory claims might be productive without being true, but, crucially, they do not conflate truth and productivity as the vital liars' claims do. This edificatory register is recognizable as something like that of the Victorian sage or, later, the public intellectual, who is invested more in prescription than descriptive contributions to knowledge. Lee's scholarly writing operates mainly in this register. As Shafquat Towheed has shown, her extensive engagement with turn-of-the-century science is marked by creative applications of as yet unproven or even discredited theories.[63] This approach differs from the sophistical deployment of scientific rhetoric to bolster such theories in that Lee emphasizes the provisionality or even figurative value of her material.

Lee is explicit about this approach in the introduction to her study, written with Anstruther-Thomson, *Beauty and Ugliness and Other Studies in Psychological Aesthetics* (1912). There she explains that she and her coauthor are bringing to aesthetics two fields of study that are just emerging as disciplines—on the one hand, "psychology," which "has only lately detached itself from general philosophy," and on the other, "the various sciences dealing with the comparison, the origin and the evolution of artistic form, and which are still dependent on ethnography and anthropology ..., on archaeology and what is called connoisseurship."[64] Thus, Lee asserts that she is offering a work of contemplation rather than of conviction: the ideas in the book will both "afford to more thorough scientific investigators real or imaginary facts for their fruitful examination" as well as "give satisfaction to the legitimate craving for philosophical speculation."[65] This is not only because of the newness of the fields she is drawing on, but because of her humanistic methods, which entail provisionality: "My aesthetics will always be those of the gallery and the studio, not of the laboratory. They will never achieve scientific certainty. They will be based on observation rather than on experiment; and they will remain, for that reason, conjectural and suggestive."[66]

This lack of "scientific certainty" is not a weakness for Lee. Rather, it maps onto her sense of what constitutes truth. In contrast to her vital liars, Lee embraces caution and provisionality, emphasizing the "rough[ness]" of her ideas, as opposed to the too smooth systems of the vital liars. In out-sophisticating these other writers, she deploys sophistication as edginess. She offers not a complete system but "trains of thought converging towards a rough philosophy of my own."[67] Lee's philosophy is purposefully fragmented in order to correspond to what she sees as the fragmentary nature of reality as it appears to humans: it is "discontinuous, discrete, because attention is intermittent, and positions, points of view are various."[68] While some of Lee's approach resembles James's pragmatism, Lee sees his project as ultimately committed to a specious standard of "satisfying," coherent truths, while her methods do not involve such resolution. This resistance to coherence can also be understood as connected to unorthodox gender practices: Hilary Fraser has argued that Lee's writing presents a "third sex authorial identity" linked to a "*becoming* identity that she fashions for herself that is not conceived as originary and fixed, but forever in process."[69]

Lee's fragmentary scholarly aesthetics are aligned with the scientific method of professional scholarship in their commitment to rationality and empiricism and positioned against the sophistry she finds in "Vital Lies" by rejecting too much coherence. These affinities and divergences are apparent in the prose of *Vital Lies* as well as of *Beauty and Ugliness*. This aesthetics is not always beautiful: *Beauty and Ugliness*'s own coauthor objected to its jargon.[70] Both books feature operational definitions, italicized key terms, and frequent quotations from sources. They earnestly perform the conventions of ambitious professional scholarship as a superior alternative both to the falsehood of "Vital Lies" and to pedantic scholarship that, while sound, had abdicated engagement with the big questions of the nature of life and its implications for ethical practice.

But, alongside its jargon, there are thrills and even fantastic imagery that connect Lee's scholarly writing back to her vivid early fiction. In particular, *Beauty and Ugliness* highlights its provisionality through figures of the fantastic, to pleasurable effect. Lee and Anstruther-Thomson evoke the uncertainty of their study using an archeological metaphor: "we two have noticed odd, enigmatic, half-hidden vestiges, which might be (and might also not be!) walls, terraces, and roadways."[71] In this depiction of their study as a strange cityscape uncovered on an archaeological dig, Lee links their scholarly writing to the realm of the fantastic, where the past resurfaces, oddities and enigmas abound, and things "might be (and might also not be!)."[72] Importantly, unlike her detested vital liars, Lee does not claim to have uncovered definitive meanings of history or art. Instead, her approach offers glimpses of exciting ideas that may or may not prove valid, presented through vivid figures of speech. Committed to a responsible provisionality in her scholarly writing, Lee depicts encounters with uncertainty as offering their own satisfactions.

## The sophisticated amateur versus the sophists

Lee's sophisticated amateur responded to a pervasive sense of the narrowing of legitimate modes of inquiry during academic professionalization and specialization. It expanded the repertoire of scholarly practices by reworking conventionally amateur, and feminized, practices that embraced emotion and embodiment. At the advent of the modern research university, Lee thus pursued a project akin to Rita Felski's "postcritical" endeavor to encourage more wide-ranging affects, methods, and forms of professional scholarly practice, particularly those featuring "attachment" in contrast to suspicion, detachment, distance.[73] In this way, Lee and Felski each engage in a prominent tradition of using amateurism to critique and revitalize academic scholarship.

Lee's sophisticated amateur not only helps us better understand the critical force of amateurism but may also offer a resource for exploring postcritique's capacity for political engagement. One objection to postcritical methodologies has been a charge of quietism.[74] Lee, by contrast, deploys her sophisticated amateurism explicitly to political ends. Her criticism concerns the political implications of scholarship that proffers coherent narratives, which yield emotional rewards, even if those narratives are not empirically true. As we have seen, Lee links such approaches to emerging fascist politics. In this way, Lee's sophisticated amateurism offers a timely perspective on the interconnections of scholarly style and political events in our own era, when a new set of vital lies, of too-coherent accounts of history and current events, are promulgated in close connection with anti-democratic politics.

By attending particularly to the aesthetics of scholarly practice, and the feelings one might have in response to those aesthetics, Lee's sophisticated amateurism may help us better recognize sophistry today, and even persuade its fans of its illegitimacy, in ways critique does not. In Andrew Marantz's recent account in *The New Yorker* of UC Berkeley's 2017/2018 "free speech year," we see critique operating in proximity to, and sometimes against, extreme right-wing "sophist[s]"—famous for conspiracy-mongering and bigotry—invited to lecture on campus.[75] Such sophists include Milo Yiannopoulos, Ben Shapiro, Pamela Geller, and Mike Cernovich. After considering Marantz's account of critical engagement with such contemporary sophistry, I will consider how bringing sophisticated amateurism to bear might strengthen approaches that oppose these figures' rhetoric.

Covering a response to the "free speech year" programming, Marantz reports on a scene of public literary analysis, describing undergraduates annotating a poster printed with the text of a lecture recently delivered on campus by Shapiro, then the host of the top right-wing podcast in the United States.[76] Marking "fallacies" in the lecture, the students engage in a familiar form of critique.[77] Lee's sophisticated amateurism offers additional resources for engaging this material. Sophisticated amateurism's attention to the aesthetics of scholarship enables it to highlight not only fallacies but also the styles of these speeches, introducing an area where the critic and the fan of these speeches might share a recognition of their style and emotional effects. These stylistic elements consist, in the case of Shapiro, of "indignant syllogisms [spit out] in a rapid nasal delivery," and in the case of Yiannopoulos, a performance of queer sophistication signaled by "combative one-liners and protean, peroxide-blond hair" and prominent reference to his homosexuality.[78] (This description suggests how Yiannopoulos's campus speeches might fit in a lineage with Oscar Wilde's epigrammatic and aesthetic late Victorian American lectures.)

By attending to these stylistic elements, in addition to the substance of the fallacies imparted through them, today's sophisticated amateur would note how the particular aesthetic qualities suggest or reinforce substantive flaws in the content of the talks: for example, a rapidity that makes syllogisms sound like confident logic but obscures their content. Moreover, in attending to the emotions signaled by the style of these speeches, the sophisticated amateur might be able to imagine the satisfaction some people find in them—in the one-liners with their suggestion of superior wit or the emotionally satisfying performance of logic in "indignant syllogisms." To focus on the emotion performed and fostered through the style of these speeches is to go beyond disproving false content on the level of argument. This focus enables the critic to acknowledge the appeal of the style of these speeches for their fans and to recognize these fans' attachments to the speakers; this recognition, then, may enable another kind of engagement. With reference to style even before substance, the critic may discredit the speech by pointing out how certain smooth styles indicate the presence of false content. In this exchange of impressions and ideas, today's sophisticated amateur is attuned not only to the faults of sophistry but to its appeal—both of which are crucial to its anti-democratic effects.

## Notes

1 See Stefan Collini, *Absent Minds: Intellectuals in Britain* (New York: Oxford University Press, 2006).

2 Vernon Lee, *Vital Lies: Studies of Some Varieties of Recent Obscurantism*, 2 vols. (London: John Lane, 1912).

3 Vernon Lee, "Harrison Unanimisim Lecture: War, Group=Emotion and Art," Handwritten MS (June 3, 1915): 24 small notebook pages and 132 pages, Vernon Lee Collection, Colby College Special Collections, Waterville, Maine, 91.

4 Joseph Litvak, *Strange Gourmets: Sophistication, Theory, and the Novel* (Durham, NC: Duke University Press, 1997), 19.

5 *How Soon Is Now?: Medieval Texts, Amateur Readers, and the Queerness of Time* (Durham, NC: Duke University Press, 2012).

6 Talia Schaffer, *The Forgotten Female Aesthetes: Literary Culture in Late-Victorian England* (Charlottesville: University of Virginia Press, 2000).

7 For reader response, see Christina Zorn, "*The Handling of Words*: Reader Response Victorian Style," in *Vernon Lee: Decadence, Ethics, Aesthetics*, ed. Catherine Maxwell and Patricia Pulham (New York: Palgrave, 2006); for cultural studies, see Shaffer, *Forgotten Female Aesthetes*, 62; for New Criticism, see Benjamin Morgan, *The Outward Mind: Materialist Aesthetics in Victorian Science and Literature* (Chicago: University of Chicago Press, 2017).

8 Meghan Clarke and Francesco Ventrella, "Women's Expertise and the Culture of Connoisseurship," *Visual Resources* 33, nos. 1–2 (2017): 1–10; Susan Lanzoni, "Practicing Psychology in the Art Gallery: Vernon Lee's Aesthetics of Empathy," *Journal of the History of the Behavioral Sciences* 45, no. 4 (2009): 330–354.

9 Faye Hammill, *Sophistication: A Literary and Cultural History* (Liverpool: Liverpool University Press, 2010), 71, 8.

10 John Kucich, *The Power of Lies: Transgression in Victorian Fiction* (Ithaca, NY: Cornell University Press, 1994), 4.

11 Ibid. With this suspicion of rhetorical smoothness, Lee was working in a Victorian tradition of what Adelene Buckland calls "anti-coherence," which rejected "a fictionalizing arrangement of parts into suspiciously plausible wholes." Adelene Buckland, *Novel Science: Fiction and the Invention of Nineteenth-century Geology* (Chicago: University of Chicago Press, 2014), 27, 62.

12 Bonnie G. Smith, *The Gender of History: Men, Women, and Historical Practice* (Cambridge, MA: Harvard University Press, 1998).

13 Ibid., 139. Smith is quoting from an English periodical of 1877.

14 Gill Perry, Anne Laurence, and Joan Bellamy, "Introduction," in *Women, Scholarship and Criticism: Gender and Knowledge, 1790–1900*, ed. Joan Bellamy, Anne Laurence, and Gill Perry (Manchester: Manchester University Press, 2000), 8.

15 Walter Pater, *The Renaissance: Studies in Art and Poetry*, ed. Donald L. Hill (1873; Berkeley: University of California Press, 1980), xix.

16 Lee to Henrietta Jenkin, October 2, 1874, in *Selected Letters of Vernon Lee, 1856–1935: Volume I, 1865–1884*, ed. Amanda Gagel (London: Taylor and Francis, 2016), 176.

17 Smith, *Gender of History*, 197.

18 Ibid., 185.

19 Ibid., 21.

20 Dinshaw, *How Soon Is Now?*, 29.

21 Vernon Lee, *Hauntings and Other Fantastic Tales* (1890; Peterborough, ON: Broadview, 2006), 63.
22 Ibid., 38.
23 See, for example, Kelefa Sanneh, "Jordan Peterson's Gospel of Masculinity," *The New Yorker*, March 5, 2018, and Alan Burdick, "Looking for Life on a Flat Earth," *The New Yorker*, May 30, 2018. Available online: https://www.newyorker.com/magazine/2018/03/05/jordan-petersons-gospel-of-masculinity (accessed January 4, 2019) and https://www.newyorker.com/science/elements/looking-for-life-on-a-flat-earth (accessed January 4, 2019).
24 Ibid., 40.
25 As Stefano Evangelista notes, Lee "follows a Victorian tradition of sage and prophetic writing that runs from Ruskin to Pater, in which vision is believed to give access to a higher epistemology." Stefano Evangelista, *British Aestheticism and Ancient Greece: Hellenism, Reception, Gods in Exile* (New York: Palgrave Macmillan, 2009), 64. For more on shifts in these kinds of authority, see Anne DeWitt, *Moral Authority, Men of Science, and the Victorian Novel* (New York: Cambridge University Press, 2013).
26 Vineta Colby, *Vernon Lee: A Literary Biography* (Charlottesville: University of Virginia Press, 2003), 93–94; Kristy Martin, *Modernism and the Rhythms of Sympathy: Vernon Lee, Virginia Woolf, D.H. Lawrence* (New York: Oxford University Press, 2013), 59.
27 Vernon Lee, *Louis Norbert: A Two-fold Romance* (London: John Lane, 1914), 58, 154, 22.
28 Ibid., 10, 145, 154.
29 Ibid., 9.
30 Ibid., 168.
31 Ibid., 169.
32 Ibid., 182.
33 Ibid., 182, 190, 191.
34 Ibid., 198.
35 Ibid., 196.
36 Jane Ellen Harrison, *Themis: A Study of the Social Origins of Greek Religion* (1912; 2nd edn. 1927; Cambridge: Cambridge University Press, 2010), 494.
37 Ibid., 491.
38 This divine, friendly femininity can also be seen as connected to the "saintly" sexuality Dennis Dennisoff finds in Lee's *Miss Brown*, which is associated with a Joan-of-Arc-like androgyny or in Lee's own terms, a "sexless[ness]" that is associated with a desire to serve humanity rather than to be wife to a particular man. Dennisoff, *Aestheticism and Sexual Parody: 1840–1940* (Cambridge: Cambridge University Press, 2006), 54. This gender practice can also be seen as linked

with the early twentieth-century "humanist" rather than "feminist" political identity that Lee embraced. Patricia Pulham, "A Transatlantic Alliance: Charlotte Perkins Gilman and Vernon Lee," in *Feminist Forerunners: (New) Womanism and Feminism in the Early Twentieth Century*, ed. Ann Heilmann (London: Pandora Press, 2003), 38.

39 These depictions often involved a lack of putatively normal, active heterosexuality, as in Browning's grammarian who is "dead from the waist down," or the presence of links between scholarship and homosexuality, as in the queer circle of men investigating the identity of Shakespeare's addressee in Wilde's "The Portrait of Mr. W. H."

40 Heather Love, *Feeling Backward: Loss and the Politics of Queer History* (Cambridge, MA: Harvard University Press, 2007), 74. As Leela Gandhi has shown, the late Victorian sexologist and activist Edward Carpenter—who once observed that Lee and her lover Kit Anstruther-Thomson would make an admirable addition to his study of "inverts"—theorized friendship as a perfected love without sex and as a foundation for radical political alliances. Leela Gandhi, *Affective Communities: Anticolonial Thought, Fin-de-Siècle Radicalism, and the Politics of Friendship* (Durham, NC: Duke University Press, 2006). Benjamin Hudson's discussion of Edward Fitzgerald points to an even earlier site of the union of these traditions: building on Dinshaw, Hudson suggests certain practitioners of amateur scholarship may also practice a queer "amateur sexuality" that pursues "flirtation for its own sake" alongside friendship, rather than sex and marriage. Benjamin Hudson, "The Exquisite Amateur: FitzGerald, the *Rubaiyat*, and Queer Dilettantism," *Victorian Poetry* 54, no. 2 (2016): 161, 168.

41 Dinshaw, *How Soon Is Now?*, 31.

42 Gandhi, *Affective Communities*, 58.

43 Lee, *Louis Norbert*, 102.

44 Ibid., 103.

45 Ibid., 85.

46 Lee's own language conflated friendship and romantic love in regard to these women. For example, writing of Robinson to Anstruther-Thomson, Lee recalled the former as "the first great friendship and love of my life." Lee to Anstruther-Thomson, August 18, 1904, quoted in Phyllis F. Mannochi, "Vernon Lee and Kit Anstruther-Thomson: A Study of Love and Collaboration between Romantic Friends," *Women's Studies* 12 (1986): 129–148. For more on Lee's queer relationships, see Sally Newman, "The Archival Traces of Desire: Vernon Lee's Failed Sexuality and the History of the Interpretation of Letters in Lesbian History," *Journal of the History of Sexuality* 14, nos. 1–2 (2005): 51–75.

47 Lee, *Vital Lies*, 2:100.

48 Ibid., 1:iii, 2:100, 2:205, 2:152.
49 Vernon Lee, *Studies in the Eighteenth Century in Italy*, 2nd edn. (1880; London: Fisher Unwin, 1907), xix.
50 Ibid., 1.15.
51 Ibid., 1.51. Lee is careful, in criticizing James and some aspects of pragmatism, to praise other elements of James's work and pragmatism more broadly. As a polemical but sometimes appreciative critic of pragmatism, Lee might be further recovered as a voice to include in recent work on the broad history of pragmatism and its value for literary studies today. See, for example, Nicholas Gaskill, "What Difference Can Pragmatism Make for Literary Study?" *American Literary History* 24, no. 2 (2012): 374–389.
52 Lee, *Vital Lies*, 1.208.
53 Ibid., 2:205.
54 Ibid., 1:165, 37.
55 Ibid., 1:35.
56 Ibid., 1:48.
57 Ibid., 1:201.
58 Vernon Lee, Notebook of March–April 1926, Notebooks (holograph manuscripts, 1926–1935, 27 vol.), Vernon Lee Collection, Colby College Special Collections, Waterville, Maine.
59 Vernon Lee, "Art and religion" (article, 1916, 3 p.): Lee's review of *Apotheosis and Afterlife: Three Lectures on Certain Phases of Art and Religion in the Roman Empire*, by Mrs. Arthur Strong, *The Nation*, April 1, 1916: 20 and 22, Vernon Lee Collection, Colby College Special Collections, Waterville, Maine, 2.
60 Lee, *Vital Lies*, 1:244, 1:245.
61 Mark A. Schneider, *Culture and Enchantment* (Chicago: University of Chicago Press, 1993), 12.
62 Ibid., 203–204.
63 Shafquat Towheed, "The Creative Evolution of Scientific Paradigms: Vernon Lee and the Debate over the Hereditary Transmission of Acquired Characters," *Victorian Studies* 49, no. 1 (2006): 33–61.
64 Vernon Lee and Clementina Anstruther-Thomson, *Beauty and Ugliness and Other Studies in Psychological Aesthetics* (London: John Lane, 1912), 2.
65 Ibid., viii.
66 Ibid.
67 Lee, *Vital Lies*, 2:119.
68 Ibid., 2:176.
69 Hilary Fraser, "Interstitial Identities: Vernon Lee and the Spaces In-between," in *Marketing the Author: Authorial Personae, Narrative Selves and Self-fashioning, 1880–1930*, ed. Marysa Demoor (New York: Palgrave Macmillan, 2004), 115, 121.

70 Diana Maltz, "Engaging 'Delicate Brains': From Working-class Enculturation to Upper-class Lesbian Liberation in Vernon Lee and Kit Anstruther-Thomson's Psychological Aesthetics," in *Women and British Aestheticism*, ed. Talia Schaffer and Kathy Alexis Psomiades (Charlottesville: University of Virginia Press, 2000), 220.
71 Lee and Anstruther-Thomson, *Beauty and Ugliness*, viii.
72 Ibid.
73 Rita Felski, *The Limits of Critique* (Chicago: University of Chicago Press, 2015), 180.
74 A recent anthology exploring "postcritique" addresses these criticisms, arguing both that "it is no longer feasible [... ] to assume that critique is synonymous with leftist resistance or that rethinking critique implies a retreat into aestheticism, quietism, belle-lettrism, or other much maligned 'isms' of literary studies." Elizabeth S. Anker and Rita Felski, *Critique and Postcritique* (Durham, NC: Duke University Press, 2017), 15.
75 Andrew Marantz, "Fighting Words," *The New Yorker*, July 2, 2018, 37.
76 Ibid., 39.
77 Ibid.
78 Ibid., 39, 34, 36.

# Bibliography

Anker, Elizabeth S., and Rita Felski, *Critique and Postcritique*. Durham, NC: Duke University Press, 2017.

Buckland, Adelene. *Novel Science: Fiction and the Invention of Nineteenth-century Geology*. Chicago: University of Chicago Press, 2014.

Burdick, Alan. "Looking for Life on a Flat Earth." *The New Yorker*, May 30, 2018. Available online: https://www.newyorker.com/science/elements/looking-for-life-on-a-flat-earth (accessed January 4, 2019).

Clarke, Meghan, and Francesco Ventrella. "Women's Expertise and the Culture of Connoisseurship." *Visual Resources* 33, nos. 1–2 (2017): 1–10.

Colby, Vineta. *Vernon Lee: A Literary Biography*. Charlottesville: University of Virginia Press, 2003.

Collini, Stefan. *Absent Minds: Intellectuals in Britain*. New York: Oxford University Press, 2006.

Dennisoff, Dennis. *Aestheticism and Sexual Parody: 1840–1940*. Cambridge: Cambridge University Press, 2006.

DeWitt, Anne. *Moral Authority, Men of Science, and the Victorian Novel.* Cambridge: Cambridge University Press, 2013.

Dinshaw, Carolyn. *How Soon Is Now?: Medieval Texts, Amateur Readers, and the Queerness of Time.* Durham, NC: Duke University Press, 2012.

Evangelista, Stefano. *British Aestheticism and Ancient Greece: Hellenism, Reception, Gods in Exile.* New York: Palgrave Macmillan, 2009.

Felski, Rita. *The Limits of Critique.* Chicago: University of Chicago Press, 2015.

Fraser, Hilary. "Interstitial Identities: Vernon Lee and the Spaces In-between." In *Marketing the Author: Authorial Personae, Narrative Selves and Self-fashioning, 1880–1930*, edited by Marysa Demoor, 114–133. New York: Palgrave Macmillan, 2004.

Gagel, Amanda, ed. *Selected Letters of Vernon Lee, 1856–1935: Volume I, 1865–1884.* London: Taylor and Francis, 2016.

Gandhi, Leela. *Affective Communities: Anticolonial Thought, Fin-de-Siècle Radicalism, and the Politics of Friendship.* Durham, NC: Duke University Press, 2006.

Gaskill, Nicholas. "What Difference Can Pragmatism Make for Literary Study?" *American Literary History* 24, no. 2 (2012): 374–389.

Hammill, Faye. *Sophistication: A Literary and Cultural History.* Liverpool: Liverpool University Press, 2010.

Harrison, Jane Ellen. *Themis: A Study of the Social Origins of Greek Religion.* 1912. 2nd edn. 1927. Cambridge: Cambridge University Press, 2010.

Hudson, Benjamin. "The Exquisite Amateur: FitzGerald, the *Rubaiyat*, and Queer Dilettantism." *Victorian Poetry* 54, no. 2 (2016): 155–177.

Kucich, John. *The Power of Lies: Transgression in Victorian Fiction.* Ithaca, NY: Cornell University Press, 1994.

Lanzoni, Susan. "Practicing Psychology in the Art Gallery: Vernon Lee's Aesthetics of Empathy." *Journal of the History of the Behavioral Sciences* 45, no. 4 (2009): 330–354.

Lee Collection. Colby College Special Collections. Waterville, Maine, USA, 1866–1960.

Lee, Vernon. *Hauntings and Other Fantastic Tales.* 1890. Peterborough, ON: Broadview, 2006.

Lee, Vernon. *Louis Norbert: A Two-fold Romance.* London: John Lane, 1914.

Lee, Vernon. *Studies in the Eighteenth Century in Italy.* 1880. 2nd edn. London: Fisher Unwin, 1907.

Lee, Vernon. *Vital Lies: Studies of Some Varieties of Recent Obscurantism.* 2 vols. London: John Lane, 1912.

Lee, Vernon, and Clementina Anstruther-Thomson. *Beauty and Ugliness and Other Studies in Psychological Aesthetics*. London: John Lane, 1912.

Litvak, Joseph. *Strange Gourmets: Sophistication, Theory, and the Novel*. Durham, NC: Duke University Press, 1997.

Love, Heather. *Feeling Backward: Loss and the Politics of Queer History*. Cambridge, MA: Harvard University Press, 2007.

Martin, Kristy. *Modernism and the Rhythms of Sympathy: Vernon Lee, Virginia Woolf, D.H. Lawrence*. New York: Oxford University Press, 2013.

Maltz, Diana. "Engaging 'Delicate Brains': From Working-class Enculturation to Upper-class Lesbian Liberation in Vernon Lee and Kit Anstruther-Thomson's Psychological Aesthetics." In *Women and British Aestheticism*, edited by Talia Schaffer and Kathy Alexis Psomiades, 211–229. Charlottesville: University of Virginia Press, 2000.

Mannochi, Phyllis F. "Vernon Lee and Kit Anstruther-Thomson: A Study of Love and Collaboration between Romantic Friends." *Women's Studies* 12 (1986): 129–148.

Marantz, Andrew. "Fighting Words." *The New Yorker*, July 2, 2018, 34–43.

Morgan, Benjamin. *The Outward Mind: Materialist Aesthetics in Victorian Science and Literature*. Chicago: University of Chicago Press, 2017.

Newman, Sally. "The Archival Traces of Desire: Vernon Lee's Failed Sexuality and the History of the Interpretation of Letters in Lesbian History." *Journal of the History of Sexuality* 14, nos. 1–2 (2005): 51–75.

Pater, Walter. *The Renaissance: Studies in Art and Poetry*, edited by Donald L. Hill. 1873. Berkeley: University of California Press, 1980.

Perry, Gill, Anne Laurence, and Joan Bellamy, "Introduction." In *Women, Scholarship and Criticism: Gender and Knowledge, 1790–1900*, edited by Joan Bellamy, Anne Laurence, and Gill Perry, 1–15. Manchester: Manchester University Press, 2000.

Pulham, Patricia. "A Transatlantic Alliance: Charlotte Perkins Gilman and Vernon Lee." In *Feminist Forerunners: (New) Womanism and Feminism in the Early Twentieth Century*, edited by Ann Heilmann, 34–43. London: Pandora Press, 2003.

Sanneh, Kelefa. "Jordan Peterson's Gospel of Masculinity." *The New Yorker*, March 5, 2018. Available online: https://www.newyorker.com/magazine/2018/03/05/jordan-petersons-gospel-of-masculinity (accessed January 4, 2019).

Schaffer, Talia. *The Forgotten Female Aesthetes: Literary Culture in Late-Victorian England*. Charlottesville: University of Virginia Press, 2000.

Schneider, Mark A. *Culture and Enchantment*. Chicago: University of Chicago Press, 1993.

Smith, Bonnie G. *The Gender of History: Men, Women, and Historical Practice*. Cambridge, MA: Harvard University Press, 1998.

Towheed, Shafquat. "The Creative Evolution of Scientific Paradigms: Vernon Lee and the Debate over the Hereditary Transmission of Acquired Characters." *Victorian Studies* 49, no. 1 (2006): 33–61.

Zorn, Christina. "*The Handling of Words*: Reader Response Victorian Style." In *Vernon Lee: Decadence, Ethics, Aesthetics*, edited by Catherine Maxwell and Patricia Pulham, 174–192. New York: Palgrave, 2006.

Zorn, Christina. *Vernon Lee: Aesthetics, History, and the Victorian Female Intellectual*. Athens: Ohio University Press, 2003.

PART THREE

# The Critic as Amateur in Old and New Media

# 8

# Dorothy Richardson and *Close Up*: Amateur and Professional Exchanges in Film Culture

*Zlatina Nikolova and Chris Townsend*

In 1927 the novelist Dorothy Richardson joined the film journal *Close Up* as a regular contributor, publishing over twenty essays before publication ceased in December 1933. Best known as the author of the serial novel *Pilgrimage*, written in thirteen volumes between 1912 and 1946, Richardson was unfamiliar with the technical language of filmmaking. Although rarely considered as a film critic, she was nonetheless a crucial contributor to the magazine. Richardson agreed to contribute following an invitation from her friend, the author Bryher (Annie Winifred Ellerman), who was also *Close Up*'s benefactor and coeditor.[1] Initially amateur critics themselves, Bryher and her husband, the Scottish artist Kenneth Macpherson, along with their companion H.D., founded *Close Up* under the aegis of their Swiss-based publishing project POOL. The journal's aim was to introduce new audiences to film art and encourage their engagement with experimental film practices, from diverse viewpoints; *Close Up* was also advertised as encouraging amateurs. Such sponsorship apparently extended to its own contributions: Marianne Moore would characterize the first issue as founded in well-meaning amateurism.[2] Yet, as we show, *Close Up* was from a very early point a terrain of reciprocal flow and circulation between amateur and professional critics and practitioners that problematizes its categorization as typical, modernist "little magazine."

*Close Up* is often understood as dominated by literary modernists who, even as they expanded the avant-garde's ambitions into mass culture, were hostile toward its formal conventions, and material and institutional practices.[3] H.D., Gertrude Stein and indeed Richardson are frequently cited as typifying the kind of writer the magazine attracted. However, analysis shows that *Close Up*'s principal contributors were neither established modernist writers nor amateur critics. Rather, exemplified by Robert Herring (a film critic), Jean Lenauer (a critic based in Paris), and Oswell Blakeston (a studio cinematographer), they were mostly professionals in the nascent media industries.[4]

We argue that *Close Up*, and the POOL Group's wider network, might in fact be seen as a locus for different forms of amateurism, where contributors from diverse fields exchanged or intercalated roles. Thus, media industry professionals such as Herring and Blakeston used the exchange with the avant-garde that *Close Up* fostered to enter the literary domain as experimental writers and as influencers. Extra-cinematic writing in *Close Up—the critical or promotional textual supplement to film*—by both established literary practitioners and industry professionals is paralleled elsewhere in POOL's activities by a body of para-cinematic writing—*the transposition of cinematic effects into text*—produced by the "professional" critics. Macpherson, Herring, and Blakeston all published "cinematic" fiction under POOL's aegis. Richardson, as a professional novelist but "amateur" critic, acted differently: she deployed the established technique of detailed, realistic social observation typical of her novels in her film criticism. She manifests her engagement with film through reception rather than production, through "anthropology" rather than aesthetics. We therefore challenge arguments made for the influence of film aesthetics on Richardson's writing and suggest that this dynamic may be inverted:

her "amateur" approach to film criticism is in fact defined by the social commentary that emerges in her fiction writing.[5]

We further question what being an amateur film critic means in a journal that hybridized the ideas of editors from the modernist avant-garde with those of industry professionals. For, if Richardson shares common positions and learning processes as a critic they are, oddly, often located within popular culture and shared with middlebrow professionals. We therefore establish parallels between Richardson's approach and those of her contemporaries who simultaneously fashioned careers as professional critics in the mass media and modernist literary stylists in avant-garde magazines. These include Bryher, the Imagist poet Iris Barry at the *Daily Mail* and *Spectator*, the novelist Olive Moore at the *Daily Sketch*, and Caroline ("C.A.") Lejeune at the *Guardian* and later the *Observer*, as well as Herring, who replaced Lejeune at the *Guardian*. With the exception of Herring, these early critics were women, writing out of and about a gendered experience of spectatorship. Like Richardson, they lacked any formal qualification beyond an enthusiasm for the movies.

However much of an amateur we might deem Richardson to be, that status is less distinctive, and far less pejorative, than seems at first to be the case. She publishes in a journal that fosters exchanges between amateurs and professionals, between literary and media practitioners, and blurs distinctions between them so that professionals in one activity become tyros in the other. In the early years of *Close Up*'s publication, Bryher and Macpherson have enthusiasm but no experience of filmmaking or film criticism. Their industry contacts are limited with German acquaintances such as G. W. Pabst the principal entry to professional networks. The early commissioning of material from professionals such as Blakeston, Herring, and Eric Elliott, who had proven credentials as freelance writers, was perhaps a conscious attempt to acquire both technical competencies and a formal lexicon that the editors lacked. It was also a way of gaining access to the promotional networks of production companies. Paradoxically, this turn to the industry meant that many of *Close Up*'s writers were amateurs, approaching their material from a different direction—not as novelists and poets writing about film but cinematographers and editors writing about films rather than shooting or editing them.

The transformation of the British film industry after the Cinematograph Act (Quota Act) of 1927 created new pathways to enter an increasingly professionalized practice. The Quota Act prompted a rapid increase in film production, witnessing a growth in studio facilities and the registration of over two hundred production companies, mostly in and around London. This stimulus provided the basis of the new media industries on which *Close Up*'s editors drew for formal and technical expertise.[6] While those opportunities were often in technical or production roles, there were openings for writers, which increased once the introduction of sound technologies demanded scripted dialogue rather than gesture as the animating force of narratives. Furthermore, exhibition formats changed, responding to demographic shifts and the more varied use of leisure time. Cinemas ranged from large theaters in the West End with full orchestras and cafés to small spaces with a single pianist in poorer areas.[7] Since her articles focus on the period immediately following the introduction of the Cinematograph Act, Richardson effectively acts as an anthropologist of film culture in 1920s Britain.

The promotion and reception of films also led to the development of film criticism as a profession. As Haidee Wasson observes of the early 1920s, "both in the United States and in the United Kingdom, film struck an increasingly serious pose in periodicals and daily newspapers; professionalised and dedicated 'film critics' became regular contributors."[8] Yet this was a profession unaccompanied by the necessity of qualification. That looseness of condition meant that critical roles could be opened to those prepared to seize their opportunity: this included individuals who were perhaps otherwise marginalized from mainstream modernist activity—notably women.

C. A. Lejeune became a writer at the *Guardian* in 1921 through family connections to C. P. Scott, the newspaper's editor. Initially a music critic, she would later reflect: "Why should I not turn my pleasure into profit and earn my living by seeing films? The profession of film criticism had not yet come into being."[9] Like her peers, Lejeune established her craft by formulating an acceptable critical discourse in the public sphere and negotiating a path between endorsement and critique within the promotional apparatuses of the production companies. Her language was grounded in the experience of spectatorship and space, rather than in formal analysis. When Lejeune moved in 1928 from the *Guardian* to the *Observer*, her column "The Week on Screen" passed to Robert Herring. He had begun as a critic in 1926–1927 with titles including the literary magazine the *London Mercury, Drawing and Design: The Magazine of Taste*, and indeed, *Close Up*, first publishing with Bryher and Macpherson in November 1927. Although he was not an industry professional, graduating from Cambridge in English in 1924, and first working on J. C. Squire's middlebrow literary magazine *The London Mercury*, Herring's writing quickly becomes more attentive to the spatial organization, camera work, and lighting of films than any of the other critics considered here.

While Herring negotiated a path into mainstream writing on film from freelance contributions to a range of magazines, there began, at this point, a productive exchange between middlebrow titles such as the BBC's *The Listener* and avant-garde journals such as *Close Up*. Herring's *Guardian* column would variously address Pabst's *Pandora's Box* (1929), the work of the vanguard film composer Edmund Meisel, and Eisenstein's *October* (1927). All of this was material that might have been included in *Close Up*—and sometimes was. Herring's *Guardian* feature on "negro films" in 1928 would lead to his introduction to the actor Paul Robeson and, eventually, *Close Up*'s seminal issue on the topic in August 1929.[10]

Olive Moore had a wider remit as a writer in the mass media than Lejeune, Herring, or Iris Barry, writing broadly on the experience of women in modern society. We include her firstly because within this discourse she necessarily reflected on the ways in which film depicted and affected women. That is, Moore occupied precisely the thematic into which Richardson ventures as a novelist who engaged with film culture. Secondly, Moore was associated with the *Close Up* circle to the extent that in the 1930s her publication was aided by Oswell Blakeston.[11] Finally, and of particular interest given the claims made for "cinematicity" in the work of British modernist women writers, and for Richardson in particular, there is complete incongruity between Moore's writing in the public sphere and her highly experimental literary technique. If, as Renée Dickinson suggests, Moore is a novelist who reimagines the modernist text in contingent response to changes in the lives and subjectivities of women in interwar Britain, that formal experiment does not extend to her widest contact with those women as readers, even as her themes remain consistent.[12] In contrast, Richardson's formal exploration of similar themes remains consistent across fiction and public discourse.

Iris Barry typified an initial amateurism that turned to professionalism. Denied Oxford entry by the accident of the First

World War she fashioned a career as a minor poet, publishing in Harold Monro's *Poetry and Drama* and Harriet Monroe's *Poetry*.[13] An ability to write clear and entertaining prose led to regular articles in the *Spectator* from 1923 and film criticism in the *Adelphi* and *Vogue*—a similar, if slightly more prestigious mix to Herring's early portfolio—before she was hired by the *Daily Mail*, then the highest circulation national newspaper in Britain.[14] As early as 1926 Barry was being described as a "whole-time professional cinema critic."[15] Although this nomination came in one of the magazines for which she was a reviewer, its distinction between amateur and professional is notable precisely because it promotes critical authority. Yet Barry did not address film in formal terms: rather, her concerns were very like Richardson's and Lejeune's. Hankins observes of her work at the *Adelphi* that it "anchors her analysis in her immediate experience as a thoughtful spectator."[16] As Wasson points out, her address was often to "an explicitly gendered subset" of the national audience, talking to women about a shared experience of cinema-going.[17] That new audience was certainly important to newspapers, as a target for their advertisers, and the critic's approach was not pedagogical but rather grounded in a mutual fascination with films as fashionable topics of conversation and consumption. Richardson and Barry have in common a background of marginalized literary practice and no formal knowledge of filmmaking—meaning that their subjects are fundamentally existential rather than aesthetic. However, where Barry and indeed Lejeune and Herring differ from Richardson is in their preparedness to engage directly with the promotional apparatus of the industry. This was something that Richardson eschewed, whereas other *Close Up* contributors worked routinely with that apparatus and used their connections with major studios to develop particular articles and supply the magazine with promotional stills for illustration.

Laura Marcus argues that Richardson's articles are characterized by a defense of "the movies" and popular cinema, contrasting this with other *Close Up* critics.[18] While this contrast perhaps oversimplifies positions that evolved through the magazine's life, we can recognize Richardson's approach as interested in cinema as popular culture, premised upon education and spectatorship rather than aesthetics. Throughout her writing for *Close Up*, Richardson takes the position of a spectator and a social commentator. She discusses the audiences who frequent the cinema most often, the films they are most likely to see, the spaces in which they watch, and the medium's effect on them. Characterized by a "universal hospitality," the cinema is a "refuge" for "weary women of all classes," "sensitives," "elders," and a "charming girl."[19] Alongside these observations, Richardson gives opinions on inter-titles, musical accompaniment, and sound technology. These reflections on the experience of spectatorship and the audience's engagement with cinema's evolving apparatus lead to a distinctive understanding of film culture.

Richardson shows that film appeals to audiences from all social classes. The cinema is a sanctuary from the troubles of daily life, unifying spectators into a cohesive community. As she visited film theaters across London, Richardson chronicled the formation of this community of filmgoers and the changing attitudes to the new art of the "photoplays" in England.[20] Her first article describes the "repulsive" cinema "whose plaster frontages and garish placards broke a row of shops in a strident, north London street."[21] The "tired women … and small children" is a stereotype that recurs in her later essays on audiences, "The Increasing Congregation" and "The Front Rows."[22] Her record of stereotypes continues in "There's No Place Like Home" where the seats of the garage-shaped hall of the cinema are taken by "the leaning lady" and "the solitary, motionless middle-aged man."[23] Each of these characters visits the cinema for a different reason: either to find solace from their daily chores, like the women and mothers Richardson notices in the audiences, or to be entertained like the small children. "Cinema in Arcady" adds that film spectatorship may be one's "admission to a generalised social life" or one's only "escape from ceaseless association" of urban life.[24] Richardson thus records the changing atmosphere of the cinema in the arcade, the slums, the tenement, or the village, as well as the experience of familiarity when one enters the cinema.[25]

Alongside these observations on cinema's function as a space of entertainment, social association, or even solitude, Richardson chronicled changing attitudes toward spectatorship and perceptions of film as art in Britain. At first, Richardson treated film as an alternative to theater.[26] Perceptions of lower cultural status were manifest in her early articles. The public's understanding of silent cinema was dominated not by narrativity but by seeing films as a continuous performance of moving images merged with musical accompaniment that one could enter and leave at any time. This conception of film discouraged serious critical engagement and led to the popularity of genres that privileged set pieces rather than progressively developing scenarios. Although "prime favourites" with audiences, the melodrama and the "farcical comedy" were understood to be of little artistic value, unlike the works largely privileged by other *Close Up* critics.[27] Yet the apparent stereotypes of Richardson's articles are sensitive records of audiences, acknowledging film's reflection of their taste.[28] Larger theaters in central London became venues for social exchange, as Richardson shows in "The Cinema in Arcady" while smaller cinemas were places of solitude and escape for the working classes.[29]

Richardson's record of changing attitudes toward film continued in her reflections on the emergence of sound technologies. Both Tim Armstrong and James Donald have explored the question of sound as one of the key discourses in *Close Up*.[30] Donald explains the journal's concern with sound with its search for "pure cinema" and the clear definition of film as a medium.[31] H.D. claimed that sound "welded" to the moving image underscored film's artificiality and hindered immersive experience.[32] While the projection of voice and image worked in perfect unison, they remained separate entities that fulfilled "different mechanical requirements."[33] Several leading correspondents for the journal wrote with concern of a return to static theatricality as a consequence of sound technology.[34] As the technology developed, so these positions changed. Macpherson reflected on the benefits of sound technology in October 1929, pointing to Hitchcock's *Blackmail* (1929) as a successful use of the medium.[35] Herring had already done this in a *Manchester Guardian* piece in April (about *The Doctor's Secret*) and a BBC talk in August; Blakeston and Hugh Castle also took up the topic in the August and September 1929 issues of *Close Up*. Macpherson sought an aesthetic that incorporated the new technology and used it to experiment with narrative.[36] Lenauer's "The Sound Film: Salvation of Cinema" of April 1929 had already promulgated this idea, claiming that having reached its zenith, silent film was about to die out and be replaced by sound film.[37] While Ian Christie describes *Close Up* as a rear-guard defense of the aesthetics of silent art cinema the journal was in actuality the site of heated debate and progressive endorsement.[38] It is clear from Herring's and Blakeston's writing in particular that the positions on sound in *Close Up* evolved beyond the reactionary shortly after spring 1929.[39]

Richardson entered this discussion by distinguishing between live musical accompaniment and the new sound technology. In her first article she remarked that "Music is essential," arguing that while a good orchestra can highlight specific moments and effects, "a piano played by one able to improvise ... is preferable."[40] Her article on musical accompaniment described in detail the improvisations of a pianist whose talent merged the picture and the music into one continuous performance.[41] Richardson clearly preferred screenings in the poorer areas and the suburbs, where silent films were more likely to be accompanied by a single pianist rather than an orchestra. Recording the growing prosperity of metropolitan cinemas in the immediate pre-sound era and before the economic depression of the early 1930s, Richardson noted the pianist's replacement with a small orchestra, a practice that typified larger cinemas.[42] She concluded that live musical accompaniment was essential to film spectatorship, regardless of the musicians' talent. The unity of the moving image and the musical accompaniment elicited the "stillness and concentration" necessary for the audience's immersion into the experience of film spectatorship.[43] The moving image on its own is "obscene" and "makes no personal demand upon the onlooker."[44]

Although "Almost Persuaded" suggests some enthusiasm for sound film, "Dialogue in Dixie" only a few months later makes clear Richardson's reservations.[45] The addition of synchronized sound to the moving picture distorted the viewing experience with a demand for concentration that distracted from film's visual essence.[46] Despite the "good to excellent" cinematography and the actors' performances in Paul Sloane's *Hearts in Dixie* (1929), its images were obstructed by the slow speech and imperfections of sound technology as sound and "dead" silence alternated throughout the "film opera."[47] In "Film Gone Male" the binary of silent versus sound film becomes a metaphor for the novelist's observations on society's gender dynamics. Sound film's mission of "becoming audible and ... a medium of propaganda" is a "masculine destiny."[48] By contrast, silent film's "innocence" is "essentially feminine."[49] Women, whom "men call womanly ... are silent as the grave."[50] Despite their incessant "chattering," they use speech not as a form of communication but as a "facade" that disguises their "spiritual nakedness."[51] Along with their social commentary, the two articles reveal that Richardson considered sound film superficial and dangerous. While it possessed some limited artistic properties, sound could be exploited to limit the audience's imagination and enforce a specific interpretation of the moving image.

Although she attended less to social and gender stereotypes, Bryher shared Richardson's concern for film's effect on audiences, specifically children. Following her reviews of cinematic treatments of the First World War in the early numbers of *Close Up*, she turned her attention to the pedagogical possibilities for film in two articles: "Films in Education: The Complex of the Machine" and "Films for Children." "Films in Education," listed under the alternative title "Education and Cinema," adumbrated the public's moral concerns with cinema: "Films teach crime, are bad for the eyesight, cinemas breed germs, movies are responsible for all the evils and the restlessness of the modern age."[52] Film's mechanical nature and entertainment appeal were products of the frenetic pace and mechanization of the modern era. Many people related the medium to the industrialization of labor and the machines that had robbed an entire generation of "a sense of power" over their employment and place in modern society.[53] The Establishment's control over films suitable for children and various modes of film censorship were this generation's attempt to place young people "in a state equal with themselves" by limiting film's accessibility.[54]

However, Bryher consistently argued that film could nurture intellect while functioning as entertainment.[55] Children were aware of film's properties and effects so there was no need to shield them.[56] Instead, film's inherent realism could be employed within innovative teaching methods, exploiting children's interest in "any kind of illustration or picture" and their ability to learn visually.[57] Bryher proposed lessons followed by film screenings and practical work that could replace traditional teaching approaches.[58] She further outlined the benefits of spectatorship in "Films for Children" in August 1928, presenting a list of films children should see contrary to the censors' recommendations.[59] Apart from documentaries and newsreels, the list included the short musical *Power and Beauty* (1926) and the Soviet film *Mother* (1926). In addition, Bryher mentioned Pabst's *Joyless Street* (1925) and Room's *Bed and Sofa* (1927)—which were art films dealing with "adult" topics such as prostitution and cohabitation. Bryher traced the public's prejudice against these films to state censorship and the critics' inability to form divergent opinions. Children, as well as mass audiences, should be taught to discern a film's importance by its application of experimental practices or its narrative.

In contrast to Bryher's polemic, Richardson's reflections on film's effect on children map both the advantages of their exposure to film and its negative consequences for their perception of the world. "The Front Rows" focused on three boys sitting in the front row of the cinema.[60] Instead of spending their Saturday afternoon in the streets, they choose to stay in the "coolness" of the film theater.[61] Film is an ironic "black villainy" that has drawn the boys into the stuffy cinema.[62] These popularly promulgated negative effects were balanced against film's promise as an educational medium. The children get the chance to see films that are not necessarily deemed fit by adults for children's viewing and as a result they are "learning either less than nothing or more than was good."[63]

Richardson continued in this vein in August 1928. Published alongside Bryher's "Films for Children," Richardson's article of the same title claimed that film had the potential to entertain children *and* educate them.[64] The child's relationship with film was similar to her relationship to the picture book, a parallel that Bryher also noticed.[65] However, Richardson recognized a problem, suggesting that film's capacity to manipulate space and time posed a challenge to its realistic representation of the world. Although educative, "nature" films were produced with the aim to entertain and astonish and, as a result, endowed "natural processes" with a sense of "unnatural smooth swiftness and reality."[66] At this point, unusually, Richardson made aesthetic rather than moral judgments or anthropological observations, suggesting that editing created a false impression of the reality of biological processes as the egg and the chicken became nothing more than "a conjuring trick."[67] While Richardson challenged cultural skepticism toward the new medium, she cautioned against misunderstandings latent in the temporal-spatial malleability it promises. Bryher omitted such considerations in her reflections on film's potential. Although she largely refrained from discussions of filmmaking practices, the thematic scope of Richardson's essays in *Close Up* demonstrates her awareness of film's cultural, artistic, and educational potential. She comments on the flourishing culture of cinema-going and film spectatorship but also chronicles the development of British society's understanding of the medium and its multiple applications.

Eschewing the technicalities of film's production and promotion, Richardson examined the social routines and habits that film culture encouraged. Such elision of the filmic apparatus marginalizes her in the context of *Close Up*'s focus on international film industries, filmmaking practices, and theories. While Richardson shared concerns about film's place in education, spectatorship, and censorship with Bryher, Bryher became more knowledgeable about filmmaking practices through her connections with European filmmakers like Pabst and Sergei Eisenstein. That research fed into her articles on Pabst's films, as well as her exploration of the Soviet industry in *Film Problems of Soviet Russia* (1929).[68] Richardson's commentary on film's role in culture was instead fueled by her observations and experiences as a spectator. Her analysis of the viewing experience informs the subjectivity of the commentary in *Pilgrimage*.

Although organized according to what she considered central concepts of cinema-going culture, such as the cinema's democratic space and the diverse "congregation" of social types in its audiences, Richardson's articles also recorded her own experiences of film. Richardson regularly described her personal impressions of entering the film theater or watching the continuous performance of moving images. This descriptive prose mirrors Miriam's observations in *Pilgrimage* and what McCracken and Pritchett describe as the central protagonist's "hyperaesthesia."[69] They see *Pilgrimage*'s self-awareness of its own sociocultural context originating in Miriam's acute awareness of the "sensorium of the visual, the musical, and the haptic" of the narrative world.[70] This sensitivity to experience forges a connection between Miriam and the reader.[71] That is, Miriam behaves very much like a "professional" critic, like an Iris Barry, C. A. Lejeune, or Olive Moore establishing a rapport with their largely female audience. Richardson's focus on her protagonist's consciousness and the sensuous description of Miriam's life has led to comments on the "cinematic" nature of *Pilgrimage*—this despite the fact that much of the series was written well before Richardson wrote about film.

Jane Garrity draws parallels between Richardson's fiction and her *Close Up* articles: she compares Miriam's "shifting perspective" to "the roving eye of a camera."[72] Narrative subjectivity destabilizes the readers' position as it entwines them with the protagonist's personal sense of events and abolishes the interferences of other consciousness. Garrity notes that Richardson considers the film-viewing experience to be almost "alchemical" as it produces another form of consciousness that engages the spectator.[73] Film's "alien" consciousness and its relationship to its audience can be related to the relationship between the reader and Miriam informed by the subjectivity of *Pilgrimage*'s prose. Yet Richardson's writing in *Pilgrimage* does not employ the para-cinematic manipulation of time and space that characterizes the experimental fiction of Macpherson, Blakeston, or Herring—an editorial manipulation that Richardson indeed critiques as a filmic practice.

Richardson's articles were informed by the same approach that structured the readers' relationship to Miriam's experiences rather than the formalized position of a filmmaker. Although her film writing appears "amateur" when compared to the technical sophistication that underpins many other *Close Up* critics' texts, it established her as an anthropologist of early film culture in Britain. Richardson aligns herself with the gendered cinematic audience just as Miriam articulates the thoughts and problems of young women in early twentieth-century society. She writes: "We go ... We emerge, glitter for a moment in the brilliant light of the new flamboyant foyer, and disappear for the evening in the queer faintly indecent gloom."[74] Richardson recorded her hopes for and disappointment with the talkies in a similar collective voice: "We would make allowances. We were about to see the crude, the newly-born. We grew willing to abandon our demand for the frozen window-sill in favor of a subscription for a comfortable cradle."[75] Her impressionistic approach distanced her from the technically authoritative voices of critics like Blakeston, Herring, Macpherson, and even Bryher and rendered her texts more appealing to the audiences that *Close Up* tried to educate about the new film art.

Richardson's film criticism, the tone of her articles, and the issues she discussed placed her in a unique position as intermediary between professional filmmakers and film critics on the side and spectators and laymen on the other. She acknowledged film's cultural and artistic potential, even if she had no technical expertise with the medium, nor with the discourses and apparatuses of the industry. Yet her articles remain important for mirroring the spectator's sensitivity to cinematic experience. Richardson defined the relationship between the popular audience and film's technologies and forms. While other *Close Up* critics theorized the effects of cinema, Richardson dwelled on those effects at first-hand and, like the middlebrow critics of the mainstream press, turned them into the central topic of her writing.

## Notes

1 Dorothy Richardson to Bryher, 1927. Bryher Papers GEN MSS 97 Series I Correspondence Box 52, Folder 1915, Granted by permission of the Beinecke Rare Books and Manuscript Library, Yale University on behalf of the Schaffner Family Foundation.

2 Advertisement for *Close Up, Transition* (July 1927): n.p., Marianne Moore, "Comment," *The Dial* 83 (November 1927): 449–450, Kenneth Macpherson, "As Is," *Close Up* I, no. 1 (July 1927): 15, and "As Is," *Close Up* I, no. 2 (August 1927): 6–13.

3 James Donald, Anne Friedberg, and Laura Marcus, *Close Up, 1927–1933. Cinema and Modernism* (Princeton, NJ: Princeton University Press, 1998), vii.

4 Betsy van Schlun, *The POOL Group and the Quest for Anthropological Universality* (Berlin: De Gruyter, 2017); Chris Townsend, "A Deeper, Wider POOL: Reading *Close Up* through the Archives of Its Contributors," *Papers on Language and Literature*, forthcoming, 2019.

5 Jane Garrity, *Step-daughters of England: British Women Modernists and the National Imaginary* (Manchester: Manchester University Press, 2003).

6 Steve Chibnail, *Quota Quickies* (London: BFI Publishing, 2007), 18–19.

7 Laraine Porter, "Temporary American Citizens: British Cinema in the 1920s," in *The Routledge Companion to British Cinema History*, ed. I. Q. Hunter, Laraine Porter and Justin Smith (London: Routledge: 2017), 42–43.

8 Haidee Wasson, "The Woman Film Critic: Newspapers, Cinema and Iris Barry," *Film History* 18, no. 2 (2006): 155.

9 C. A. Lejeune, *Thank You for Having Me* (London: Hutchinson, 1964), 69.

10 Robert Herring, "Negro Films," *Manchester Guardian* (December 15, 1928): 11. Herring to Bryher, December 21, 1928. Bryher Papers GEN MSS 97 Series I Bryher Correspondence, Box 18, Folder 703. Granted by permission of the Beinecke Rare Books and Manuscript Library, Yale University on behalf of the Schaffner Family Foundation.

11 Oswell Blakeston, "Appointment with X," undated typescript, Oswell Blakeston Collection, Harry Ransom Center, University of Texas at

Austin. Series II. Works, 1927–1985. Box 4, Folder 1–2, 33. Having used *Close Up* as a portal to the literary world, Blakeston established his own networks of influence. In this manuscript he claims to have helped place Silvia Dobson's *The Happy Philistine* (Duckworth, 1937), Moore's *The Apple Is Bitten Again* (Wishart, 1934) and Dallas Bower's *Plan for Cinema* (Dent, 1936).

12 Renée Dickinson, *Female Embodiment and Subjectivity in the Modernist Novel: The Corporeum of Virginia Woolf and Olive Moore* (London: Routledge, 2009), 3.

13 Robert Sitton, *Lady in the Dark: Iris Barry and the Art of Film* (New York: Columbia University Press, 2014).

14 Leslie Hankins, "Iris Barry, Writer and Cinéaste, Forming Film Culture in London 1924–1926: The *Adelphi*, the *Spectator*, the Film Society and British *Vogue*," *Modernism/Modernity* 11, no. 3 (September 2004): 488–515.

15 "The Metaphysic of the Movies," review of Iris Barry, *Let's Go to the Pictures* (1926), *Spectator*, November 13, 1926: 84. Cited in Hankins, "Iris Barry," 490.

16 "Iris Barry," 495.

17 "The Woman Film Critic," 157.

18 Laura Marcus, "Continuous Performance: Dorothy Richardson," in Donald, Friedberg and Marcus, *Close Up 1927–1933*, 152.

19 Dorothy Richardson, "The Increasing Congregation," *Close Up* I, no. 6 (December 1927): 61–65.

20 "Continuous Performance," (July 1927): 35.

21 Ibid.

22 Ibid.; "The Increasing Congregation," 64; Dorothy Richardson, "The Front Rows," *Close Up* II, no. 1 (January 1928): 60.

23 Dorothy Richardson, "There's No Place like Home," *Close Up* I, no. 5 (November 1927): 45.

24 Dorothy Richardson, "The Cinema in Arcady," *Close Up* III, no. 1 (July 1928): 52–57.

25 "There's No Place like Home," 44–47; Dorothy Richardson, "The Cinema in the Slums," *Close Up* II, no. 5 (May 1928): 58–62; "The Cinema in Arcady," 52–57.

26 "Continuous Performance," 34–35.

27 "The Cinema in Arcady," 56.

28 Anthony Aldgate and Jeffrey Richards, *Best of British: Cinema and Society from 1930 to the Present* (London: I. B. Tauris, 2009), 1–4.

29 "The Cinema in Arcady," 55.

30 Tim Armstrong, *Modernism, Technology and the Body: A Cultural Study* (Cambridge: Cambridge University Press, 1998), 231–233; James Donald, "From Silence to Sound," in Donald, Friedberg and Marcus, *Close Up 1927–1933*, 80–82.

31 "From Silence to Sound," 80.
32 H.D., "The Mask and the Movietone," *Close Up* I, no. 5 (November 1927): 20.
33 Ibid., 21.
34 Oswell Blakeston, *Daily Telegraph*, July 5, 1928. Robert Herring, "The Talkies," *The London Mercury* XIX (November 1926): 110, 201.
35 Kenneth Macpherson, "As Is," *Close Up* V, no. 4 (October 1929): 257–262.
36 Ibid., 262.
37 Jean Lenauer, "The Sound Film: Salvation of the Cinema," *Close Up* IV, no. 4 (April 1929): 18–21.
38 Ian Christie, "Introduction," in *The Film Factory: Russian and Soviet Cinema in Documents, 1896–1939*, ed. Ian Christie and Richard Taylor (London: Routledge, 1994), 6.
39 Robert Herring, "Barrie on the Sound Film," *Manchester Guardian*, April 27, 1929; Robert Herring, "Film Criticism," *BBC 2LO*, August 2, 1927, see Robert Herring to Bryher, Bryher Papers GEN MSS 97 Series II, Writings Box 19, Folder 706, "Sunday" (an internal reference to a comment in the *Manchester Guardian* dates this letter to August 4, 1927); Hugh Castle, "Elstree's First 'Talkie'," *Close Up* V, no. 2 (August 1929): 133; Oswell Blakeston, "Russia's New Pictures," *The Bioscope* 1193 (August 14, 1929): 27; Oswell Blakeston, "One Swallow," *Close Up* V, no. 3 (September 1929): 244–245; Oswell Blakeston, "The Russian Film, part II," *The Educational Screen* VIII, no. 8 (October 1929): 232.
40 "Continuous Performance," 37.
41 Dorothy Richardson, "Musical Accompaniment," *Close Up* I, no. 2 (August 1927): 59.
42 Ibid., 59–60.
43 Ibid.
44 Ibid., 61.
45 Dorothy Richardson, "Almost Persuaded," *Close Up* IV, no. 6 (June 1929): 36; Dorothy Richardson, "Dialogue in Dixie," *Close Up* V, no. 3 (September 1929): 211–218.
46 "Dialogue in Dixie," 215.
47 Ibid., 213–214.
48 Dorothy Richardson, "Film Gone Male," *Close Up* IX, no. 1 (March 1932): 38.
49 Ibid., 37.
50 Ibid.
51 Ibid., 36.
52 Bryher, "'Education and Cinema'/'Film in Education: The Complex of the Machine'," *Close Up* I, no. 2 (August 1927): 51.

53 Ibid.
54 Ibid.
55 Bryher, "Dope or Stimulus," *Close Up* III, no. 3 (September 1928): 60.
56 "'Education and Cinema'/'Film in Education'," 51.
57 Ibid., 51, 53–54.
58 Ibid., 54.
59 Bryher, "Films for Children," *Close Up* III, no. 2 (August 1928): 16–18.
60 "Front Rows," 59–64.
61 Ibid., 60.
62 Ibid.
63 Ibid.
64 Dorothy Richardson, "Films for Children," *Close Up* III, no. 2 (August 1928): 23.
65 Ibid., 24; "'Education and Cinema'/'Film in Education'," 53.
66 Ibid., 25.
67 Ibid.
68 Bryher, "'Education and Cinema'/'Film in Education'"; Bryher, "Films for Children"; "G.W. Pabst: A Survey," *Close Up* I, no. 4 (December 1927); Bryher, *Film Problems of Soviet Russia* (Territet: POOL Reflections, 1929).
69 Scott McCracken and Elizabeth Pritchett, "Plato's Tank: Aestheticism, Dorothy Richardson and the Idea of Democracy," *Pilgrimages: The Journal of Dorothy Richardson Studies* 6 (2013–2014): 94–99.
70 Ibid., 94.
71 Ibid.
72 *Step-daughters of England*, 91.
73 Ibid., 93.
74 "The Increasing Congregation," 62.
75 "Dialogue in Dixie," 212.

# Bibliography

Aldgate, Anthony and Jeffrey Richards. *Best of British: Cinema and Society from 1930 to the Present*. London: I. B. Tauris, 2009.

Anonymous - "The Metaphysic of the Movies," review of Iris Barry, *Let's Go to the Pictures* (1926), *The Spectator*, November 13, 1926: 84, cited in Hankins, Leslie. "Iris Barry, Writer and Cinéaste, Forming Film Culture in London 1924–1926: the *Adelphi*, the *Spectator*, the Film Society and British *Vogue*." *Modernism/ Modernity*, 11, no. 3, (September 2004): 488–515.

Armstrong, Tim. *Modernism, Technology and the Body: A Cultural Study*. Cambridge: Cambridge University Press, 1998.

Blakeston, Oswell. "Appointment with X," undated typescript, Oswell Blakeston Collection, Series II: Works, 1927–1985, Box 4, Folder 1–2, 33. Harry Ransom Center, University of Texas at Austin.

Blakeston, Oswell. "Russia's New Pictures." *The Bioscope*, 1193, August 14, 1929.

Blakeston, Oswell. "The Russian Film, part II." *The Educational Screen* VIII, no. 8, October 1929.

Blakeston, Oswell. "Approach to Sound." *Kinematograph Weekly* 158, April 24, 1930.

Bryher. "'Education and Cinema'/'Film in Education: The Complex of the Machine'." *Close Up* I, no. 2 (August 1927): 49–54.

Bryher. "G.W. Pabst: A Survey." *Close Up* I, no. 4 (December 1927): 56–61.

Bryher. "Films for Children." *Close Up* III, no. 2 (August 1928): 16–20.

Bryher. "Dope or Stimulus." *Close Up* III, no. 3 (September 1928): 59–61.

Bryher. *Film Problems of Soviet Russia*. Territet: POOL, 1929.

Chibnail, Steve. *Quota Quickies*. London: BFI Publishing, 2007.

Christie, Ian. "Introduction." In *The Film Factory: Russian and Soviet Cinema in Documents, 1896–1939*, edited by Ian Christie and Richard Taylor. London: Routledge, 1994.

Dickinson, Renée. *Female Embodiment and Subjectivity in the Modernist Novel: The Corporeum of Virginia Woolf and Olive Moore*. London: Routledge, 2009.

Donald, James, Anne Friedberg, and Laura Marcus. *Close Up, 1927–1933. Cinema and Modernism*. Princeton, NJ: Princeton University Press, 1998.

Donald, James. "From Silence to Sound." In *Close Up 1927–1933, Cinema and Modernism*, ed. James Donald, Anne Friedberg, and Laura Marcus, 79–82. Princeton, NJ: Princeton University Press, 1998.

Garrity, Jane. *Step-daughters of England: British Women Modernists and the National Imaginary*. Manchester: Manchester University Press, 2003.

Hankins, Leslie. "Iris Barry, Writer and Cinéaste, Forming Film Culture in London 1924–1926: the *Adelphi*, the *Spectator*, the Film Society and British *Vogue*." *Modernism/ Modernity*, 11, no. 3, (September 2004): 488–515.

H.D. "The Mask and the Movietone." *Close Up* I, no. 5 (November 1927): 18–31.

Herring, Robert. "The Movies." *The London Mercury* XV, November 1926.

Herring, Robert. "Negro Films." *Manchester Guardian*, December 15, 1928.
Herring, Robert. Robert Herring to Bryher, December 21, 1928. Bryher Papers GEN MSS 97, Series I, Bryher Correspondence, Box 18, Folder 703, Herring, Robert, 1927–1928. Beinecke Rare Books and Manuscript Library, Yale University on behalf of the Schaffner Family Foundation.
Herring, Robert. "Barrie on the Sound Film." *Manchester Guardian*, April 27, 1929.
Kraszna-Krausz, Andor. "The First Russian Sound Films." *Close Up* VIII, no. 4 (December 1931).
Lenauer, Jean. "The Sound Film: Salvation of the Cinema." *Close Up* IV, no. 4 (April 1929): 18–21.
Lejeune, C. A. *Thank You for Having Me*. London: Hutchinson, 1964.
Macpherson, Kenneth. "As Is." *Close Up* I, no. 1 (July 1927): 5–15.
Macpherosn, Kenneth. "As Is." *Close Up* I, no. 2 (August 1927): 5–17.
Macpherson, Kenneth. "As Is." *Close Up* V, no. 4 (October 1929): 257–262.
Marcus, Laura. *The Tenth Muse. Writing about Cinema in the Modernist Period*. Oxford: Oxford University Press, 2007.
McCracken, Scott and Elizabeth Pritchett. "Plato's Tank: Aestheticism, Dorothy Richardson and the idea of Democracy." *Pilgrimages: The Journal of Dorothy Richardson Studies* 6 (2013–2014): 84–106.
Marianne Moore. "Comment." *The Dial* 83 (November 1927): 449–450.
Porter, Laraine. "Temporary American Citizens: British Cinema in the 1920s." In *The Routledge Companion to British Cinema History*, edited by I. Q. Hunter, Laraine Porter and Justin Smith. London: Routledge: 2017.
Richardson, Dorothy. Dorothy Richardson to Bryher, 1927. Bryher Papers GEN MSS 97 Series I Correspondence Box 52, Folder 1915. Granted by permission of the Beinecke Rare Books and Manuscript Library, Yale University on behalf of the Schaffner Family Foundation.
Richardson, Dorothy. "Musical Accompaniment." *Close Up* I, no. 2 (August 1927): 58–62.
Richardson, Dorothy. "There's no Place like Home." *Close Up* I, no. 5 (November 1927): 44–47.
Richardson, Dorothy. "The Increasing Congregation." *Close Up* I, no. 6 (December 1927): 61–65.
Richardson, Dorothy. "The Front Rows." *Close Up* II, no. 1 (January 1928): 59–64.
Richardson, Dorothy. "The Cinema in the Slums." *Close Up* II, no. 5 (May 1928): 58–62.
Richardson, Dorothy. "The Cinema in Arcady." *Close Up* III, no. 1 (July 1928): 52–57.
Richardson, Dorothy. "Films for Children." *Close Up* III, no. 2 (August 1928): 21–27.

Richardson, Dorothy. "Almost Persuaded." *Close Up* IV, no. 6 (June 1929): 31–37.

Richardson, Dorothy. "Dialogue in Dixie." *Close Up* V, no. 3 (September 1929): 211–218.

Richardson, Dorothy. "The Censorship Petition." *Close Up* VI, no. 7 (January 1930): 7–11.

Richardson, Dorothy. "Film Gone Male." *Close Up* IX, no. 1 (March 1932): 36–37.

Schlun, Betsy van. *The POOL Group and the Quest for Anthropological Universality*. Berlin: De Gruyter, 2017.

Sitton, Robert. *Lady in the Dark: Iris Barry and the Art of Film*. New York: Columbia University Press, 2014.

Townsend, Chris. "A Deeper, Wider POOL: Reading *Close Up* through the Archives of Its Contributors." *Papers on Language and Literature*, 2019.

Wasson, Haidee. "The Woman Film Critic: Newspapers, Cinema and Iris Barry." *Film History* 18, no. 2 (2006).

# 9

# New Judgments: Literary Criticism on Air

*Emily Bloom*

The BBC producer Stephen Potter entered the world of broadcasting as a refugee from academia. He spent his early career as a lecturer in English at the University of London, writing books on Coleridge and D. H. Lawrence. In 1937 he wrote a book titled *The Muse in Chains*, which articulated his displeasure with the academic study of English. His primary critique was with the growing disconnection between the esotericism of academic criticism and the everyday experience of readers outside of the ivory tower. In 1941 Potter launched a radio series called "New Judgment" that attempted to bridge this divide by offering accessible literary criticism to radio's mass publics.[1] The program invited contemporary writers to create innovative programs explicating the work of literary and cultural figures from the past. Despite differences across the series, the "New Judgment" formula involved a multi-generic blending of criticism, biography, drama, and readings that were intended to make literary criticism accessible and entertaining to the common reader or, in this case, the common listener.

While it is an academic truism that mid-century critics professionalized literary criticism as it is now practiced in universities across the globe, the idea of a popular literary criticism intended for mass audiences and performed through mass media has largely faded from cultural memory. These broadcasts reveal how writers during the Second World War adapted literary criticism for mass publics through the hybrid style of the feature broadcast, which was pioneered by Potter and his colleagues in the Features Department. Potter's series not only fulfilled his goal of wresting literary criticism from the specialized vocabularies of experts, but it also encouraged professional writers to learn radio writing, diving in as amateurs to a new and unfamiliar medium. The critic's status as an amateur radio writer, however, was conferred against the backdrop of radio's increasing professionalization. As the medium moved from its preprofessional era—when radio was operated by amateur enthusiasts—to its mid-century "golden age" of consolidation and professionalization, radio practitioners were especially keen to assert their newfound expertise.[2] In the case of the "New Judgment" series, we see the fulcrum shifting as literary critics embrace amateurism just as broadcasters were exerting their newfound status as experts.

Focusing on the "New Judgment" series, this essay describes how the exigencies of war and the opportunities of new media enabled critics to experiment with unfamiliar techniques that popularized literary criticism for vast listening audiences at a time when paper restrictions on publishers and the existential threat of Blitz bombings made literary traditions seem more fragile than ever. The correspondence surrounding two programs by Stephen Spender on Walt Whitman (1941) and Seán O'Faoláin on Oliver Goldsmith (1942) reveal the fraught dynamics that emerged between the respective roles of the producer, writer, and listener as critics; the question of how to pitch of the programs in terms of intellectual difficulty; and the role of audience appreciation in determining value.

Before joining the BBC, Potter outlined his critique of the academic study of English Literature in his book *The Muse in Chains*. Potter uses the portmanteau "Inglit" to describe the established version of English literary scholarship, whose practitioners he describes as "anecdotalists, antiquarians, hero-worshippers, pedants, and collectors."[3] He goes on to define three versions of the professional Literary Man that he found most pernicious: the categorizer and simplifier of literature into periods and movements; the critic obsessed with authorial biography; and "the note-man or surface creeper."[4] All these versions, he argued, separated literature from the creative process and from critical thought and distanced the literary past from the contemporary world of writers and readers. He feared that this growing divide between the Inglit Man and readers and writers would destroy literary appreciation, turning it into either rote knowledge, a celebrity fixation on canonical authors, or a merely pedantic activity that distanced readers from the works themselves.

*The Muse in Chains* is part jeremiad and part satire; Potter's attacks on the Inglit Man, while broad and wide-ranging—covering everyone from the university professor to the journalistic man of letters—are consistent in their focus on the evils of specialization and genius-worship. Potter writes:

> The growing up of the impression among "book-lovers"—a fairly good word for those who are subdued into trance-like receptivity, rather than stimulated to activity, by the contact of genius—that they are all of them perfectly competent critics, but that real "creative" writing is impossible for them unless they are flukily presented at birth with something vague, something supernatural, called genius.[5]

Here Potter attacks abstract notions of literary genius as well as the practice of literary appreciation as a passive activity. Instead, he demands a readership that considers the text from creative and critical points of view. He also implies that readers don't deserve to think of themselves as critics without earning the distinction by being "stimulated to activity." Written in the 1930s, on the verge of war in Europe, the book suggests an immanent critique of fascism in literary studies. Potter sees himself as standing against both technocratic and "great man" approaches to literature that either limit literary criticism to a small pool of experts speaking a specialized vocabulary or that insist on the exceptionality of the literary genius who stands apart from the common writer and reader.

Potter's intervention in literary studies was contemporary with the emergence of New Criticism and shares some of its features, including pushing back against the dominance of specialized philological and literary-historical approaches to literature. In *Literary Criticism: A Concise Political History*, Joseph North calls for a reconsideration of the political value of New Criticism for the intellectual Left. North argues that I. A. Richards, in his formulation of practical criticism, sought to "cultivate the aesthetic capabilities of readers" and that, unlike later New Critics such as F. R. Leavis, he focused his criticism on the relationship between the work of art and its audience rather than the formalist approach that was later attributed to him.[6] Later versions of New Criticism, according to North, enshrined the critic as expert and perverted Richards's goal of making critics of all readers. However, Christopher Hilliard notes that for F. R. Leavis, as well, "thinking about literature was intimately connected with thinking about living."[7] This emphasis on the practical value of criticism meant that Leavis was invested in considering literary judgment from the perspective of the present; as Leavis himself argued, "the crucial test of a knowledge of the past is to be able to apply judgment in the present."[8] This language mirrors Potter's articulation of the aims of his "New Judgment" program. What Richards, Leavis, and Potter reacted to in academic literary scholarship was the divide that had emerged between literature and life, and all sought, in different ways, to foster in literary criticism forms of judgment that could be extended to everyday life.

*The Muse in Chains* shares with New Criticism a critique of specialization, an attack on biographical fallacies, and an emphasis on the need for readers to cultivate their own critical skills. Potter wanted readers to feel empowered to make new judgments about canonical texts but also to be receptive to contemporary literature and capable of evaluating works in the present. Potter's contributions to New Criticism have been overlooked, in part, because of the marginalization of the radio medium in which he put his ideas into practice. Conversations about the rise of mid-century criticism have tended to focus on literary journals such as *Scrutiny*, academic institutions in the United States and UK, and adult education initiatives, but rarely on mass media.[9] And yet radio was a vibrant medium for reconsidering the role of criticism in everyday life. The BBC was, from its inception, committed to an Arnoldian version of culture that aimed to disseminate "the best that has been thought and said" and would therefore provide fertile ground for attempts to bring literary criticism to broad listening publics.[10]

When Potter joined the BBC in 1936, he brought with him an agenda to turn literary studies away from the Inglit Man. He began in Schools Broadcasting with literature programs aimed at schoolchildren on Chaucer, Johnson, Keats, Shakespeare, Spenser, and William Morris. By 1941, in the early days of the Second World War, he had moved to the Features Department where he pitched an idea for a series of literary broadcasts that invited contemporary writers to offer a "new judgment" on a writer from the literary past. The programs aimed to foreground the relationship between canonical literary works and the present moment. Using the lens of the present, Potter also sought to democratize literary criticism, making it more relevant and approachable for mass publics. If the Inglit Man represented hierarchical reading practices—what we might today call "the sage on the stage"—then the "New Judgment" critics adopted a radically leveling approach, addressing canonical literary figures on a human scale. Oliver Goldsmith, for instance, became for Seán O'Faoláin a lover of low society and Walt Whitman, for Stephen Spender, was not timeless but responded to the current events of his time. The program was also polyphonic, interspersing the voice of the critic and the canonical author with other voices, including various personifications of the "common reader." Listeners were encouraged to adopt a democratizing, contemporary lens with which to view literary history and were introduced to living writers who showcased these critical approaches.

The "New Judgment" series moved criticism away from either the professor or the man of letters and into the institutional structures of the radio medium, which demanded collaboration between the critic and the producer and called for new approaches to the audience. At its most ambitious, the "New Judgment" series positions radio as an essential medium for imagining mass publics for literary criticism at mid-century. Theodor Adorno famously argued that mass media such as radio produces passive consumers and, by undermining the active reading practices of the print-era public sphere, has a deleterious effect on contemporary democracy. He singles out radio as especially prone to authoritarianism and passive reception: "Above all on the radio the authority of society standing behind every speaker immediately addresses its listeners unchallenged."[11] My argument here, in contrast, adopts a less deterministic understanding of the medium to show how a producer such as Potter and the writers whom he commissioned approached radio as a medium with critical potential. In other words, they believed that radio could offer the space for a critical conversation about literature and, in the process, create publics capable of not only hearing but also making new judgments.

In the still-nascent field of radio modernism—which brings together radio studies and modernist studies—attention has focused on programs that borrow from journalistic genres of criticism such as the book review. From its origin, the BBC had a difficult time distinguishing radio programming from print journalism, which led to conflicts with the press over rights. Debra Rae Cohen describes radio's "intermediality" and points to the BBC's magazine the *Listener* as an example of how radio needed print journalism to engage audiences unfamiliar with the medium and to "assuage anxieties about broadcasting."[12] Programs such as George Orwell's "Voice" or E. M. Forster's "Some Books" brought writers to the microphone to talk about contemporary literature but did not differ much, in terms of genre, from traditional book reviews, lectures, or critical essays other than their shorter length, more colloquial style, and in some cases, use of dialogue between commentators.[13] It is notable that Virginia Woolf, as Randi Koppen observes, referred to her radio talks as articles and complained about the radio-specific "talks element."[14] The dialogue format that emerged in the BBC's Talks Department under Hilda Matheson tried to steer writers away from literary prose and toward the intimacy of face-to-face conversation. What we see in Potter's programs, however, is an attempt neither to replicate journalistic models nor to downplay the interceding medium through an emphasis on intimate address; rather, Potter brings the medium itself to the forefront in his attempt to invent a radiogenic mode of literary criticism.

These programs brought together an eclectic combination of talk, dramatic dialogue, reenactment, and readings and, in so doing, formally reimagined literary criticism for a new medium. In a letter to Seán O'Faoláin, Potter makes the distinction explicit: "Each author is of course given complete freedom in his treatment of his theme, with the one reservation, that it is a 'feature' and not a talk; that is to say, a proportion—and rather the larger proportion—of the half-hour is dramatic scenes."[15] Laurence Gilliam, Director of the Features Department, defined the radio feature as distinct from a film feature or a journalistic feature, but instead, a mode of documentary radio-writing that merges actuality with imaginative drama. Gilliam writes, "The significance of the feature programme is, then, that it is the form of statement that broadcasting has evolved for itself, as distinct from those other forms, which it has borrowed or adapted from other arts or methods of publication. It is pure radio, a new instrument for the creative writer and producer."[16] Though Gilliam overstates the purity of the feature—one might say that it is, rather, a hybrid mixture of existing forms— it is notable that he defines the genre as an attempt to understand the medium on its own terms. Criticism by the Features Department would, therefore, attempt to create new forms of criticism best suited for the medium and its publics.

"New Judgment" ran for ten years from 1941 to 1951 with thirty-nine total programs. Programs included V. S. Pritchett on Daniel Defoe, J. B. Priestley on Charles Dickens, and two by Elizabeth Bowen on Jane Austen and Anthony Trollope.[17] At a time of wartime paper rationing, BBC programs such as "New Judgment" offered a rare platform for literary criticism in a highly constricted publishing landscape. Robert Hewison describes paper restrictions and conscription in the Second World War as giving rise to the "grand slaughter of magazines."[18] The lack of publishing opportunities, the BBC's generous fees to writers for their work, and the unparalleled audience size made offers from the broadcasting corporation hard for writers to resist.[19]

Despite its origins in the Second World War, "New Judgment" was not explicitly designed as a propaganda series. In fact, several of the contributors noted how much they enjoyed working on a series that they did not perceive to be propaganda. For example, BBC producer Mary Hope Allen, who produced Rosamond Lehmann's George Eliot script, wrote to the actress Dorothy Holmes-Gore, "I have been working on propaganda programmes, mostly about factory workers, and to do a literary script again, with acting parts is bliss."[20] Although the series was not overtly propagandistic, Potter pitched the original idea in nationalist terms, describing it as "series of literary programmes in which English writers of the past will be presented, criticised or appraised by outstanding English men and women of the present."[21] By 1942, the series would move away from the strictly literary framework to include programs on musicians, actors, political figures, and even a mountaineer; however, the initial outline focused on the patriotic vantage of great men and women of English literary history.

Moreover, some of the programs seemed to align nearly perfectly with Ministry of Information policy directives. For instance, the first broadcast in the series, Stephen Spender on Walt Whitman, corresponded with a wave of broadcasts aimed at fostering sympathetic bonds between the UK and the United States at a time when the United States had not yet joined the war. Broadcast just a month before Pearl Harbor, the script originally contained the following lines: "Walt Whitman designed his work to be the poetry of democracy as consciously as Americans are laying down the keels of liners to bring arms to the aid of democracy today."[22] This line was later cut, perhaps because it was unwise to broadcast information about the neutral United States shipping arms to the UK or because it struck the writer or producer as too propagandistic. Potter often seemed anxious to distance these literary programs from propaganda broadcasting, in one instance complaining that there was an incomplete transition between a "New Judgment" program and what Potter refers to as "the feeblest piece of propaganda I have ever heard," which he feared would lead listeners to assume that the two were linked.[23]

In line with other cultural endeavors during the war, the series justified itself as a heritage program highlighting the best of British culture past and present. In a 1941 memo, Potter outlines the proposed series as follows:

> They are half-hour programmes and the author will be required to provide a script which will contain about 45 per cent. original narration, 20 per cent. suggestions for passages to be read, and the remainder, suggestions, material and framework for two or three acted scenes. In addition to this, the authors will in most cases be asked to speak their own narrative material. They will, in fact, be responsible for the whole programme, except that in the case of the acted scenes the adaptation and dialogue will be done in collaboration with me.

In this memo, collaboration comes up as a potentially thorny issue. Each author was told to provide a script with very specific parameters for the distribution of material, and while they were trusted to write the narration and offer "suggestions" for the literary passages to be read, Potter was less confident that they would be able to handle radio drama. In fact, fee structures for "New Judgment" were determined by how much the author wrote on his or her own—those writers who wrote the entire script tended to receive higher fees, while those for whom the BBC brought in additional radio writers received less. The critics, while experts in their literary genres, were handled cautiously as promising amateurs in radio writing.

The professional identity of the radio producer was new, but it is perhaps because of this novelty that people like Potter quickly claimed the role of specialists. Radio introduced a new range of technical experts who needed training to work in the medium; several high-profile writers and critics such as William Empson, George Orwell, and Louis MacNeice, attended the BBC's training school in order to become producers.[24] If Potter was uneasy with specialization in literary studies, he seems to have taken for granted specialization in broadcasting. As the producer, Potter served as each program's technical expert, supervising and guiding the amateur radio critics.

Evidence for Potter's heavy hand is apparent in the first program in the series, "Stephen Spender on Walt Whitman." Spender's script for this program includes a character called "Inglit Man" who is an amalgam of all three types of literary man—the categorizer, biographer, and "surface creeper"—that Potter caricatures in *The Muse in Chains*. Spender and Potter both receive billing on the program, the former as the headliner and the latter as presenter. Spender spoke for the narrative sections and is accompanied by seven other actors playing different parts such as Whitman and Emerson; an American who enters to correct Spender on points relating to Whitman's American identity; and of course, the Inglit Man, who one presumes would have spoken in a posh Ox-Bridge accent.[25]

The Inglit Man provides a foil for Spender, setting up his new judgments of Whitman against a series of stuffy interjections. When Spender argues that "Whitman designed his work to be the poetry of democracy," the Inglit Man protests: "Poets aren't machines, they don't design their work like you do a ship or a house, surely. Isn't it true that they should grow like leaves on a tree?"[26] While the Inglit Man's perspective is not written to be convincing, the program stages a debate between Spender's committed poetics, motivated by a sense of persuasion, and the Inglit Man's denial of authorial intention and his belief that political design is a corruption of the integrity of the work. This was a live debate in the 1930s and 1940s and Spender was very much a partisan in the debate, arguing for a Left poetics to address the urgent conflicts of the time.[27] Spender believed that the Left offered artists a sense of moral purpose in a historical moment defined by crisis, but he was also adamant about the autonomy of the artist who must be free to pursue literary forms without bending them to political orthodoxy. Samuel Hynes argues that for Spender and other members of the Auden circle:

> Criticism is taken to be a function of the movement of history, and so … it is correct and necessary that writers should be political. But even if criticism is understood to be determined by history, even if the necessary subject is understood to be politics, the traditional literary considerations still remain.[28]

The new judgment that Spender offers on Whitman assimilates him into a committed poetics that mirrors Spender's own.

Spender also comes as close as he can on air to championing Whitman's most explicitly sexual sections from *Leaves of Grass*, "L'Enfants d'Adam." As Spender tells the audience: "Love for him was a wide all-embracing amorphous emotion not attached to any one person, and friendship with him—friendship for the soldiers whom he nursed in the war—is really as intense a feeling as his love."[29] The inclusion of these passages draws listeners' attention to Whitman's sexuality and offers a new judgment that undermines what Spender describes as the "moral disapproval" of Whitman's critics. Spender also uses the opportunity of the broadcast to champion a homoerotic poem that had been suppressed or dismissed. As a queer, socialist poet, Spender rehabilitates a Whitman in his own image, one who lays a clear foundation for his own poetic project. With "New Judgment," Potter created a platform for writers to articulate a version of the literary past most amenable to their goals and ambitions for contemporary literature. Potter was clearly an active collaborator in a script like Spender's, down to the inclusion of his own creation, the Inglit Man, but the critical approach to Whitman is Spender's own and reflects his politics and poetics.

When Spender wrote to Potter concerned that the audience wouldn't know enough about Whitman and that he should explain more, Potter wrote back to say:

> I think to a great extent you can forget the size of your audience. I am reminded to say this by some question you asked, "would such and such a point be too subtle"; and am fearful that you may think it obligatory to do too much "writing down"—something which, except in certain good senses of that phrase, you would never normally do.[30]

Writing his first feature broadcast, Spender expressed concern about how to pitch the program to radio's unseen masses.[31] Would the program be too subtle, too literary, lacking the proper framing for a public who may or may not be familiar with Whitman's work? Spender was not the only one to stumble upon the question of audience, and Potter's response, though confident, betrays a deeper anxiety about whether such literary criticism was appropriate to radio at all.

The audience for "New Judgment" programs was difficult to gauge, especially in the days before the postwar Third Programme offered a station explicitly for such "highbrow" programming. These programs went out on the Home Service and reached a large and undifferentiated public. By 1936, the BBC had established a Listener Research Department to assess listener responses to programs. The department was headed by Robert Silvey who began his career in the statistical department for an advertising firm where he began using the public opinion research techniques then being honed in the United States by George Gallup and others.[32] Previously, the BBC handled public opinion research, such as it was, by sifting through the letters that listeners wrote in. Under Silvey's leadership, Listener Research adopted what were, at the time, cutting-edge sampling techniques to estimate audience size and to collect evaluative judgments on programming.[33]

In 1942 the department produced a report for Seán O'Faoláin's "New Judgment" on Oliver Goldsmith. According to the report, the "Appreciation Index" for this program was only sixty-five—the average for all Features programs on the BBC was seventy-five and Bowen's earlier "New Judgment," Potter's favorite, was rated a seventy-two. On a survey card that was sent to listeners, one can see that a major concern for the "New Judgment" series was whether the audience was already familiar with the literary work and how this impacted their appreciation for the program. The survey asked listeners: "Before you heard this broadcast, how far were you familiar with the works of Oliver Goldsmith?" It also gave two options for listeners: one for those who felt "sufficiently familiar with the works of Oliver Goldsmith to express an opinion" and one for those who "do not feel competent" to evaluate O'Faoláin's criticism but were instead asked whether "the broadcast did arouse your interest in Goldsmith's works."[34] The programs were judged by two parallel metrics: the value of the criticism to an informed listener and the ability of the program to spark interest for listeners unfamiliar with the author.

O'Faoláin's script reveals less of Potter's overt influence than Spender's. The script begins with the fanciful conceit of a statue of Goldsmith outside of Trinity College coming to life and examining the state of his posthumous reputation. O'Faoláin advocates for a populist Goldsmith, one who was a man of the people, intensely interested in common life. Audience responses to the program are striking for the loquaciousness of the respondent's own judgments. As the BBC researcher notes, "The majority of the opinions expressed were critical, though not unsympathetic." If Potter's goal was to foster critical listening practices, then the audience reports reveal a certain degree of success. Listeners, perhaps primed by other broadcasts in the series, were often frustrated with O'Faoláin's biographical approach to Goldsmith's life, which they thought distracted from a proper focus on his works. As one listener reported, it was "a study of a writer with the writings left out, Hamlet without the Prince."[35] Another listener wrote in to say:

> I think the author's idea—that Goldsmith's real métier was the sympathetic delineation of low life—was interesting, and has a good deal of probability, but the way it was presented was not effective, only occasionally, and as it were accidentally, was it supported by reference to his works. The author ably suggested what Goldsmith might have done, but hardly considered what he did do.[36]

Here we see not the passive listener that Adorno and others describe as an outcome of mass media. Instead, the listener takes on the role of critic, responding with judicious judgments to a literary program. Some listeners felt that O'Faoláin's take on Goldsmith was not very new and compared it to Samuel Johnson's. Even those respondents who claimed ignorance of Goldsmith offered critical assessments of the program. One wrote, "The arguments were too clever for me. The impression I got was cleverness of the author but not much substance in the arguments."[37] This listener doesn't simply profess ignorance but rather offers his or her own judgment that the O'Faoláin's script was clever without substance.

One outcome we see in the "New Judgment" series is the emergence of mass media's participatory culture. The final critics in this series become not the producer or the author but the audience members who participate in surveys and voluntarily write to the broadcasting service to express their own judgments. Although these research reports were never public documents, they clearly fulfilled a desire among listeners to participate in the programs as critics. The programs themselves modeled this participation, including listener-figures within the broadcasts and otherwise highlighting modes of active listening. As Potter demotes the professionalized Inglit Man in favor of the voice of the contemporary writer, we see here that the last word is given to the citizen-critic, the listener-in who wants a share of the action. As a collaborative medium, radio points to the origins of a participatory culture in which, suddenly, everybody's a critic. What often went without saying, however, is that this acceptance of the critic as amateur often went hand in hand with the rise of the technical expert. These new experts claimed positions of authority by wielding access to technology and statistics. Anyone can be a critic, they maintained, but only the trained expert could be a radio producer like Potter or public opinion researcher like Silvey. The amateurs enthusiastically contributing to radio's participatory culture, whether the critic crafting a first radio script or the listener writing survey responses, were both carefully shepherded along by newly minted technical experts. On the tilting scales of amateurism and expertise, the role of literary critic became increasingly accessible to all at the same moment that new professional experts emerged to direct how this criticism would be disseminated and assessed. In this sense, we are still living in the world of amateur criticism that programs like "New Judgment" created. The expansion of criticism to the everyday reader on review sites like *Goodreads* or Amazon is made possible by computer programmers, today's foremost technical experts, who create the algorithms that shape our experience of reading today.

## Notes

1 Special thanks to the BBC Written Archives Centre at Caversham for access to the "New Judgment" Production File and especially to Matthew Chipping for his invaluable assistance. Different participants in the series used variant spellings of Judgment (or Judgement).

2 The language of a "golden age," of course, reveals a bias in favor of radio's professionalization. In contrast, Jesse Walker's *Rebels on the Air: An Alternative History of Radio in America* (New York: New

York University Press, 2001) offers a counter-narrative that laments the triumph of professionals over amateurs in the battle over the airwaves. Walker describes regulatory measures in the United States in the 1910s through 1930s as leading to "a series of enclosures, in which the spectrum rights held by hams, non-profit broadcasters, and small entrepreneurs were expropriated by powerful private interests and the state," 47.

3 Stephen Potter, *The Muse in Chains: A Study in Education* (London: Jonathan Cape, 1937), 17.

4 Ibid., 25.

5 Ibid., 37.

6 Joseph North, *Literary Criticism: A Concise Political History* (Cambridge, MA: Harvard University Press, 2017), 15.

7 Christopher Hilliard, *English as Vocation: The Scrutiny Movement* (Oxford: Oxford University Press, 2012), 25.

8 Qtd in ibid., 31.

9 For instance, in the seventh volume of the *Cambridge Companion to Literary Criticism: Modernism and the New Criticism. Volume 7. Modernism and the New Criticism*, ed. A. Walton Litz, Louis Menand, and Lawrence Rainey (New York: Cambridge University Press, 2008) there are no references to radio or discussions of the BBC as an institution for criticism (this, despite there being a section on "The Critic and the Institutions of Culture"). For more on *Scrutiny*, adult education, and Cambridge see Hilliard's *English as Vocation*. Scholars of American Literature have shown how the Southern Agrarians helped establish New Criticism in American universities. As Paul Lauter writes, following their failure to bring about change in the broader public sphere, the Southern Agrarians "were amazingly successful in establishing the hegemony of their ideas in the culture of the academy at its apogee" ("Versions of Nashville, Visions of American Studies," *American Quarterly* 47, no. 2 [1995]: 191).

10 For more on the influence of Matthew Arnold's *Culture and Anarchy* on the BBC, see Todd Avery, *Radio Modernism: Literature, Ethics and the BBC, 1922–1938* (New York: Ashgate, 2006). Avery aligns the first general manager of the BBC, John Reith, with New Critics such as F. R. and Q. D. Leavis as an "Arnoldian cultural theorist" and the BBC as an "Arnoldian institution," 25.

11 Theodor Adorno, "The Schema of Mass Culture," in *The Culture Industry: Selected Essays on Mass Culture* (New York: Routledge, 2001), 96.

12 Debra Rae Cohen, "Intermediality and the Problem of the *Listener*," *Modernism/Modernity* 19, no. 3 (2012): 585.

13 Henry Mead notes that George Orwell modeled "Voice" on little magazines like *The Adelphi* and *Horizon*. Henry Mead, "'Keeping Our Little Corner Clean": George Orwell's Cultural Broadcasts at the BBC," in *Broadcasting in the Modernist Era*, ed. Matthew Feldman, Erik Tonning, and Henry Mead (London: Bloomsbury, 2014), 183. For more on E. M. Forster's "Some Books," see Daniel Ryan Morse's "Only Connecting?: E.M. Forster, Empire Broadcasting and the Ethics of Distance," *Journal of Modern Literature* 34, no. 3 (2011): 87–105.

14 Randi Koppen, "Rambling Round Words: Virginia Woolf and the Politics of Broadcasting," in *Broadcasting in the Modernist Era*, ed. Matthew Feldman and Erik Tonning (London: Bloomsbury, 2014), 140.

15 Letter from Stephen Potter to Seán O'Faoláin, February 18, 1942, New Judgment Production File, 1941–1946, R19/822/1, BBC Archives, Caversham.

16 Laurence Gilliam, *BBC Features* (London: Evans Brothers Limited, 1950), 10. Gilliam's book is an edited anthology that collects exemplary models of the Features genre, including one example from the "New Judgment" series on Cardinal Manning by Christopher Sykes. In editing Features programs for the page, however, Gilliam rendered them in essayistic prose, which obscures their generic complexity.

17 Elizabeth Bowen's contributions to "New Judgment" are available in published form: the Jane Austen script can be found in *Listening In*, edited by Allan Hepburn (Edinburgh: Edinburgh University Press, 2010), and the Anthony Trollope script is in *The Mulberry Tree*, edited by Hermione Lee (New York: Harcourt Brace Jovanovich, 1986), and was also published by Oxford University Press in 1946. For more on Bowen's contributions to "New Judgment," see my chapter "Elizabeth Bowen's Spectral Radio," in *The Wireless Past, Anglo-Irish Writers and the BBC, 1931–1968* (Oxford: Oxford University Press, 2016).

18 Hewison, Robert, *Under Siege: Literary Life in London, 1939–1945* (Oxford: Oxford University Press, 1977), 11.

19 A few writers who Potter approached and who expressed interest such as Rebecca West, Desmond McCarthy, and Kenneth Clark decided not to participate in the end.

20 Letter from Mary Hope Allen to Dorothy Holmes-Gore, August 12, 1942, New Judgment Production File, 1941–1946, R19/822/1, BBC Written Archives Centre, Caversham. The George Eliot broadcast involved women as producer, writer, and subject; however, the series generally veered much more heavily toward men. Only four

programs were by women writers (in addition to Rosamon Lehmann on George Eliot, there were the two by Elizabeth Bowen, as well as Edith Evans on Mrs. Siddons).

21 Letter from Stephen Potter to Lord David. October 14, 1941, New Judgment Production File, 1941–1946, R19/822/1, BBC Written Archives Centre, Caversham.

22 Stephen Spender, "New Judgment: Stephen Spender on Walt Whitman," November 2, 1941, Scripts Library, BBC Archives Centre, Caversham.

23 Stephen Potter, Memo on the Guedalla Froude Programme, January 12, 1942, New Judgment Production File, 1941–1946, R19/822/1, BBC Written Archives Centre, Caversham.

24 These writers all took BBC training courses during the Second World War when there was a large wave of hiring to supply the new demands for propaganda writing. William Empson and George Orwell both attended the BBC's training course, titled "General Broadcasting Technique," which was run at Bedford College, University of London. See John Haffenden's *William Empson: Against the Christians*, vol. 2 (Oxford: Oxford University Press, 2006), 23 and D. J. Taylor's *George Orwell: A Life* (New York: Macmillan, 2003), 304. Louis MacNeice described his experience at the BBC training school as a gradual turn away from his earlier cynicism about the BBC and a growing appreciation of the skill involved in broadcasting, which he found "technically fascinating." See MacNeice, *Letters of Louis MacNeice*, ed. Jonathan Allison (London: Faber and Faber, 2010), 439.

25 There are no recordings of the "New Judgment" series in the BBC Sound Archives. The BBC only recorded a small fraction of its programming and during the war it is more likely that these resources would have been allocated to programs of importance to national security.

26 Spender, "Walt Whitman," 2.

27 Spender refers to himself as a "democrat" in the program but does not, of course, mention that he had joined the Communist Party in 1937. He would later famously revoke his affiliation as a contributor to *The God That Failed* (New York: Harper, 1949), a collection of personal testaments against Communism.

28 Samuel Hynes, *The Auden Generation: Literature and Politics in England in the 1930s* (London: Bodley Head, 1976), 161–162.

29 Spender, "Walt Whitman," 16.

30 Stephen Potter, Letter to Stephen Spender, September 27, 1941, New Judgment Production File, 1941–1946, R19/822/1, BBC Written Archives Centre, Caversham.

31 Previously to "New Judgment," Spender's poems had appeared in poetry anthology programs; he had given one talk for Schools Broadcasting on William Wordsworth (March 12, 1935) and had participated in a discussion on poetry with Walter de la Mare and Desmond Hawkir (November 8, 1940).

32 Silvey was hired to create the Listener Research Department (late the Audience Research Department) on the strength of a report he did for his advertising agency, the London Press Exchange, that surveyed the British public's newspaper reading habits. Robert Silvey, *Who's Listening? The Story of BBC Audience Research* (London: George Allen & Unwin Ltd, 1974), 16.

33 Silvey describes these techniques, which were still new in the UK when the Listener Research Department was formed, as a combination of Probability Sampling and Quota Sampling. He attributes both systems to public opinion researchers in the United States: the former to Rensis Likert's Survey Research Center at the University of Michigan and the latter to George Gallup. Silvey, *Who's Listening?*, 51.

34 BBC Listener Research Department, Survey on "New Judgment: Sean O'Faolain on Oliver Goldsmith," New Judgment Production File, 1941–1946, R19/822/1, BBC Written Archives Centre, Caversham.

35 "New Judgment: Sean O'Faolain on Oliver Goldsmith," Listener Research Report, New Judgment Production File, 1941–1946, R19/822/1, BBC Written Archives Centre, Caversham.

36 Ibid.

37 Ibid.

# Bibliography

Adorno, Theodor. "The Schema of Mass Culture." In *The Culture Industry: Selected Essays on Mass Culture*, 61–97. New York: Routledge, 2001.

Allen, Mary Hope. Letter to Dorothy Holmes-Gore. August 12, 1942. New Judgment Production File, 1941–1946. R19/822/1. BBC Written Archives Centre, Caversham.

Avery, Todd. *Radio Modernism: Literature, Ethics and the BBC, 1922–1938*. New York: Ashgate, 2006.

BBC Listener Research Department. Report on "New Judgment: Sean O'Faolain on Oliver Goldsmith." New Judgment Production File, 1941–1946. R19/822/1. BBC Written Archives Centre, Caversham.

BBC Listener Research Department. Survey on "New Judgment: Sean O'Faolain on Oliver Goldsmith. New Judgment Production File, 1941–1946. R19/822/1. BBC Written Archives Centre, Caversham.

Bloom, Emily. *The Wireless Past: Anglo-Irish Writers and the BBC, 1931–1968*. Oxford: Oxford University Press, 2016.

Cohen, Debra Rae. "Intermediality and the Problem of the *Listener*." *Modernism/Modernity* 19, no. 3 (2012): 569–592.

Gilliam, Laurence. *BBC Features*. London: Evans Brothers Limited, 1950.

Haffenden, John. *William Empson: Against the Christians*. Vol. 2. Oxford: Oxford University Press, 2006.

Hepburn, Allan. *Listening In: Broadcasts, Speeches, and Interviews by Elizabeth Bowen*. Edinburgh: Edinburgh University Press, 2010.

Hewison, Robert. *Under Siege: Literary Life in London, 1939–1945*. Oxford University Press, 1977.

Hilliard, Christopher. *English as a Vocation: The Scrutiny Movement*. Oxford: Oxford University Press, 2012.

Hynes, Samuel. *The Auden Generation: Literature and Politics in England in the 1930s*. London: Bodley Head, 1976.

Lauter, Paul. "Versions of Nashville, Visions of American Studies." *American Quarterly* 47, no. 2 (1995): 185–203.

Litz, A. Walton, Louis Menand, and Lawrence Rainey. *Cambridge Companion to Literary Criticism: Modernism and New Criticism*. Vol. 7. New York: Cambridge, 2008.

Koppen, Randi. "Rambling Round Words: Virginia Woolf and the Politics of Broadcasting." In *Broadcasting in the Modernist Era*, edited by Matthew Feldman and Erik Tonning, 137–154. London: Bloomsbury, 2014.

MacNeice, Louis. *Letters of Louis MacNeice*, edited by Jonathan Allison. London: Faber and Faber, 2010.

Mead, Henry. "'Keeping Our Little Corner Clean': George Orwell's Cultural Broadcasts at the BBC." In *Broadcasting in the Modernist Era*, edited by Matthew Feldman, Erik Tonning, and Henry Mead, 169–194. London: Bloomsbury, 2014.

Morse, Daniel Ryan, "Only Connecting?: E.M. Forster, Empire Broadcasting and the Ethics of Distance." *Journal of Modern Literature* 34, no. 3 (2011): 87–105.

North, Joseph. *Literary Criticism: A Concise Political History*. Cambridge, MA: Harvard University Press, 2017.

Potter, Stephen. Letter to Lord David. October 14, 1941. New Judgment Production File, 1941–1946. R19/822/1. BBC Written Archives Centre, Caversham.

Potter, Stephen. Letter to Sean O'Faolain. February 18, 1942. New Judgment Production File, 1941–1946. R19/822/1. BBC Written Archives Centre, Caversham.

Potter, Stephen. Letter to Stephen Spender. September 27, 1941. New Judgment Production File, 1941–1946. R19/822/1. BBC Written Archives Centre, Caversham.

Potter, Stephen. Memo on the Guedalla Froude Programme. New Judgment Production File, 1941–1946. R19/822/1. January 12, 1942, BBC Written Archives Centre, Caversham.

Potter, Stephen. *The Muse in Chains: A Study in Education*. London: Jonathan Cape, 1937.

Silvey, Robert. *Who's Listening? The Story of BBC Audience Research*. London: George Allen & Unwin Ltd, 1974.

Spender, Stephen. "New Judgment: Stephen Spender on Walt Whitman." November 2, 1941. Scripts Library. BBC Written Archives Centre, Caversham.

Taylor, D. J. *George Orwell: A Life*. New York: Macmillan, 2003.

Walker, Jesse. *Rebels on the Air: An Alternative History of Radio in America*. New York: New York University, 2001.

# 10

# The Small Press and the Feminist Critic

*Melanie Micir*

Florence Howe knew next to nothing about publishing when she founded The Feminist Press in 1970. After being approached by several university presses to write a biography of Doris Lessing, she had countered with a different sort of project, one that would "produce one hundred small biographies about the lives and work of important women in literature and history."[1] She planned to enlist a number of contemporary writers, including Lessing, in this project, and various editors were initially interested. But whenever her pitch reached the ears of "financial managers," it got voted down for the same reason: "There's no money in it."[2] For a time, she gave up on the idea, but unbeknownst to her, word of the project spread quickly through newsletters of women's liberation groups across the country, and Howe received "about a hundred letters" from women who "wrote that they were eager to work on this project, either by writing it or by buying the finished products."[3] She then invited these women to attend a meeting at her house, which is how, on November 17, 1970, Florence Howe ended up hosting fifty people in her living room, and The Feminist Press was born:

> Most of the meeting was taken up with introductions. Leah Heyn said she was there because her seven-year-old daughter had asked

> for a book that depicted a woman doctor … She had searched bookstores and libraries, and had found nothing, though she knew that women had been doctors since the nineteenth century. As we went around the room, it was clear that, while no one had experience in publishing, no one seemed awed by the tasks before us. The room crackled with energy.[4]

Howe did not concern herself overmuch with the obviously amateur nature of this collective undertaking. She thought that, as a "movement project," it would only last a few years, and she "imagined that 'regular publishers' would seize on the idea once they saw it in action."[5] She was entirely wrong on the first count—the press is still in operation today—but she was only somewhat wrong on the second. While more traditional publishing presses did not line up to collaborate with Howe, the transformation from idealistic project to functioning press only happened after Howe took an academic position in New York and suddenly found herself surrounded by "publishing professionals."[6] The financial managers of the big presses still stayed away, but individual women working in publishing flocked to the project. Many had already heard about The Feminist Press, and one such "publishing professional," Verne Moberg, "volunteered to work full time as unpaid staff" to take care of the many "matters [Howe] knew nothing about."[7] For years, many members of the staff were volunteers. The "Reprints Advisory Committee" consisted of "a large group of young academic teachers of literature and history, all of whom are now well-known scholars," and even the readers were considered part of the larger undertaking, as "during the first decade and into the second, we knew our enthusiastic audience personally."[8] The project was a labor of love for virtually everyone involved.

Howe's description of the founding of The Feminist Press focuses on energy and enthusiasm, not expertise or even experience. The "essential goal" during the early years of the press, according to Howe, was "to publish so that college students could read texts written by women, as part of their literary education."[9] The women in Howe's living room were motivated not by a potential profit margin but by the collective sense that they had to do it—sometimes explicitly for their daughters, as in Heyn's introductory testimony—or it simply would not be done. The small press thus became an urgent matter for modern feminism. As feminists adopted journalist

A. J. Liebling's dictum that "freedom of the press is guaranteed only to those who own one," they formed their own presses—at times in their own living rooms.[10] And although many feared that feminist politics would be warped by traditional publishing structures—indeed, Julia Penelope, a lesbian feminist activist and academic, suggested in 1985 that "no reconciliation seems possible between political conscience and economic survival"[11]—The Feminist Press continues to be the oldest women's publishing house in existence today.

Despite this longevity, there have been relatively few studies of the significance of independent feminist presses for literary, cultural, and political history. According to literary historian Simone Murray, whose *Mixed Media: Feminist Presses and Publishing Politics* offers a British-focused corrective, feminist publishing studies is a "phantom discipline—commented upon as much for its absence as for its contributions."[12] And while Murray's 2004 monograph is primarily concerned with print culture, her title suggests that any current iteration of feminist publishing studies would necessarily encompass the growing terrain of feminist media history as well. Whether asked of old or new media, however, Murray's underlying question remains relevant: why have professional scholars routinely dismissed or given only "glancing acknowledgment" to the significance of feminist presses?[13] Even in scholarship focused on women and literature, and even within the field of women's studies, feminist publishing has been ignored, marginalized, or only briefly acknowledged.[14] Howe's reflection on her work with The Feminist Press ends with a question about the nature of this critical neglect: "Does it matter that young people know nothing of the history I have outlined in this essay?"[15]

My answer, however surprising, is: not necessarily. Although I of course share Howe's belief in the importance of understanding history, especially feminist history, the truth is that it may not always matter whether "young people" know much about this history before embarking on their own publishing projects. Not knowing may have certain advantages. In the case of contemporary feminist publishing, George Santayana's haunting aphorism—that those who cannot remember the past will be condemned to repeat it—is actually a good thing. Maybe every generation gets the independent feminist publishing project it needs. Because although The Feminist Press remains operational, we still live in a publishing world dominated by straight white men, as the annual VIDA Count makes abundantly clear.[16] And in the last decade or so, a number of women, crackling with energy once again, have followed Howe's lead and founded feminist and/or woman-focused presses of their own.

But this is all the more reason to push back against the idea that, categorically, "young people" don't know this history. What Howe's question, published in an academic journal, reveals is that it is *scholars* who have not always acknowledged the significance of feminist publishing's long history. As Murray demonstrates, the "widespread academic obliviousness to the dynamics of feminist publishing" is a peculiarly vexing issue given that, in the non- or sometimes para-academic "arena of public literary debate," feminist publishers have frequently enjoyed a relatively "high public profile."[17] And in contrast to their professional, academic counterparts, these feminist publishers tend to know this history very well indeed—not as scholars but as critical practitioners.

In this chapter, I offer case studies of several contemporary feminist publishing projects—presses, subscription services, collections—in order to suggest that the act of literary curation and publication is a mode of criticism inflected and even buoyed by enthusiasm, an almost excessive devotion, and the kind of unruly desire Carolyn Dinshaw describes as hallmarks of an "amateur sensibility."[18] This label of amateurism is not a derogatory term; if it points to a lack of training or professionalization, it does so while highlighting the generative possibilities made available by this openness. Elsewhere in this collection, Ragini Tharoor Srinivasan refers to this kind of openness as "suggestion," a term she uses in opposition to the sometimes deadening qualities of expertise. Amateurism, she writes, is "a mode of thinking, being, and writing untethered to formal license or qualification." And as Saikat Majumdar, citing Marjorie Garber's notion of "magisterial unprofessionalism," reminds us, "Amateur status as a critic can just as effectively be a postprofessional as a pre- or unprofessional state."[19] In this chapter, the critical amateurism I see in these projects is largely para-professional; the founders' slow accrual of experience and even expertise in feminist publishing occurs alongside a continued willingness to describe the projects in the vernacular of amateurism. This paradoxically persistent amateur spirit is rooted in a kind of feminist determination, a bias toward the small and self-sufficient rather than the big, male-dominated institutions of the publishing world.

These independent, woman-run projects—Dorothy, a publishing project; Emily Books; and The Second Shelf; among others—were each founded by women writers, and they continue to exist alongside their founders' ongoing work in other spheres. Danielle Dutton (Dorothy's founding editor) is a novelist and tenured professor. Ruth Curry and Emily Gould (Emily Books' two founding curators-turned-editors) are cultural critics; Gould is also a novelist. A. N. Devers (founder of The Second Shelf) is an arts journalist and cultural critic. The backgrounds of these founding editors, by and large, were not steeped in the practices of professional publishing; instead, these presses and projects began as side hustles, labors of love, amateur affairs. Each has an explicitly feminist publishing model: Dorothy publishes "works of fiction or near fiction or about fiction, mostly by women"; Emily Books is devoted to promoting and now publishing "weird books by women"; and The Second Shelf collects and sells "rare books, modern first editions, manuscripts, & rediscovered works by women."[20] As Urmila Seshagiri has written about Persephone Books, a London-based press that reprints "neglected fiction and non-fiction by mid-twentieth century (mostly) women writers," these small undertakings bring "a deliberate transparency to the institutional vectors of literary production, promotion, and circulation."[21] And, even beyond this transparency, they invoke an unusual intimacy between publisher, writer, and reader, so much so that *The Atlantic* likened the Dorothy catalog to the "ringing endorsement of writers you've never heard of by a friend whose taste you can absolutely trust," and *Brooklyn Magazine* described Emily Books as "a collection of titles by women that feels more like a secret handshake than a business plan."[22] These descriptions might well be taken as further examples of how women's writing is too often denigrated within a publishing world dominated by men. But in these intimations of cultish friendships and secret handshakes, they also highlight the comparative cool of the scrappily amateur project.

Throughout this chapter, curation is understood to be a form of criticism, and these upstart projects practice an implicit ("suggestive," in Srinivasan's sense) but hugely important form of feminist criticism. Publishing, like criticism, embeds questions of judgment. These projects bring books—variously judged and dismissed as "feminist," "subversive," "weird," and "neglected"—

into print and into view, and in doing so, they hail an audience too often ignored by large presses: a feminist, subversive, weird, and neglected audience willing to support their mission by buying subscriptions and becoming members in an ad-hoc literary salon. These projects are powered by what Persephone founder Nicola Beauman described as her "inconvenient attachment" to the unpublished, under-appreciated, and/or the out of print.[23] Their acts of curation have their origins in personal obsessions, experiences, and even friendships, but they nevertheless constitute modes of criticism that revalue writers and texts that have fallen outside of the professionalizing apparatus of the program era. The work of collecting, collating, and publishing are all critical practices that remain behind the scenes, less recognized and celebrated than the (usually) solo enterprise of critical or scholarly writing. Yet heeding Lawrence Rainey's call to read institutionally means recognizing literary and artistic movements as "a social reality, a configuration of agents and practices that converge in the production, marketing, and publicization of an idiom, a shareable language in the family of twentieth-century tongues."[24]

In a feminist account of literary history, reading institutionally reveals the gendered nature of the "configuration of agents and practices" that are necessary to literary production and circulation. From Sylvia Beach, Jane Heap, and Harriet Monroe during the early decades of the twentieth century to Dutton, Curry, Gould, Devers, and so many others today, it has fallen to women editors and "agents" to perform the literary care work necessary to secure other women writers' places in our ongoing literary conversations. Writing about modernist collections (in museums and anthologies), Jeremy Braddock suggests that we should understand collecting as a form of public engagement rather than a retreat into an elite private sphere. In this view, modernist collections of literature and art were "a means of addressing the work of art to the public, modeling and creating the conditions of modernism's reception."[25] Dorothy, Emily, and The Second Shelf do this work today. More than securing publication for these marginalized or forgotten writers, these feminist projects perform a kind of curatorial sharing—the creation of networks of influence, appreciation, and even economic gain outside or in excess of the professional world of the book trade.

* * *

Though this chapter only focuses on a handful of contemporary feminist projects, I do not mean to imply that they are operating without historical precedent. Women have long been significant players in the publishing world; women—mostly straight, white women—constitute the clear majority of today's industry. According to *Publisher's Weekly*, "women represented 74% of the publishing workforce in both 2015 and 2016," and "78% of those ... are cis women, of whom 88% are heterosexual and 79% are white."[26] But with few exceptions, major presses have been and continue to be run by (straight, white) men. At a 2016 panel about women's writing organized by Emily Books, Caroline Casey, an editor at Coffee House Press, scoffed at the idea that feminists should "infiltrate and change" the big publishing institutions: "'Those institutions are already ours,' she said. '[Women] are all the people who work there. [Men] are just in charge.'"[27] Given this ongoing state of affairs, women continue to turn to smaller, independent publishing ventures for full editorial control. As Virginia Woolf, who ran the influential Hogarth Press with her husband, Leonard Woolf, from 1917 until her death in 1941, argued in *Three Guineas*, independent presses provide intellectual freedom:

> Still, Madam, the private printing press is an actual fact, and not beyond the reach of a moderate income. Typewriters and duplicators are actual facts and even cheaper. By using these cheap and so far unforbidden instruments you can at once rid yourself of the pressure of boards, policies and editors. They will speak your own mind, in your own words, at your own time, at your own length, at your own bidding. And that, we are agreed, is our definition of "intellectual liberty."[28]

Unsurprisingly, the pursuit of this intellectual freedom has been routinely cited by women throughout the twentieth (and into the twenty-first) century as their primary reason for starting their own presses.

The independent spirit, determined amateurism, and "crackling energy" Florence Howe described as characteristic of the founding meetings of The Feminist Press are common characteristics of the origin stories of these independent, woman-run presses. Just a few years after Howe's living room meeting, for example, Virago Press began "at founder Carmen Callil's kitchen table in her home in

Chelsea, ... fueled by red wine and late nights spent arguing over the politics of the emerging women's liberation movement."[29] In 1984, Urvashi Butali and Ritu Menon began Kali for Women, India's first and oldest feminist publishing house, in order to make women's voices and issues heard; after they left Kali in 2003, Butali and Menon each started a new feminist publishing project: Zubaan and Women Unlimited, respectively.[30] Lisa C. Moore founded RedBone Press in 1997 to address the lack of voices of color in feminist and queer publishing. When other presses saw "no market" for her anthology of black lesbian coming-out stories, she created a press for what she knew was an underserved but existing market: "In the face of white feminist presses who say they don't know how to sell work by women of color, Moore goes to where Black queers are, selling books at Black lesbian conferences and Black queer prides across the country."[31]

In 1998, Persephone Books "began in a room above a pub," where Nicola Beauman determined to publish "a handful of 'lost' or out-of-print books every year, most of them interwar novels by women," and the press's most important criteria continues to be that they will "only publish books that we completely, utterly love."[32] Similarly emphasizing her desire for editorial control, Rhonda Hughes described her founding of Print Vision and Hawthorne Books as rooted in the realization that "I wouldn't get what I wanted unless I left and did it myself."[33] And C. Spike Trotman, the founder of Iron Circus Comics, noted that she "didn't trust the intentions and motivations of a lot of large publishers."[34] This is an incomplete list, to be sure. Among those presses still operational today, we might just as easily focus on Aunt Lute (1982–), CALYX (1976–), Cleis (1980–), Editions des Femmes (1972–), Firebrand (1984–), Modjaji (2007–), Seal (1976–), Second Story (1972–), Tender Buttons (1989–), or Third Woman (1980–), among others. Equally influential but now shuttered presses might include Kitchen Table (1982–1989), Onlywomen (1974–2011), Press Gang (1970–2002), Shameless Hussy (1969–1989), or Sister Vision (1985–2000). And while there are many important differences—of class, race, nationality, sexuality, generation, and/or funding strategy—between the presses named here, in virtually every case, the founders cite their commitment to feminist social principles as paramount. No one thought they were going to make much, if any, money. Everyone thought they were going to make the publishing world (and the shelves of bookstores and libraries) more diverse, open, and inclusive—and, in various ways, they did.

These once upstart, now established feminist publishing projects do not just continue on, however haggardly, today; they are bolstered by a growing community of new ventures—like South Africa's Modjaji Press, founded in 2007 to publish African women writers—that spring up every year. Despite their differences, the origin stories of these new presses remain remarkably similar to those shared by the many decades of feminist publishers who came before them. And although they belong squarely within this longer history of feminist publishing, many of these new ventures continue to foreground their amateur spirit. Many but not all: the vocabularies of amateurism are deployed and received differently across racial, national, and class lines. Who can afford to be considered an amateur? And for whom does amateurism designate a youthful, anti-establishment vibrancy rather than a mode of denigration and dismissal? Like Howe before them, the women described in the following pages highlight rather than hide the ways in which their projects are undertaken in the relative absence of expertise and the overabundance of larger feminist commitments. But is the discourse of amateurism wielded proudly by the white, cis-gendered, heterosexual, highly educated, Anglo-American founders of these feminist publishing projects helpful rather than harmful to them as a direct result of this demographic privilege? Or, to put a finer point on it, to what degree is the public success of these projects—their semi-viral notoriety and the positive media attention lavished on their aesthetics of the amateur—dependent upon a media landscape that bestows an aura of professionalism even to those white women who defiantly proclaim their amateur status? In the remainder of this chapter, I will focus on the discursive similarity between three of the most well known of these contemporary feminist publishing projects. But the question of why *these* operations and their editors have come to represent a significantly more diverse movement is a question that deserves considerably more attention in both academic and nonacademic contexts.

* * *

"Hi, we're Emily Books. We make weird books by women."[35] These two lines, splashed across the page in hot pink, are the first thing you see when you visit the website of Emily Books, an ongoing experiment in feminist publishing and literary curation run by Ruth Curry and Emily Gould. Elsewhere on their website, they declare, somewhat less pithily and more expansively, that they are "passionate about the writing of women, trans people, and queer people":

> We seek out works that challenge genre distinctions, especially the distinction between memoir and fiction. We look for books that are funny, challenging and provocative. Our favorite writers are frank and unapologetic and make often-ignored or misunderstood subjectivities and points of view feel both relatable and utterly unique.[36]

But Curry and Gould have only been "making" these books since 2016, when they partnered with the more established but still independent Coffee House Press to publish two original titles per year. Initially, Emily Books was a kind of feminist subscription service, sending their loyal subscribers one e-book each month from 2011 to 2016. These books were both old and new; authors included mid-century writers like Barbara Comyns, Muriel Spark, and Sylvia Townsend Warner alongside contemporary writers such as Elena Ferrante, Eileen Myles, and Jenny Zhang. All of them were readily available elsewhere, both in print and in e-book form. And while all subscribers received these e-books in their inboxes every month, what they really signed up for was the recommendation itself, the sense that they were reading the right stuff—the books they should have known about but didn't. Emily Books wasn't helmed by Oprah or Gwyneth, but its subscribers still constituted a micro-community of fans.[37] Gould, in particular, had made quite a name for herself—not always good—within millennial New York publishing circles during the early years of the twenty-first century: she kept a popular blog, *Emily Magazine*, and she wrote for Gawker, a now shuttered gossip site. Gould's rise to fame, if not necessarily fortune, has largely coincided with the explosion of social media, and this culture of sharing, liking, and friending has made Emily Books possible. "I wanted to use my charm and charisma on behalf of other people's books," she confessed in 2014, "and that seems to, mostly, be working."[38] With the initial iteration of Emily Books, Curry and Gould were in the business of targeting and tending to what Lauren Berlant has called an "intimate public":

> An intimate public operates when a market opens up to a bloc of consumers, claiming to circulate texts and things that express people's particular core interests and desires. When this kind of "culture of circulation" takes hold, participants in the intimate public feel as though it expresses what is common among them, a subjective likeness that seems to emanate from their history and their ongoing attachments and actions. Their participation seems to confirm the sense that even before there was a market addressed to them, there existed a world of strangers who would be emotionally literate in each other's experience of power, intimacy, desire, and discontent, with all that entails: varieties of suffering and fantasies of transcendence; longing for reciprocity with other humans and the world; irrational and rational attachments to the way things are; special styles of ferocity and refusal; and a creative will to survive that attends to everyday situations while imagining conditions of flourishing within and beyond them.[39]

It is of course no accident that Berlant's primary example of an intimate public is US women's culture. The women who subscribed to Emily Books were one such world of emotionally literate strangers, interpolated but not created by Curry and Gould's picks each month. Emily Books, in its earliest days, was not a work of feminist recovery but feminist reorganization. It took literary material that already existed in the world, set it alongside and in juxtaposition with its allies and ancestors, and then opened that circle to readers. It found, and named, an intimate public that had grown organically. As a publishing imprint, it is no less invested in the continuity and sustenance of that public, rendering the often invisible arcs of feminist literary history visible by identifying new writers plotted on the same trajectories. But if Emily is and was a project rooted in curating literary collections and building intimate communities along the margins of the canon, other small feminist presses have focused on what has been lost beyond those margins.

In 2010, Danielle Dutton and her husband, Martin Riker, both experimental novelists with what Tom Lutz calls in this volume a "polymathic relation to the archive," started Dorothy, a publishing project. The pair had both worked at Dalkey Archive Press (Dutton as a book designer, Riker as Dalkey's associate director) before starting Dorothy, a press that "is dedicated to works of fiction or near fiction or about fiction, mostly by women," and this experience influenced the intertwined origin stories Dutton has told in interviews about the press. In one version, she emphasizes that she wanted to bridge the divide she saw between mainstream American literary fiction and more experimental writing. To make this happen, she intended for Dorothy to publish two "aesthetically different" books each year.[40] The first pairing consisted of Renee Gladman's experimental *Event Factory* and Barbara Comyns's *Who Was Changed and Who Was Dead*, which had first been published in England in 1954 but had been out of print for years. By offering the two books together at a discounted price, Dutton hoped to create a "crossover readership": she wanted to "encourage people to buy both when they came looking for just one—to get Renee Gladman's book into the hands of Barbara Comyns's readers and vice versa."[41] So far, there are eighteen Dorothy books, and it continues to be possible to buy each pairing together; it is also possible to buy any six Dorothy books or the entire catalog at a substantial discount. Emily Books uses the lure of social media connectivity to bolster and broaden the network of voices and readers that constitute its own intimate public; Dorothy uses the old-school apparatus of the press itself—publishing schedules, bulk discounts, inventive marketing—to constitute theirs. Dorothy takes a suggestion now mostly associated with algorithms and endows it with the thoughtful intimacy of friendship: "readers who bought Renee Gladman also bought Barbara Comyns."

But the origin story doesn't end with the art of persuasive pairing. Dutton was at least as concerned with writers as readers, and she wanted her press to be a home for under-appreciated women writers, past and present. While working at Dalkey, she "saw that the number of submissions were overwhelmingly from men," and she wanted to create space for women to submit their work. She was incensed by the lingering misogyny in literary publishing:

> Right around this time, too, I was talking about a book with a man who said to me, "I really liked it because five pages in I didn't know it was written by a woman. I couldn't tell a woman had written it." And I thought, Are you kidding me? Are we still talking about this nearly a hundred years after *A Room of One's Own*?[42]

Infuriated, she started Dorothy in order to explicitly support women's writing. And in yet another version of Dorothy's origin story, the impetus to start the press was even more specific: she wanted to support not just women's writing, in general, but the writing of one woman in particular, Renee Gladman. Dutton heard that Gladman was almost finished writing a trilogy of amazing books—known as her Ravicka books, the trilogy is now a quartet—but could not find anyone to publish them. Like Sylvia Beach offering to publish James Joyce's *Ulysses* when no other publishers would do so by turning her Left Bank bookstore and lending library, Shakespeare and Company, into a publishing house, Dutton "sent an impulsive email to Gladman, who she didn't know. 'Let me publish you, I'll start a press,' she says the email said; it was met with a miraculous response—'OK.'"[43] And, just like that, Dorothy was born.

As with Beach's Shakespeare and Company, the small size of Dorothy, as a venture, allows for quick shifts of direction, responsive adjustments of priority, even opportunistic social media blasts. The large presses, against which these small presses are defined, can use their scale and heft to establish canons, exclude marginal voices, even police those margins, but that scale can also be a disadvantage. Large presses move slowly, they must be less averse to risk, and they are less able to be guided by the kind of nimble and imaginative directorship we see in Emily and Dorothy. In these small presses, we see porous boundaries between the acts of curation, collection, design, publication, marketing, and even sales. These presses are not small because they turn away from the market; they merely see the market—their current and future readers—as indistinguishable from the books they publish. The publisher, the book, and the reader are equal parts of the same project: a transhistorical feminist community of readers and writers.

Most recently, A. N. Devers, a UK-based arts journalist and book collector, founded The Second Shelf, a business focused on "rare books, first editions, manuscripts, and other work by and about women."[44] Several years earlier, in an article entitled "The Second Shelf: On the Rules of Literary Fiction for Men and Women," novelist Meg Wolitzer had described the "second shelf" as the home of "'Women's fiction,' that close-quartered lower shelf where books emphasizing relationships and the interior lives of women are often relegated."[45] Wolitzer's essay highlights the difficulty, for women novelists, of making the "leap onto the upper shelf where certain books ... are prominently displayed and admired" by men and women alike.[46] While women read books by and about men, the reverse is not true: men too often "see most fiction by women as one soft, undifferentiated mass that has little to do with them."[47] In a subtle shift, however, Devers seems less interested in correcting men's reading and reviewing habits than in—like Emily Books and Dorothy, a publishing project—targeting a previously underserved audience of women readers and collectors. Let the books on that close-quartered shelf stay together, she suggests—just raise the whole thing up to eye level where it can be easily accessed. The idea for the project arose while Devers was attending book fairs during her early days as a collector. She noticed not only that most of the dealers and collectors around her were men but also that the prices of first editions by women authors were notably lower than those of their male peers. This was no less horrifying for being unsurprising, and she began to think about starting what would eventually become The Second Shelf. In doing so, she reimagined her role as a passive collector into one that could actively change some of the disparities she saw around her:

> Book collectors help determine which writers are remembered and canonized, and which are forgotten. The collector trade is part of a supply line, to readers' bookshelves, universities, archives and libraries. Historically it has been male-dominated (bookmen), white, and oriented around a western canon. Women, particularly women of color, are left under-recognized, their books deemed less collectable and given less space on shelves.[48]

But what if she gave them a shelf of their own, so to speak? As she began to collect women's writing with an eye toward turning her amateur undertaking into a future business, Devers was inspired by other women who entered the book business after leaving other careers. For example, Heather O'Donnell, of the Brooklyn-based Honey and Wax Booksellers, had been a successful academic before entering the rare books business. And while Honey and Wax, founded in 2011, has so far proven to be a successful business venture, O'Donnell explicitly values and encourages women's amateur contributions to the book trade by offering an annual book collecting prize. Awarded to outstanding book collections that have been conceived and acquired by young women, The Honey and Wax Book Collecting Prize was designed "to be open, as no others are, to women who are not in school ... particularly ... the many young working women—in publishing, design, bookselling, advertising, book arts, etc.—who pursue quirky and obsessive book collections for their own pleasure … [and who] are unlikely to be reached by the traditional antiquarian and academic channels."[49] The Honey and Wax prize is explicitly for amateurs; its very existence is an act of both criticism (of the existing book trade) and uplift (of those who might slowly change it).

For Devers, too, the social and historical goals of her project loom larger than its eventual bottom line, but she has admitted that she remains unsure whether it will prove to be a "viable business":

> Still, when I am at a fair and buying up books by women for The Second Shelf, I am asked by the sellers if I really think I will be able to make a profit or find a buyer. They are incredulous at my purchase of the books they have just sold me, which I take quiet note of, and let it fortify my determination to find and sell exceptional work that might have been lost due to inequality and uninterest.[50]

Despite the disbelief of her industry peers, Devers has received an outpouring of support for the project: its crowd-funded Kickstarter campaign concluded in June 2018 after receiving over six hundred contributions and exceeding its initial funding target by over 10,000 British pounds.[51] The first issue of *The Second Shelf: A Quarterly* was distributed in Fall 2018, and because the Kickstarter campaign—a mode of contemporary fund-raising, open to amateurs and professionals alike, that has become increasingly necessary in light of ongoing cuts to public funding for the arts—was so successful, Devers has already expanded the scope of The Second Shelf in ways that continue to develop. Like Emily's and Dorothy's readerships, the funders of The Second Shelf believe in the worthiness of the project itself and trust the critical vision of the woman at its helm.

In each of these projects—Emily, Dorothy, and The Second Shelf—there is an ongoing connection between amateur energy and feminist activism. Undertaken as labors of love and squeezed in around other professional commitments, these feminist publishing projects demonstrate the power of small communities to resist and transform the cultures of publishing across old and new media. To be an amateur, to nourish a small network of like-minded readers and writers, is not a mark of professional failure but a deliberate posture of challenge to the established institutions of contemporary publishing. For these women, amateurism is an occasional feminist stance. And in their hands, collecting, publishing, and otherwise circulating writing by and about women is a form of feminist criticism no less significant for its consistently devalued status in print and digital publishing scenes dominated by men.

## Notes

1 Florence Howe, "Lost and Found—and What Happened Next: Some Reflections on the Search for Women Writers Begun by The Feminist Press in 1970," *Contemporary Women's Writing* 8, no. 2 (2014): 141.
2 Ibid.
3 Ibid., 142.
4 Ibid., 143.
5 Ibid.
6 Ibid., 144.
7 Ibid. According to Howe, Moberg "set up ISBN numbers and copyright mechanisms, as well as professional design, editing, and marketing" (144).
8 Ibid., 145.
9 Ibid., 136.
10 Qtd. in Jennifer Gilley, "This Book Is an Action: A Case for the Study of Feminist Publishing," *The International Journal of the Book* 9, no. 1 (2012): 4.
11 Julia Penelope, "The Perils of Publishing," *Women's Review of Books* 2, no. 12 (1985): 3. For more on the historical context of Penelope's article as a response to the *Lesbian Nuns* publishing scandal earlier that year, see Gilley, "This Book Is an Action," 3.
12 Simone Murray, *Mixed Media: Feminist Presses and Publishing Politics* (London: Pluto Press, 2004), 22. For more recent exceptions to this "phantom discipline," see Jaime Harker and Cecilia Konchar Farr, eds., *This Book Is an Action: Feminist Print Culture and Activist Aesthetics* (Urbana, Chicago, and Springfield: University of Illinois Press, 2016), and Catherine Riley, *The Virago Story: Assessing the Impact of a Feminist Publishing Phenomenon* (New York and Oxford: Berghahn Books, 2018).
13 Ibid., 6–7.
14 Ibid.
15 Howe, "Lost and Found," 151.
16 Since 2010, VIDA: Women in Literary Arts has organized volunteers from across the country to perform their "count": they "manually,

painstakingly tally the gender disparity in major literary publications and book reviews." For more information, see http://www.vidaweb.org/the-count/.

17 Murray, *Mixed Media*, 6.

18 Carolyn Dinshaw, *How Soon Is Now? Medieval Texts, Amateur Readers, and the Queerness of Time* (Durham and London: Duke University Press, 2012), 32.

19 Saikat Majumdar, "The Critic as Amateur," *New Literary History* 48, no. 1 (2017): 22.

20 These descriptions come from the presses themselves. See http://dorothyproject.com/about/; https://www.emilybooks.com/; https://thesecondshelf.com/.

21 Urmila Seshagiri, "Making It New: Persephone Books and the Modernist Project," *Modern Fiction Studies* 59, no. 2 (2013): 244.

22 See Nathan Scott McNamara, "American Literature Needs Indie Presses," *The Atlantic*, July 17, 2016. Available online: http://www.theatlantic.com/entertainment/archive/2016/07/why-american-publishing-needs-indie-presses/491618/?utm_source=atltw. See also Kristen Evans, "We've Got Nothing to Lose: Emily Books Is Disrupting Publishing as Usual," *Brooklyn Magazine*, July 5, 2016. Available online: http://www.bkmag.com/2016/07/05/emily-books-jade-sharma-problems/.

23 In a 2012 interview with *The Guardian*, Beauman described her decision to start Persephone as one that was rooted in love: "Virago [another publisher of lost women's classics] was, and is, great as far it goes, and sometimes they did do books I suggested to them. But I had this inconvenient attachment to all these other books that they wouldn't publish. That's all I care about, really, you see: the text, the text, the text." Available online: https://www.theguardian.com/books/2012/nov/25/nicola-beauman-persephone-books-founder-interview.

24 Lawrence Rainey, *Institutions of Modernism: Literary Elites and Public Culture* (New Haven and London: Yale University Press, 1998), 4–5.

25 Jeremy Braddock, *Collecting as Modernist Practice* (Baltimore: Johns Hopkins University Press, 2012), 3. "At a time when the cultural value of modernist art was acknowledged but the mode of its institutionalization, its canon, and its relationship to society were undecided, the contest for modernism's social definition took place within this field of collections" (4).

26 Anisse Grosse, "Women Rule in Indie Publishing," *Publisher's Weekly*, April 28, 2017. Available online: https://www.publishersweekly.com/pw/by-topic/industry-news/publisher-news/article/73469-the-indie-publishing-feminist-revolution.html?utm_source=Publishers+Weekly&utm_campaign=a41addeacd-EMAIL_CAMPAIGN_2017_05_01&utm_medium=email&utm_term=0_0bb2959cbb-a41addeacd-304530177.

27 Moira Donegan, "What Is Women's Writing?: A Discussion at the Emily Books Symposium," *The Awl*, September 13, 2016. Available online: https://www.theawl.com/2016/09/what-is-womens-writing/#.33s0tjf0h. It is no coincidence that Moira Donegan, the journalist who wrote about this story for *The Awl*, is the woman who later started the "Shitty Media Men" list in October 2017. For more about this list and its ensuing scandal, see Moira Donegan, "I Started the Media Men List. My Name is Moira Donegan," *The Cut*, January 10, 2018. Available online: https://www.thecut.com/2018/01/moira-donegan-i-started-the-media-men-list.html.

28 Virginia Woolf, *Three Guineas* (1938; New York: Harcourt, 2006), 116.

29 Murray, *Mixed Media*, 34. Even after its sale to major publisher Little, Brown in 1995, Virago's influence as "the first mass-market publishers for 52% of the population—women" and its importance for feminist history is undeniable.

30 A documentary about the significance of Kali for Women, *The Books We Made*, was released in 2016. For more information about Zubaan, see Somak Ghoshal, "Urvashi Butalia: I Want to Prove Feminist Publishing Can Survive Commercially," *LiveMint*, June 14, 2013. Available online: https://www.livemint.com/Companies/595QfElEltDLfuvgNqTiOI/Urvashi-Butalia–I-want-to-prove-that-feminist-publishing-c.html.

31 Leah Lakshmi Piepzna-Samarasinha, "To Hell with 'There's No Market for You': Queer Writers of Color and Independent Publishing," *Make/Shift* (Fall/Winter 2008–2009): n.p. RedBone later expanded its mission and began to publish writing by black gay men, too.

32 See http://www.persephonebooks.co.uk/about-us/.

33 Grosse, "Women Rule in Indie Publishing," n.p.

34 Ibid.

35 See https://www.emilybooks.com/. In a subtle but interesting difference, the Twitter profile for Emily Books reads: "We sell weird books by women." The emphasis on "selling" rather than "making" in the Twitter profile may well be language from the curatorial era of Emily Books that has yet to be updated to reflect the editorial era.

36 Ibid.

37 For more about how fandoms and other kinds of collaborations and collectivities have influenced the contemporary digital publishing scene, see Aarthi Vadde, "Amateur Creativity: Contemporary Literature and the Digital Publishing Scene," *New Literary History* 48 (2017): 27–51.

38 Aaron Heckling, "Overstepping the Bounds: How Blogger Emily Gould has been Oversharing," *The Guardian*, December 14, 2014. Available online: https://www.theguardian.com/media/2014/dec/14/overstepping-bounds-blogger-emily-gould-oversharing.

39 Lauren Berlant, *The Female Complaint: The Unfinished Business of Sentimentality in American Culture* (Durham and London: Duke University Press, 2008), 5.
40 Nicole Ruddick, "Press Pass: Dorothy," *The Paris Review*, September 24, 2012. Available online: https://www.theparisreview.org/blog/2012/09/24/aunt-dorothy/.
41 Ibid.
42 Ibid.
43 Aaron Calvin, "How Small Presses Are Welcoming More Women into Publishing," *Pacific Standard*, December 21, 2016. Available online: https://psmag.com/news/how-small-presses-are-welcoming-more-women-into-publishing.
44 A. N. Devers, "Balance the Books: One Woman's Fight to Keep Great Female Writers on Shelves," *The Guardian*, May 18, 2018. Available online: https://www.theguardian.com/books/2018/may/18/the-second-shelf-an-devers-balance-the-books.
45 Meg Wolitzer, "The Second Shelf: On the Rules of Literary Fiction for Men and Women," *The New York Times*, March 30, 2012. Available online: https://www.nytimes.com/2012/04/01/books/review/on-the-rules-of-literary-fiction-for-men-and-women.html.
46 Ibid.
47 Ibid.
48 Devers, "Balance the Books," n.p.
49 Emily Temple, "Announcing a New Annual Prize for Young Female Book Collectors," *Lithub*, May 23, 2017. Available online: https://lithub.com/announcing-a-new-annual-prize-for-young-female-book-collectors/. For more information on the prize itself, see https://www.honeyandwaxbooks.com/prize.php.
50 Devers, "Balance the Books," n.p.
51 For detailed information on the current status of The Second Shelf's crowd-funded support, see: https://www.kickstarter.com/projects/writershouses/the-future-of-books-is-female-the-second-shelf-qua.

# Bibliography

Berlant, Lauren. *The Female Complaint: The Unfinished Business of Sentimentality in American Culture*. Durham and London: Duke University Press, 2008.

Braddock, Jeremy. *Collecting as Modernist Practice*. Baltimore: Johns Hopkins University Press, 2012.

Calvin, Aaron. "How Small Presses Are Welcoming More Women into Publishing." *Pacific Standard*. December 21, 2016. Available online:

https://psmag.com/news/how-small-presses-are-welcoming-more-women-into-publishing (accessed June 25, 2018).
Cooke, Rachel. "One Shade of Grey: How Nicola Beauman Made an Unlikely Success of Persephone Books." *The Guardian*. November 24, 2012. Available online: https://www.theguardian.com/books/2012/nov/25/nicola-beauman-persephone-books-founder-interview (accessed June 25, 2018).
Devers, A. N. "Balance the Books: One Woman's Fight to Keep Great Female Writers on the Shelves." *The Guardian*. May 18, 2018. Available online: https://www.theguardian.com/books/2018/may/18/the-second-shelf-an-devers-balance-the-books (accessed June 25, 2018).
Dinshaw, Carolyn. *How Soon Is Now?: Medieval Texts, Amateur Readers, and the Queerness of Time*. Durham and London: Duke University Press, 2012.
Esposito, Veronica Scott. "Independent Bookstore as Essential Political Act." *Lithub*. March 28, 2017. Available online: https://lithub.com/independent-bookstore-as-essential-political-act/ (accessed June 25, 2018).
Evans, Kristin. "We've Got Nothing to Lose: Emily Books Is Disrupting Publishing as Usual." *Brooklyn Magazine*. July 5, 2016. Available online: http://www.bkmag.com/2016/07/05/emily-books-jade-sharma-problems/ (accessed June 25, 2018).
Ghoshal, Somak. "Urvashi Butalia: I Want to Prove Feminist Publishing Can Survive Commercially." *LiveMint*. June 14, 2013. Available online: https://www.livemint.com/Companies/595QfElEltDLfuvgNqTiOI/Urvashi-Butalia–I-want-to-prove-that-feminist-publishing-c.html (accessed June 25, 2018).
Gilley, Jennifer. "This Book Is an Action: A Case for the Study of Feminist Publishing." *International Journal of the Book* 9, no. 1 (2012): 1–9.
Grosse, Anisse. "Women Rule in Indie Publishing." *Publishers Weekly*. April 28, 2017. Available online: https://www.publishersweekly.com/pw/by-topic/industry-news/publisher-news/article/73469-the-indie-publishing-feminist-revolution.html (accessed June 25, 2018).
Harker, Jaime and Cecilia Konchar Farr, eds. *This Book Is an Action: Feminist Print Culture and Activist Aesthetics*. Urbana, Chicago, and Springfield: University of Illinois Press, 2016.
Heckling, Aaron. "Overstepping the Bounds: How Blogger Emily Gould Has Been Oversharing." *The Guardian*. December 14, 2014. Available online: https://www.theguardian.com/media/2014/dec/14/overstepping-bounds-blogger-emily-gould-oversharing (accessed June 25, 2018).
Howe, Florence. "Lost and Found—and What Happened Next: Some Reflections on the Search for Women Writers Begun by The Feminist Press in 1970." *Contemporary Women's Writing* 8, no. 2 (2014): 136–153.

Majumdar, Saikat. "The Critic as Amateur." *New Literary History* 48, no. 1 (2017): 1–25.

McNamara, Nathan Scott. "American Literature Needs Indie Presses." *The Atlantic*. July 17, 2016. Available online: https://www.theatlantic.com/entertainment/archive/2016/07/why-american-publishing-needs-indie-presses/491618/ (accessed June 25, 2018).

Murray, Simone. *Mixed Media: Feminist Presses and Publishing Politics*. London: Pluto Press, 2004.

Penelope, Julia. "The Perils of Publishing." *Women's Review of Books* 2, no. 12 (1985): 3–6.

Piepzna-Samarasinha, Leah Lakshmi. "To Hell with 'There's No Market for You': Queer Writers of Color and Independent Publishing." *Make/shift* (Fall/Winter 2008–09): n.p.

Rainey, Lawrence. *Institutions of Modernism: Literary Elites and Public Culture*. New Haven and London: Yale University Press, 1998.

Riley, Catherine. *The Virago Story: Assessing the Impact of a Feminist Publishing Phenomenon*. New York and Oxford: Berghahn Books, 2018.

Ruddick, Nicole. "Press Pass: Dorothy." *The Paris Review*. September 24, 2012. Available online: https://www.theparisreview.org/blog/2012/09/24/aunt-dorothy/ (accessed June 25, 2018).

Seshagiri, Urmila. "Making It New: Persephone Books and the Modernist Project." *Modern Fiction Studies* 59, no. 2 (2013): 241–287.

Temple, Emily. "Announcing a New Annual Prize for Young Female Book Collectors." *Lithub*. May 23, 2017. Available online: https://lithub.com/announcing-a-new-annual-prize-for-young-female-book-collectors/ (accessed June 25, 2018).

Vadde, Aarthi. "Amateur Creativity: Contemporary Literature and the Digital Publishing Scene." *New Literary History* 48 (2017): 27–51.

Wolitzer, Meg. "The Second Shelf: On the Rules of Literary Fiction for Men and Women." *The New York Times*. March 30, 2012. Available online: https://www.nytimes.com/2012/04/01/books/review/on-the-rules-of-literary-fiction-for-men-and-women.html (accessed June 25, 2018).

Woolf, Virginia. *Three Guineas*. 1938. New York: Harcourt, 2006.

# Epilogue: New, Interesting, and Original—the Undergraduate as Amateur

*Kara Wittman*

> When Descartes for the first time in history made reference to a provisional morality, he created an unprecedented concept of morality by the simple act of using an adjective in a novel way. He replaced the commandments (divine, social, traditional) with elective values, rules that a person chooses to follow. To get to this point required years of critical thought, but the creation of the phrase *morale par provision* was surely instantaneous. The words simply came out that way, in unexpected juxtaposition; and as they flowed from his pen or passed through his head, he saw that they were good.
>
> —Gabriel Zaid, *The Secret of Fame*

> Nothing special was in my mind. I was just looking.
>
> —*T. J. Clark, The Sight of Death*

What Gabriel Zaid says of Descartes also is true of T. J. Clark: "When I say that I came to the paintings without previously having worked on Poussin much, this does not mean that I came to them with an open mind. I had a view of Poussin, which was no doubt all the more dogmatic for never having been spelled out—"[1] Descartes's instantaneous creation, his "unprecedented concept," and Clark's "just looking" required years of thought, of study, even of dogmatic hardening. In a moment, like lightning or wonder, appeared a new morality, a "corrective to dogma," something apparently original. The professional art historian and the philosopher were "just looking," just shifting adjectives, and something new "simply came out." But, as Zaid observes, and Clark admits: the "just," the "simply," dissemble.[2]

Our students suspected this all along. The philosopher's flash of insight from the novel adjective, the detail in Poussin's *Landscape with a Man Killed by a Snake* that "dislodge[d]" the "scholarly piling on of facts," rely on years of thinking. Seeing what is important or understanding what is worth saying—what is *original*—is not the amateur's happy accident. This is the work of experts.

Still, what seasoned critics feel for the unexpected adjective or a turned heel in a painting might nonetheless be an amateur's love. As others in this volume observe, the amateur impulse enlivens much of our work. We can appreciate the originality of Descartes's *morale par provision* or Clark's diaristic meditations on Poussin as evidence not just of scholarly achievement but also of something more personal and wonderful, freer from professional constraints, subjectively revelatory. Clark *is* a professional art historian who *was* nonetheless "just looking" and *The Sight of Death* is original because both things are true. That's hard to explain in an undergraduate classroom, and that's where I begin in this concluding chapter. The originality we ask from our undergraduates reveals the knotty heart of the critic-as-amateur. Originality does not align neatly with either amateurism or professional criticism. It requires something of both. When we ask our students to be original—and we do ask that of them—we ask them to occupy two positions at once.[3] When we ask them to be "original," (as the syllabus says, "your thesis should be original," should be "imaginative, authoritative, with original insight," "original, interesting, and relevant")[4] we ask them to walk the line between expert and tyro, professional and amateur: to be enough of a naïf to experience the wonder of "first-ness"[5] and knowledgeable enough to recognize that first-ness as such.

This contradiction emerges alongside the blossoming concern with "originality" as a literary value in eighteenth-century Europe. Françoise Meltzer captures a version of this paradox: "What emerges in the requirements for greatness in literary authorship is a paradox:

the demand for spontaneous creativity on the one hand (proof of 'natural' genius), and a work ethic that insists upon earning acquired goods or status on the other."[6] Or Paul Saint-Amour: "Originality is a property licensed by its vaunted self-sufficiency and heterodoxy but really only attainable by the most external, contingent, and generally orthodox means possible."[7] We are not perhaps asking our students to be "great" or incomparable in Wordsworthian terms, but we ask that their originality be recognizable to a critical community, which takes work. To put a finer point on it, it takes the kind of work we do as professional critics, which puts our amateur students, perforce, in an awkward position.

Considering what we ask of our students when we ask them to occupy this contradictory space allows us to reflect on how we negotiate the space between expertise and amateurism, critics and amateurs, professionals and hobbyists, epistemic confidence and unsettling wonder. These contradictions occupy the essayists in this volume, who find them in our scholarship, our relationships with our mentors, in historical figures and in virtual spaces. By spending time in the complicated space—and, in some ways, proving ground—of the undergraduate classroom I hope also to think through contradictions at the heart of our own labor, our pedagogy, and our values as literary critics. And, I should add, our desire. When we ask our undergraduates to be original we ask them to practice being professionals, but we also look for something of the wonder and self-creation that amateurs seem to represent. The historically unsettled term "original" lets us get at what we value in the amateur spirit even as it contradicts our professional values. The originality we desire, I'll end by suggesting, is perhaps akin to Benjamin's weak messianism, something that "produces the conditions" for seeing things differently, "the elusive temporal richness that promotes the indeterminacy of ever-present possibility,"[8] a way to think about "originality in secular, as opposed to magical language." Or rather what we perhaps desire is not the "originality" we name in our writing prompts and style guides but something we move steadily away from as experienced scholars and then look for in the receding category of the amateur: the promise of beginning.

The prompts, guides, and rubrics we give our undergraduate writers often ask them to be original. "Produce original interpretive work," these documents urge: "contribute original scholarship"; demonstrate "thoughts that are original"; have a thesis that is "original and interesting"; write a paper that is "imaginative, authoritative, with original insight." And so on.[9] The language, varied only slightly, proliferates; I hadn't thought much about it. That changed a few years ago when one of my colleagues and I wondered how undergraduates think about literature seminars, about our expectations, about what *they're* doing in there. So we asked them. In January 2015 we convened a working group of four English undergraduates and one graduate student and planned a series of discussions for the semester. Rather than proceed like a focus group, we took an inductive approach, letting student concerns emerge from our loose discussions about the English major and the study of literature.

What emerged was the specter of originality, something they saw haunting the relationship between our critical expertise, their passionate amateurism, and the demand that they occupy both positions at once. As one of our students put it:

> When professors tell students to come up with an "original idea" it always seems like they're asking something of me that I can never seem to achieve. I mean, what *really* is an original idea? Is it original in the sense that they've never heard it or seen it on paper before? Or original in the sense that I myself have never explored such an idea before? [...] When you find sources that support it and that seem rather similar to it, does that mean it wasn't even that original in the first place? How do I know if someone, somewhere across the world or in an alternate universe hasn't already come up with this idea? Do I need to copyright my idea for it truly to be original? Does it have to be interesting/provocative to be original?[10]

Her questions accurately represent the mood of the group, and she categorizes originality in ways that reflect this collection's concern with the poles of criticism as specialized practice and idiosyncratic pursuit, not to mention the long history of thinking about originality in literature. To be original is, perhaps, (1) something circumstantially, locally new; (2) something heretofore unuttered or unwritten; (3) something entirely personal to the thinker; (4) something unlike anything else; (5) something no one anywhere has thought before; (6) something confirmed as such by a market; (7) something judged to be interesting, something that *feels* original.[11]

Such language traces the conflicting associations of originality with, on the one hand, amateurism and, on the other, professional criticism. How we define originality informs how we train our undergraduates. Do we hope students will hold on to the aspects of their amateurism that allow them to wonder and explore without feeling constrained by professional expectation, to remain, as Roland Barthes puts it, in the epistemological "as if" of the "Amateur," the subjective and intimate "pinnacle of [their] particularity"?[12] Are we hoping instead that they will shed these traces of amateurism and win "the certification of the original"[13] adjudicated according to already recognized scholarly standards of innovation?[14]

Those expectations are confusing. And undergraduates are told as much, with some candor, by one of the most popular sources for writing and research help on the internet today. Here is the Purdue Online Writing Laboratory [OWL] on "Intellectual challenges in American academic writing":

> There are some intellectual challenges that all students are faced with when writing. Sometimes these challenges can almost seem like contradictions, particularly when addressing them within a single paper. For example, American teachers often instruct students to:
>
> Develop a topic based on what has already been said and written BUT write something new and original.
>
> Rely on experts' and authorities opinions BUT improve upon and/or disagree with those same opinions.
>
> Give credit to previous researchers BUT make your own significant contribution.
>
> Improve your English to fit into a discourse community by building upon what you hear and read BUT use your own words and your own voice.[15]

The OWL does not offer any advice for navigating these contradictions; the subsequent section is on avoiding plagiarism. And *avoiding plagiarism* returns us to one ostensible reason for our prompting students to "contribute original scholarship": intellectual property, theft, the agony of influence. But the literature on plagiarism is anything but straightforward, shot through as it is by the complexities of Western thinking about originality.

As it concerns undergraduate writing, the literature on plagiarism is vast. Extending from the comparatively banal (tutorials and handbooks on citation styles, paraphrasing, quotation sandwiches) to the menacing ("colleges, faculty, and students ... [are] equally consumed by the notion that plagiarism is widespread and uncontrollable [...] the fear that plagiarism is not only rising but attaining the status of a pandemic; that the core values of our society [such as its reverence for originality] are threatened by this virus"[16]), writing on plagiarism is anxious to make sure undergraduate writers show the proper respect for the cultural values represented in the intellectual marketplace. "Avoiding plagiarism is important," write the authors of a popular handbook on student writing, "for in Western culture *the use of someone else's words or ideas without acknowledgement and as your own is an act of academic dishonesty and can bring devastating results*" (emphasis in original).[17] According to its website, the "originality and plagiarism checking service" Turnitin.com is "trusted by over 15,000 higher education institutions in over 140 countries."[18] In other words, the anti-plagiarism juggernaut is working to professionalize students, to prepare them to be recognized in and by a culture that will reward "original expression" or "the absence of verbatim copying and the demonstrable presence of a modicum of creativity."[19] Part of the professionalization effort is about avoiding plagiarism and thus demonstrating a student's capacity for original thought; the other part is about citing sources accurately and consistently and thus honoring the originality of others. Both aspects participate in the implicit belief that originality can be sniffed out, tracked, and measured so that the student can pass through this extensive security clearance into the scholarly community.

But worries about plagiarism and professionalization are only part of the desire for students to "demonstrate thoughts that are original." The advice for undergraduate writers in the Purdue OWL enjoins students to account for what they have learned but then rates that learning according to its capacity to exceed itself, to generate something new. And the newness is cast in terms that predate—and also underwrite—the modern intellectual property marketplace: the language of genius, originality, and self, language that imagines something "new and original" immanent in "your own words and your own voice."

In his essay "The Critic as Amateur," Saikat Majumdar recounts the story of Pankaj Mishra's "failure to write an original piece on Edmund Wilson," the self-doubt attending that scholarly failure, and Mishra's subsequent turn to a more personal narrative about the critic. We might see that "failure to write an original piece" as a professional failure, an inability to enter the marketplace of ideas, but neither Majumdar nor Mishra sees it that way. For Mishra, failure was the result of writing in someone else's voice, from someone else's perspective. A recent graduate, living in a provincial, decolonized city, Mishra wanted to learn and to honor the American critic from whom he had already learned so much, but his twinned anxiety about not having read enough, and having read just enough to write in someone else's voice without realizing it, made him feel he could not be original. "Original" here sounds much like the originality celebrated by anti-plagiarism invectives, but the originality at which Mishra in fact arrived looks more like the originality of Edward Young's *Conjectures on Original Composition*. What Mishra produces out of his own sense of failure, Majumdar tells us, is a "remarkable," even beautiful story of *Bildung*, "an unlikely story of autodidacticism," an "essay about reading, and, particularly, engaging with literary criticism," motivated by a narrative impulse emerging from a ravenous desire to learn and Mishra's "unexpected" perspective.[20] This is Young's celebrated originality: "they had but little learning, and few books; yet may the most learned be struck with some astonishment at their so singular natural sagacity, and most exquisite edge of thoughts," an unexpected group of luminaries burning with "*cœlestis origo*."[21] What Mishra eventually authors, Majumdar contends, he could only author "not as a professional scholar, but as an amateur."[22]

If the professional scholar's originality manifests in the avoidance of plagiarism (Mishra: "What I wrote seemed to me too much like a reprise of what a lot of other people had already said"), something in which we are certainly training our students, we seem also to be looking for a slightly different originality from them. This other originality indexes learning while also revealing what Young called "vegetable" genius.[23] Originality is perhaps not entirely about the marketplace but also about our desire to see that our students are learning. We register that learning by asking them to refract what they've encountered through something in themselves and thus originate something new. David Matheson writes that "ideas produced *from a student's own point of view* can sometimes produce a new insight."[24] This is not exactly "creation *ex nihilo*," but, as Robert Macfarlane reminds us, neither was Young's.[25] What persists from Young's work (and the Romantic theories it inspired) is the notion of the individual whose compositions exceed "mere imitation" by virtue of the tendrils from that original "vital root" or bulb of genius that emerge from within. "Use your own words and your own voice," the Purdue OWL catechizes, to make something "new and original."

We cultivate our students' ability to pass learning through the prism of their own "words and voices" and so to be original. In doing so we ask them to occupy paradoxes articulated by Saint-Amour and Meltzer: to be at once preprofessional scholars, able to navigate with some acumen the vast body of ideas that exist, and originals, creators with something new to contribute. That new thing, we suggest, will be at once the ticket to entering an existing marketplace of ideas and the measure of some internal process—learning, perhaps. But not just learning, because metrics for learning are easy and various. Asking our students to inflect their learning with their own words and voices suggests we're looking for something *in addition* to learning, some mark of an original self, some sign of individuality, some human desire. Our work as professional critics sets us up to register the second according to the terms of the first: originality only appears in an extant, known field against which it can bear the mark of the singular. How we recognize it as original depends in large part on our own scholarship. William Duff, publishing his *Essay on Original Genius* (1767) eight years after Edward Young's *Conjectures*, recognized in what terms his own originality would be judged:

> In an Essay on Original Genius, Originality of Sentiment will naturally, and may, no doubt, justly be expected [ … T]he Author begs leave to subjoin a caution to his Readers: It is, that they would not expect to meet with original sentiments in those parts of this Essay, where it is scarce possible they should be discovered. […] In what degree Originality of Sentiment is really discovered … must be left to the determination of the intelligent and impartial Reader. The Author, for his own part, can at least declare, that he is not conscious of having borrowed his observations on these subjects from the Writings of any other person whatever.[26]

Duff's mea culpa locates him clearly, and not without good company, in the period's contradictory messaging about originality—messages we echo in the imperatives we issue our undergraduates. For example, when that ostensive champion of original genius, Percy Shelley, writes in a letter to William Godwin after publishing *The Revolt of Islam*, "I exercised myself in the despair of producing any thing original," he says this not in response to some failure of the poem but because it failed in the marketplace.[27] Although he takes pains in the "Author's Preface" to assure his readers that the worth of the poem emerges from his not imitating "any style of language or versification" peculiar to any other poet, the true adjudicator of its worth—and perhaps thus of its originality—appears to be, for him, the paying public.[28]

Just as, for Majumdar, Mishra's turn from producing scholarship on Edmund Wilson to his unconventional, deeply personal, intellectual-coming-of-age narrative marks a turn from professional to amateur, so do the shifting values that attend "originality" map a tension between the professional critic and the amateur. The heavily cited book of literary criticism marks its originality relative to a field, whereas the originality of the sparsely researched book must be congenital, *sui generis*. "Among scholars … footnote citation indexes are used as a measure of comparative value," Marjorie Garber observes; "the absence of footnotes is a bold, in-your-face declaration of professional amateurism in its most magisterial form."[29] In short, our profession valorizes two mutually constitutive but perhaps finally inconsonant manifestations of originality. Professional originality takes the form of the idea made recognizable in its newness by its divergence from existing scholarship and vetted by peers according to those terms, the idea that can then be published and copyrighted. What we might call amateur originality sprouts from uncultivated soil of self, voice, "some vision of the work as having been made entirely from scratch, happening this time and this time only, in perfect synchronicity with its own becoming."[30] This amateur originality is not about origination as pioneering or trailblazing, about the "newness" that only an extant field can register, but rather is about discovering a wondering, feeling "I."[31]

The originality we demand from our students asks them to comprehend both, to "be informed about critical debates and literary theories" and yet also to "find their own way into a literary work, not to parrot the interpretations of others."[32] As fledgling preprofessional critics, our students demonstrate in the carefully cited papers that flag their own contributions among the parenthetical and superscript "mark[s] of professional display"[33] that they are able to ratify and uphold the regimes that undergird our profession. As amateurs, their incipient textual sovereignty gives us access to "the passion that comes from investment in one's work, pride of authorship of writing one owns and loves," the "exhilarating, creative, [and] fun" that gives our work and our teaching meaning.[34]

As I've been suggesting, the tension between professional and amateur criticism this volume explores plays out in the terms of the originality we want, at least as our learning outcomes, rubrics, and style guides have it, from our students. But is this really what we want, or are there different desires at work here? What if this slippery notion of originality gets in the way of our valuing amateurism on its own terms and understanding the amateur impulses that linger in our own professional criticism? And what if studying our desire for student originality helps us to understand that both our notions of professionalism and amateurism—terms that rely on each other—have obscured for us what it means to be a critic and a student? Originality, as Young took pains to establish, is aspirational; "nature" might, as he puts it, create originals, but in order not to "die Copies," we require a lifetime of becoming, not being, that seedling original. As Anis Bawarshi shows us, the distinction between "what is known and what is new" is generically, historically, and culturally specific; the "supposedly original writer" works with "inherited lexical, grammatical, and semantic encounters"; originality might, in fact, simply be ongoing displacement, "a name for an endless, perhaps occasionally violent, substitution of one experience for another."[35] As Paul Valéry puts it,

> We say that an author is *original* when we cannot trace the hidden transformations that others underwent in his mind […] there are … works of which the relation with earlier productions is so intricate that we become confused and attribute them to the direct intervention of the gods.[36]

Or, in less vaunted terms, Jonathan Lethem offers this in the "Key" to his breathtaking plagiarism *The Ecstasy of Influence*:

> Though in truth by the time I'd finished, his words were so utterly dissolved within my own that had I been an ordinary cutting-and-pasting journalist it never would have occurred to me to give Dahlen a citation. The effort of preserving another's distinctive phrases as I worked on this essay was sometimes beyond my capacities; this form of plagiarism was oddly hard work.[37]

In his essay on Modernist citation, Kevin Dettmar puts it in terms that hit perhaps closest to where our undergraduates live: "To put it crudely: Stephen [Dedalus] wants to be Byron when he grows up, but it is starting to look like there will not be any openings by the time he is ready to go on the market."[38]

So maybe we can never be original. But considering the tension between the professional and the amateur in terms of originality allows us to view both categories not in their impossible contingencies but in terms of the desire that animates our work as critics. We need neither be what Darren Hick calls "originality deniers," nor to tack between the dependent terms "professional" and "amateur" to get at the love and wonder that might still linger in our criticism.[39] Our students, not ready to be original in the marketplace and maybe not original geniuses (is anyone?), offer us something beyond the "professional amateur," or the "critic as amateur" or the imagined "interesting and original" author of a million term papers. They are, simply, beginners.

There's a curious moment in Plato's *Theaetetus* in which Socrates—normally the confident "midwife" for his young students' learning—talks himself into a corner about the nature of knowledge and pulls back, annoyed at his own garrulity, frustrated that his incontinent desire to get at the true nature of knowledge led him so far down a false path that he convinced himself he'd arrived at something new. "I am not only annoyed," he tells Theaetetus, "I am alarmed. I am afraid of what I may say if someone asks me, 'So Socrates, you've discovered false judgment have you?' [...] I believe I am very likely to say 'yes,' with an air of flattering myself upon our having made some beautiful discovery."[40] Socrates gets so uncomfortable with the disorienting lostness and wonder necessary to philosophy, that he persuades himself he's discovered something that is in fact just *wrong*. This is bad, he tells Theaetetus; we have "to go back to the beginning."[41] Once there, the interlocutors come to the conclusion that they don't know what knowledge is, that everything they've produced has been a "wind-egg," and that *this was the lesson*. Beautiful discoveries are nothing, Socrates tells Theaetetus; the point is to be able again and again to deliberate, to cast aside dogma, to ask new questions. And so, "in freeing the young philosopher from his own fledgling doctrines," Mary-Jane Rubenstein writes, "Socrates [frees] him *for* the aporetic vertigo of wonder," the "only beginning of philosophy."[42]

The lesson of *Theaetetus*, a key text for the Romantics in its affirmation of the wonder they understood as immanent in poetic genius, is in fact not about *origination* at all. It's about teaching a young student to begin. "Every student of literature," Edward Said offers in his 1975 *Beginnings*, "necessarily deals with originality and with the related subject of influences and sources; yet very few critics have systematically tried to examine originality in secular, as opposed to magical, language."[43] Said is interested in the weak messianism of beginnings as "opposed to originalities, or to those ideal Presences whose ideal originality Yeats called 'self-born mockers of man's enterprise.'" A beginning, he continues, "is what I think scholarship ought to see itself as, for in that light scholarship or criticism revitalizes itself. [...] For the scholar or researcher, a beginning develops when the conditions of his reality become equal to the generosity of his, of everyman's, intellectual potential."[44] In other words, a beginning is a choice; it is active; it renews itself; it "promotes the indeterminacy of ever-present possibility."[45]

Shifting the terms of our pedagogical expectations and injunctions from originality to beginning allows us to reconcile some of the paradoxes that attend originality and in doing so to understand the value of amateurism, the amateur spirit not in its impossible contingencies, or in any bad faith disavowals of our compensation, our expertise, or our professional status. To see the critic as *beginner* rather than as professional or indeed as amateur is to see her as finding in her own critical position what Said sees as "the possibility of freedom, of a new cleanness, of prospective achievement, of special and novel appropriation," to see her perpetually "transformed by the renewing of [her] mind."[46]

Our two-part fascination with originality—as, on the one hand, the market-friendly avoidance of plagiarism and, on the other, evidence of organic thinking and an individual mind—crystallizes something about what we value in both the professional and the amateur critic. Our students rightly see the contradictions in our desires: "When professors tell [us] to come up with an original idea," my student said, "it always seems like they're asking something of me *that I can never seem to achieve*." Of course we are. Because they are, *ipso facto*, amateurs, they can stand in for the love, the wonder not yet deformed by the strictures of professionalism and scholarly rectitude that make our lives worth it, while also upholding our professional values. Originality circulates between these things because we've accepted the opposition between amateur and professional in these terms: the amateur critic is a vegetable genius; the professional is very good at footnotes.

The challenge is to think of the student as something other than an amateur or a professional while taking from each the values of both and, in doing so, holding onto something that we want from originality not *as* originality but as a sustained beginning. I think Derek Attridge is right when he suggests that "the best hope for a new emphasis on the amateur impulse in literary studies, perhaps, lies in the classroom," because the students in our classrooms are amateurs, yes, but more importantly they are beginners. If we can teach them not to be "original," but to begin, perhaps we can get at what we want from the amateur without needing to disavow its opposite, to revivify our work without making a stalking horse of professional criticism.

"If originality as a conception," writes Said, "has had the power for too long of depressing time backwards into lost primacy at best, and regained utopias at worst, this is a good reason for reorienting our study systematically toward the future."[47] What that will mean, for Said, is turning toward thinking about beginnings and in the concept of beginning finding a way to reconcile the antipodes of originality: "an obligation to practical reality," to one's "concrete" circumstances, to learning, to one's field of study, and "to sympathetic imagination," writing into what "cannot be known except by inventing it, exactly, intentionally, autodidactically."[48] For Barthes, this describes the epistemological position of the "Amateur":

> It is important for me to act *as if* I were to write this utopian novel. And here I regain, to conclude, a method. [...] I proceed to another type of knowledge (that of the Amateur) and it is in this that I am methodical. "As if": is not this formula the very expression of scientific procedure, as we see it in mathematics? I venture a hypothesis and I explore, I discover the wealth of what follows from it.[49]

Said, too, in his 1993 Reith lecture "Professionals and Amateurs," finds in the amateur the salutary, disruptive, and radical qualities of the resolved beginner:

> An amateur is what today the intellectual ought to be, someone who considers that to be a thinking and concerned member of a society one is entitled to raise moral issues at the heart of even the most technical and professionalized activity as it involves one's country, its power, its mode of interacting with its citizens as well as with other societies. In addition, the intellectual's spirit as an amateur can enter and transform the merely professional routine most of us go through into something much more lively and radical; instead of doing what one is supposed to do one can ask why one does it, who benefits from it, how can it reconnect with a personal project and original thought.

In 1984, he called that amateur a beginner: "But if there is some especially urgent claim to be made for criticism ... it is in that constant re-experiencing of beginning and beginning again whose force is neither to give rise to authority nor to promote orthodoxy but to stimulate self-conscious and situated activity, activity with aims non-coercive and communal."[50] In other words, the extra-institutional force and prerogative of the amateur have less to do with "de-professionalization" and more to do with flexibility, transformation, and the possibility of beginning again and again without *or within* the academy, the corporate body.[51]

We don't want our students "to parrot the interpretations of others" when they begin to engage a literary text. We want something we're calling original thought. That mandate, as we've seen, assumes a set of preexistent relationships: to the germ of a coherent, original self; to the field, the discipline, the market. Socrates's brief philosophical panic can be helpful for us here: originating something, falling back on those preconditions, might give us a way out of aporetic wonder, a way to demonstrate knowledge, but it can also be a devil's bargain. The danger is in originating, he says to Theaetetus; what we need is to begin.

If I can tell my student—who wants to know "what *really* is an original idea" and how do I know if I'm having one and according to whom?—that actually *no*, I don't care so much about the original idea, I don't care so much about plagiarism or the market or whether she's harboring some bulb of vegetable genius, my classroom will, I think, look different. It will look more like what it is, a classroom of beginners, but beginning will take on new meaning as an important part of the animating spirit of criticism, as an anti-authoritarian, open, ethical value. Whereas both "professional" and "amateur" suggest ontologies, and certainly so does the notion of origins, "beginning" is epistemological—a spirit of potential, of "articulation" in Ernesto Laclau and Chantal Mouffe's sense, where what students learn changes both what they read *and* their own selves.

How would asking students simply to begin, "to write in and as an act of discovery,"[52] as opposed to asking them to "have original thoughts," or write something "interesting and original," change the way we create our prompts? How might it change the way we articulate our goals for a course? Or the writing assignments we produce? Or find in imitation not the misdeed of plagiarism but a kind of intervention or even resistance? For many of us, the shift might seem subtle, but as I've learned, our students feel even these spectral presences. For me, turning toward criticism as beginning has meant freeing my students from the strictures of thesis statements and even more so from conclusions; it has allowed me to spend much more time on questions, even unanswerable ones; it has meant turning to the form of the essay that we inherit not from Francis Bacon's allergy to wonder but Michel Montaigne's embrace of it. "What I write here is not my teaching, but my study"; he muses, "it is not a lesson for others, but for me."[53]

A common thread running through this volume is this notion of a constant reexperiencing of beginning and beginning again. "An amateur reading," writes Attridge, "involves an openness to whatever the work, on a particular occasion, will bring—a readiness to have habits and preconceptions challenged and a willingness to be changed by the experience." It will involve a perpetual process of "learning and unlearning, as well as a constant making and unmaking of critical language," suggests Peter McDonald. The boy who can calm the wild steed, for Tom Lutz, is not an amateur, not really—he needs not disavow the professional to become himself. The boy simply falls in love "over and over again," his love only and always beginning. "Non-knowing is an enabling condition of [this] work," writes Ragini Srinivasan. "If we don't know what we don't know, we are free to know otherwise." "By trading 'certainty for uncertainty,'" she writes of Jhumpa Lahiri, "she is able to 'learn, again, to write.'" Mimi Winick finds something like this beginning in Vernon Lee's "conjectural and suggestive" aesthetic, her "*becoming* identity ... forever in process." It's even present in the image of Dorothy Richardson talking about films from the position of a spectator, someone, we take it, always walking into the cinema filled with anticipation to see a film for the first time, like Stephen Potter's audiences coming to the literary criticism they heard over the airwaves as beginners, or Pramatha Chauduri, "an essayist, in relation to the literary field," and as an essayist always at the infinitive beginning of the experiment, trying.

What we can take from our students is that they are neither professionals nor amateurs: they're beginning. It's a worthwhile place to be, as this essayists in this volume suggest: at the beginning of something, again and again. Asking our students to be original casts them at once backward to some theological origin of their own nebulous self and forward into a marketplace of ideas in which they will have attended carefully, professionally, to their intellectual brand. If as professional critics we've lived for a long time in the marketplace, our amateur impulses suggest a deep desire to shuttle back toward the origin, the vegetable and creative self. But our students allow us to think something else: perhaps we do not need to be amateur critics or critics as amateurs. Perhaps we can just, and again, begin.

## Notes

1 T. J. Clark, *The Sight of Death: An Experiment in Art Writing* (New Haven, CT: Yale University Press, 2006), 12.

2 Gabriel Zaid, *The Secret of Fame: The Literary Encounter in an Age of Distraction* (Philadelphia: Paul Dry Books, 2008), 169.

3 The "we" here can, of course, never be all of us. This "we" is comprised of the preponderant expectations for originality in the learning outcomes advertised by Departments of English; disciplinary trade handbooks and style guides casting "originality" as that to which student writers should aspire; individual and departmental grading rubrics; assignment prompts and course descriptions. This "we" also comprehends the near-universal institutional anxiety about originality's opposite: plagiarism.

4 Janet E. Gardner, *Writing about Literature: A Portable Guide* (New York: Macmillan, 2009), 18; *English Literature Writing Guide* (University of Edinburgh, 2017), 19. Available online: https://www.ed.ac.uk/files/imports/fileManager/English%20Literature%20Writing%20Guide%20final.pdf; Maralee Harrell, "Grading according to a Rubric," *Teaching Philosophy* 28, no. 1 (March 2005). See also, for just a small sample of literature programs using the language of student "originality," the Department of English learning outcomes for the University of Oregon, Kansas State University, Pomona College, Duke University, Carnegie Mellon University, and the University of California, Berkeley.

5 "Wonder [seems] premised on 'first-ness': the object that appears before the subject is encountered for the first time, or *as if* for the first time." Sara Ahmed, *The Cultural Politics of Emotion* (Edinburgh: Edinburgh University Press, 2014), 179.

6 Françoise Meltzer, *Hot Property: The Stakes and Claims of Literary Originality* (Chicago: Chicago University Press, 1994), 4.

7 Paul St. Amour, *The Copywrights: Intellectual Property and the Literary Imagination* (New York: Cornell University Press, 2003), 8.

8 Russ Castronovo, "The Function of Criticism at a Different Time," in *Critique and Postcritique*, ed. Elizabeth Anker and Rita Felski (Durham, NC: Duke University Press, 2017), 247.

9 Eric Dugdale, "Essay Rubric"; Sophia McClennan, "General Evaluation Rubric for Papers"; "Courses Guide," Literature Program, University of Pittsburgh; "Example of an Analytical Research Paper," University of Richmond Writing Center; Donna Campbell, "Literary Studies Paper with Possible Points"; Sara Spurgeon, "Guidelines for Seminar Paper: Topic Proposal, Abstract, Paper." All materials publicly available: see Works Cited.

10 Catherine Zinski, Blackboard Discussion. Mills College, Spring 2015. Quoted with permission.

11 Cf. Sianne Ngai's work on the category of the "interesting": she traces the tensions that "interesting" undergirds: between "individual and system," "unknown and known," "individuation and standardization." Perhaps unsurprisingly, "original" and "interesting" often show up together in our instructions for undergraduate literary criticism. Sianne Ngai, *Our Aesthetic Categories: Zany, Cute, Interesting* (Cambridge: Harvard University Press, 2012).

12 Roland Barthes, "Longtemps, je me suis couché de bonne heure ...," in *The Rustle of Language*, trans. Richard Howard (Berkeley: University of California Press, 1989), 289.

13 Rosalind Krauss, *The Originality of the Avant Garde and Other Modernist Myths* (Cambridge: The MIT Press, 1986), 162.

14 Michel Foucault, *The Archaeology of Knowledge* (New York: Routledge, 1989).
15 OWL: The Purdue Online Writing Lab, "Intellectual Challenges in American Academic Writing." Available online: http://owl.purdue.edu/owl/resource/589/01/ (accessed May 2018).
16 Linda Adler-Kassner, Chris Anson, and Rebecca Moore Howard, "Framing Plagiarism," in *Originality, Imitation, and Plagiarism: Teaching Writing in the Digital Age*, ed. Caroline Eisner and Martha Vicinus (Ann Arbor: The University of Michigan Press, 2008), 231.
17 Andrea A. Lunsford and John J. Ruszkiewicz, *Everything's an Argument* (New York: Bedford/St. Martin's, 2004), 404.
18 Turnitin.com. Available online: http://turnitin.com/en_us/higher-education (accessed May 2018).
19 Saint-Amour, *Copywrights*, 7.
20 Saikat Majumdar, "The Critic as Amateur," *New Literary History* 48, no. 1 (2017): 2.
21 Edward Young, *Conjectures on Original Composition*, ed. Edith J. Morley (Manchester: Manchester University Press, 1918), 16–17.
22 Majumdar, "Critic," 2.
23 Young, *Conjectures on Original Composition*, 7.
24 David Matheson, *An Introduction to the Study of Education* (New York: Routledge, 2008), 347 (my emphasis).
25 Robert Macfarlane, *Original Copy: Plagiarism and Originality in Nineteenth-century Literature* (Oxford: Oxford University Press, 2007), 18n1.
26 William Duff, *An Essay on Original Genius and Its Various Modes of Exertion in Philosophy and the Fine Arts, Particularly in Poetry* (London: Forgotten Books, 2015), xv.
27 Macfarlane, *Original*, 30.
28 Percy Bysshe Shelley, "Author's Preface," in *The Revolt of Islam* (London: John Brooks, 1829). That he equates market failure with his own failure to be original does not mean that he turned all value judgments over to the consuming public—only that he saw a relationship between market failure and his own capacity to be original.
29 Marjorie Garber, *Academic Instincts* (Princeton, NJ: Princeton University Press, 2001), 40–42.
30 Eric Hayot, *The Elements of Academic Style: Writing for the Humanities* (New York: Columbia University Press, 2014), 138.
31 "Pleasure" comes up often in this volume as something to which an amateur has perhaps more, or at least different, access than the professional.
32 Rita Felski, *Uses of Literature* (Oxford: Blackwell, 2008), 11.

33 Garber, *Instincts*, 41.
34 For more on "textual sovereignty" see Meltzer, *Hot Property*, 4.
35 Anis Bawarshi, "Genres as Forms of In(ter)vention," in *Originality, Imitation, and Plagiarism: Teaching Writing in the Digital Age*, ed. Eisner and Vicinus (Ann Arbor: Michigan University Press, 2008), 79; Steiner qtd in Macfarlane, *Original*, 4; Edward Said, "On Originality," in *Uses of Literature*, ed. Monroe Engel (Harvard: Harvard University Press, 1973), 53.
36 Edward Said, *Beginnings: Intention and Method* (New York: Columbia University Press, 1985), 15.
37 Jonathan Lethem, *The Ecstasy of Influence: Nonfictions, etc.* (New York: Vintage Books, 2011), 117.
38 Kevin Dettmar, "The Illusion of Modernist Allusion and the Politics of Postmodernist Plagiarism," in *Perspectives on Plagiarism and Intellectual Property in a Postmodern World*, ed. Lise Buranen and Alice M. Roy (New York: SUNY Press, 1999), 103.
39 Darren Hick, *Artistic License: The Philosophical Problems of Copywright and Appropriation* (Chicago: Chicago University Press, 2017), 6.
40 Plato, *Theaetetus*, ed. Bernard Williams, trans. M. J. Levett (Indianapolis: Hackett, 1992), 195c.
41 Ibid., 199d.
42 Mary-Jane Rubenstein, *Strange Wonder: The Closure of Metaphysics and the Opening of Awe* (New York: Columbia University Press, 2008), 7. Rubenstein's work first alerted me to the real discomfort Socrates evinces in his conversation with Theaetetus. There is much to be said beyond the scope of this essay about wonder in this "postcritical" moment. Rita Felski evokes wonder in her discussion of "enchantment" in *Uses of Literature*, but especially as it concerns Plato and Aristotle, wonder and enchantment must be kept separate.
43 Said, *Beginnings*, 14.
44 Ibid., 380.
45 Castronovo, "Function of Criticism," 247.
46 Said, *Beginnings*, 35.
47 Said, "On Originality," 65.
48 Said, *Beginnings*, 349.
49 Barthes, "Longtemps," 289.
50 Said, *Beginnings*, xiv.
51 See Rosinka Chauduri in this volume on "de-professionalization."
52 Said, *Beginnings*, 379.
53 Michel Montaigne, *The Complete Works: Essays, Travel Journal, Letters* (New York: Knopf, 2003), 331.

# Bibliography

Adler-Kassner, Linda, Chris M. Anson, and Rebecca Moore Howard. "Framing Plagiarism." In *Originality, Imitation, and Plagiarism: Teaching Writing in the Digital Age*, edited by Caroline Eisner and Martha Vicinus. Ann Arbor: The University of Michigan Press, 2008.

Ahmed, Sara. *The Cultural Politics of Emotion*. Edinburgh: Edinburgh University Press, 2014.

Barthes, Roland. "Longtemps, je me suis couché de bonne heure ...." In *The Rustle of Language*, trans. Richard Howard. Berkeley: University of California Press, 1989.

Barthes, Roland. *The Preparation of the Novel: Lecture Courses and Seminars at the College de France* (1978–1979 and 1979–1980), trans. Kate Briggs. New York: Columbia University Press, 2011.

Bawarshi, Anis. "Genres as Forms of (In)tervention." In *Originality, Imitation, and Plagiarism: Teaching Writing in the Digital Age*, edited by Caroline Eisner and Martha Vicinus. Ann Arbor: The University of Michigan Press, 2008.

Castronovo, Russ. "The Function of Criticism at a Different Time." In *Critique and Post Critique*, edited by Elizabeth Anker and Rita Felski. Durham, NC: Duke University Press, 2017.

Campbell, Donna. "Literary Studies Paper with Possible Points." Available online: https://public.wsu.edu/~campbelld/litstudiespercent.docx (accessed May 2018).

Clark, T. J. *The Sight of Death: An Experiment in Art Writing*. New Haven, CT: Yale University Press, 2006.

"Courses Guide." Literature Program. University of Pittsburgh. Available online: http://www.englishlit.pitt.edu/undergraduate/courses-guide (accessed May 2018).

"Curriculum Map." Department of English, University of Oregon. Available online: https://cas.uoregon.edu/wp-content/uploads/2014/03/English-Curriculum-Map.pdf (accessed May 2018).

"Department of English." *2017–2018 Course Catalog*. Carnegie Mellon University. Available online: http://coursecatalog.web.cmu.edu/dietrichcollegeofhumanitiesandsocialsciences/departmentofenglish (accessed May 2018).

Dettmar, Kevin J. H. "The Illusion of Modernist Allusion and the Politics of Postmodern Plagiarism." In *Perspectives on Plagiarism and Intellectual Property in a Postmodern World*, edited by Lise Buranen and Alice M. Roy. New York: State University of New York Press, 1999.

Duff, William. *An Essay on Original Genius and Its Various Modes of Exertion in Philosophy and the Fine Arts, Particularly in Poetry*. London: Forgotten Books, 2015 (1767).

Dugdale, Eric. "Essay Rubric [Classics]" Writing across the Curriculum. Gustavus Adolphus College. Available online: https://gustavus.edu/wac/faculty/documents/Dugdale-rubric-essay.pdf (accessed May 2018).

*English Literature Writing Guide*. University of Edinburgh, 2017. Available online: https://www.ed.ac.uk/files/imports/fileManager/English%20Literature%20Writing%20Guide%20final.pdf (accessed May 15, 2018).

Enteen, Jillana. "Close Reading for Your Posts and Essays." Available online: nuwrite.northwestern.edu/communities/firstyear/.../Close_reading_assignments.doc (accessed May 2018).

"Example of an Analytical Research Paper." University of Richmond Writing Center. Available online: http://writing2.richmond.edu/writing/wweb/english/example1.html (accessed May 2018).

Felski, Rita. *Uses of Literature*. Oxford: Blackwell Publishing, 2008.

Foucault, Michel. *The Archaeology of Knowledge*. New York: Routledge, 1989.

Garber, Marjorie. *Academic Instincts*. Princeton, NJ: Princeton University Press, 2001.

Gardner, Janet E. *Writing about Literature: A Portable Guide*. New York: Macmillan, 2009.

"Goals and Learning Objectives." Department of English, Duke University. Available online: https://english.duke.edu/undergraduate/goals-learning-objectives (accessed May 2018).

Harrell, Maralee. "Grading according to a Rubric." *Teaching Philosophy* 28, no. 1 (March 2005): 3–15.

Hayot, Eric. *The Elements of Academic Style: Writing for the Humanities*. New York: Columbia University Press, 2014.

Hick, Darren. *Artistic License: The Philosophical Problems of Copyright and Appropriation*. Chicago: University of Chicago Press, 2017.

Krauss, Rosalind. *The Originality of the Avant-garde and Other Modernist Myths*. Cambridge: The MIT Press, 1986.

"Learning Goals." Department of English, Pomona College. Available online: https://www.pomona.edu/academics/departments/english/courses-requirements (accessed June 2018).

Lethem, Jonathan. *The Ecstasy of Influence: Nonfictions, etc*. New York: Vintage Books, 2011.

Lunsford, Andrea A. and John J. Ruszkiewicz. *Everything's an Argument*. New York: Bedford/St. Martin's, 2004.

Macfarlane, Robert. *Original Copy: Plagiarism and Originality in Nineteenth-century Literature*. Oxford: Oxford University Press, 2007.

Majumdar, Saikat. "The Critic as Amateur." *New Literary History* 48, no. 1 (2017): 1–25.

Matheson, David. *An Introduction to the Study of Education*. New York: Routledge, 2008.

McClennan, Sophia. "General Evaluation Rubric for Papers." August 10, 2004. Available online: http://www.personal.psu.edu/users/s/a/sam50/rubric.htm (accessed May 2018).

Meltzer, Françoise. *Hot Property: The Stakes and Claims of Literary Originality*. Chicago: University of Chicago Press, 1994.

Montaigne, Michel de Eyquem. *The Complete Works: Essays, Travel Journal, Letters*. New York: A. A. Knopf, 2003.

Ngai, Sianne. *Our Aesthetic Categories: Zany, Cute, Interesting*. Harvard: Harvard University Press, 2012.

OWL: The Purdue Online Writing Lab. "Intellectual Challenges in American Academic Writing." Last modified October 10, 2014. Available online: https://owl.english.purdue.edu/owl/resource/589/01/ (accessed May 2018).

Plato. *Theaetetus*. Edited by Bernard Williams, trans. M. J. Levett. Indianapolis: Hackett, 1992.

Rubenstein, Mary-Jane. *Strange Wonder: The Closure of Metaphysics and the Opening of Awe*. New York: Columbia University Press, 2008.

Said, Edward. *Beginnings: Intention and Method*. New York: Columbia University Press, 1985.

Said, Edward. "On Originality." In *Uses of Literature*, edited by Monroe Engel. Cambridge: Harvard University Press, 1973.

Said, Edward. "Professionals and Amateurs," from "The Reith Lectures: Representations of the Intellectual." July 1993. Available online: https://www.bbc.co.uk/programmes/p00gmx4c (accessed May 2018).

Saint-Amour, Paul. *The Copywrights: Intellectual Property and the Literary Imagination*. New York: Cornell University Press, 2003.

Shelley, Percy Bysshe. "Author's Preface." In *The Revolt of Islam*. London: John Brooks, 1829.

Spurgeon, Sara. "Guidelines for Seminar Paper: Topic Proposal, Abstract, Paper." Available online: https://www.depts.ttu.edu/english/general_info/directory/faculty_profile_pages/Spurgeon_Students_Files/Spurgeon_Guidelines_for_Seminar_Paper.pdf (accessed May 2018).

"Student Learning Outcomes for English Majors in the Department of English at Kansas State University." Department of English, Kansas State University. January 29, 2015. Available online: https://www.kstate.edu/english/programs/ugrad/slos.html (accessed May 2018).

Turnitin for Higher Education. Available online: http://turnitin.com/en_us/higher-education (accessed May 2018).

"Undergraduate Student Learning Initiative Report." Department of English, University of California at Berkeley. November 6, 2008. Available online: https://english.berkeley.edu/undergraduate/usli (accessed May 2018).

Young, Edward. *Conjectures on Original Composition*. Edited by Edith J. Morley. Manchester: Manchester University Press, 1918.

Zaid, Gabriel. *The Secret of Fame: The Literary Encounter in an Age of Distraction*. Philadelphia: Paul Dry Books, 2008.

# INDEX